DAN PONTOW
1010 N. Spruce
Creston, Iowa 50801
782-7778

THE AMERICAN HISTORY AND ENCYCLOPEDIA OF MUSIC

W. L. HUBBARD
EDITOR IN CHIEF

EMIL LIEBLING
GEO. W. ANDREWS
ARTHUR FOOTE
EDWARD DICKINSON
ASSOCIATE EDITORS

EDITORIAL CONTRIBUTORS

G. W. CHADWICK
FRANK DAMROSCH
FREDERICK STOCK
CARL FAELTEN
W. J. HENDERSON
H. E. KREHBIEL
FREDERICK STARR
CLARENCE DICKINSON
THEODORE SPIERING
FRANZ KNEISEL
EDWARD M. BOWMAN
OSCAR SAENGER
GEORGE C. GOW
FREDERIC W. ROOT
W. S. B. MATHEWS
BERNHARD LISTEMANN
HARRISON M. WILD
ARNOLD DOLMETSCH

IRVING SQUIRE
NEW YORK

THE METROPOLITAN, NEW YORK

New York possesses in the Metropolitan an opera house which ranks with the most important in the world. It faces on Broadway and extends from Thirty-ninth Street to Fortieth Street. It is severely plain and practical in design but none the less spacious and imposing. Including the seventy-three boxes it has a seating capacity of 3500, the auditorium being unsurpassed in convenience of arrangement. The stage is one hundred feet in length, ninety feet in depth and one hundred and fifty feet in height. The cost of the Metropolitan was $1,500,000. The two tiers of boxes and three balconies make in all five galleries. The Metropolitan was opened Oct. 22, 1883, with Henry E. Abbey as manager. "Faust" was sung with Campanini and Nilsson as principals in the cast. The Metropolitan was built and managed by a corporation composed largely of men who were unable to secure boxes at the Academy of Music, then the only opera house in the city.

THE AMERICAN HISTORY AND ENCYCLOPEDIA
OF MUSIC

HISTORY
OF
AMERICAN MUSIC

WITH

INTRODUCTIONS

BY

GEORGE W. CHADWICK

AND

FRANK DAMROSCH

W. L. HUBBARD

EDITOR

IRVING SQUIRE

Toledo

New York Chicago

Copyright 1908 by
IRVING SQUIRE
Entered Stationers' Hall
LONDON

CONTENTS

LIST OF ILLUSTRATIONS

AMERICAN COMPOSERS

G. W. CHADWICK.

Theodore Thomas once remarked that he thought the prestige of Boston as a musical city during the last twenty-five years was largely due to the influence of Harvard University. It is not probable that he meant the direct educational influence, since Harvard has at no time encouraged the study of "applied" music or influenced her students to become professional musicians by offering technical training in singing or the playing of musical instruments. Rather is it to be inferred that he had in mind the refining influence of the fine arts, and that broad, general culture which Harvard offers in such large measure, and of which it is so easy for the citizens of Boston to take advantage.

Nevertheless, Harvard was the first University in America to add music to its curriculum as a serious study. For many years an orchestral society of undergraduates, known as the Pierian Sodality, had flourished in the college, and out of this grew later, in Boston, the Harvard Musical Association. This society, originally organized largely of Harvard graduates, kept orchestral music alive in Boston for more than fifteen years; in fact, from 1865 until 1881, when the Boston Symphony Orchestra was founded. From this time its activity as a concert-giving organization practically ceased, but it still exists and flourishes as a social organization, numbering among its members most of the musical Harvard alumni as well as the principal professional musicians who live in Boston, and its fine library is a power for good.

It was largely through the influence of this Association that John K. Paine was appointed instructor in music at Harvard in 1862. Later, in 1875, the department was organized with him at its head as full professor. He had acquired a good education in Germany under Haupt and Wieprecht, and his Mass for chorus and orchestra had been performed with success in Berlin. His duties at Harvard allowed him time to give some organ concerts and historical lectures outside of the University. His oratorio, "St. Peter," was performed in Portland, his native town, in 1873, and extracts from it had been given at the Peace Jubilee of 1869; but it was with his first symphony in C minor that he first gained recognition as a romantic composer of high ideals and genuine imagination.

This melodious and fluent work was performed by Theodore Thomas at one of his Boston concerts in 1876 and at once attracted attention by its interesting melodic material, its masterly use of the symphonic form and its sonorous orchestration. The simple and benighted music lovers of those days had not been taught by blasé critics that the sonata form was a worn-out fetich, that noble and simple melody was a relic of the dark ages, and that unresolved dissonance was the chief merit of a musical composition. It was therefore no wonder that this work, warmly endorsed by Theodore Thomas, and performed in a manner to reveal and enhance all its beauties, should have been a stimulus and an inspiration to more than one ambitious musician of that time.

Professor Paine's second ("Spring") symphony in A major, performed in 1880, is a much more elaborate and ambitious work than that in C minor, but is hardly superior to the earlier work in genuine inspiration or spontaneous flow of ideas.

Sophocle's tragedy, " Œdipus Tyrannus," with Professor Paine's music was given at Harvard University in 1881, and afterwards in New York and Boston by a professional company. The classic dignity of the tragedy is well reflected in Professor Paine's music, which also contains much of deeply tragic significance.

His opera, "Azara," on which he spent the last fifteen years of his life, still awaits a production. A concert performance of it by the Cecilia Society of Boston revealed many beauties of thought and much interesting instrumentation.

The first representative Harvard man to adopt music was James C. D. Parker. Shortly after his graduation in 1848 he went to Leipsic, where he studied with Moscheles and Hauptmann, and became an excellent pianist and organist. Returning to Boston he was appointed organist of Trinity Church, which position he held for more than twenty-six years. He frequently appeared as soloist at the concerts of the Harvard Musical Association and at chamber concerts. He founded an excellent club, which included most of the good singers of Boston, and for this society he translated many of the shorter choral works of Mendelssohn, Gade, and others, and performed them for the first time in America. In composition his efforts were mostly confined to choral works and church music, although an overture by him (" Hiawatha") was performed by Theodore Thomas in New York and at the Peace Jubilee of 1872. At the Triennial Festival of the Handel and Haydn Society in 1877 Parker's " Redemption Hymn" was performed and received with much enthusiasm. Though not a pretentious work, it combined a scholarly harmonic and contrapuntal structure with profoundly touching religious expression, and its production may be regarded as one of the landmarks in the history of the Handel and Haydn Society. This hymn has since found its way into the repertory of nearly all the choral societies of the United States.

The most important event in the modern musical history of Boston was the founding in 1881 of the Boston Symphony Orchestra by Henry L. Higginson. Its influence, at first only local, has now become national and its reputation world-wide. The first conductor of the orchestra, Georg Henschel, himself an excellent composer, took much interest in the efforts of the Boston composers, and during the three years of his incumbency several of their orchestral works were performed. His good example was followed by his successor, Wilhelm Gericke, who from the beginning showed himself friendly to the growing coterie of young American composers, and most of them owe him gratitude to this day not only for making their works known to the public but for the invaluable counsel and advice in matters of orchestral technique, which his vast experience enabled him to give them.

In 1887 he performed the overture, "In the Mountains," by Arthur Foote, and with such success that it was repeated the following year. Previous to this Foote had produced some chamber music and a serenade for string orchestra, which contained many charming and effective passages. He had taken the musical courses under Paine at Harvard after his graduation and made an admirable translation of Richter's treatise on Fugue. He was one of the first to earn the degree of Master of Arts, it having been the custom to bestow it on Bachelors of Art a certain number of years after graduation.

It is perhaps by his chamber music and songs that Foote is at present best known. Some of the latter have achieved a wide popularity not only in this country but in England. His local influence and popularity as a teacher have been great, and his interest in all useful musical enterprises have made him a force in the community.

In 1884-1885 two other Boston boys, Horatio Parker and Arthur Whiting, were studying in the Munich Music

School under Rheinberger. Parker, who had made a pretty good start under Boston teachers, showed from the first the same interesting harmonic ideas, facility in expression and fluent lyric style which have since distinguished his compositions. These qualities, as well as a refined sense of orchestral coloring, were shown in his first work for choral and orchestra, "King Trojan," which was performed in the music school at his graduation in 1885. On his return to America he assumed the direction of the department of music of the Garden City School, at the same time filling various positions in New York City as organist and choirmaster.

In 1893 he composed his "Hora Novissima," a work which has become a permanent addition to the repertories of the best choral societies of America and England, and has gained a wider popularity than any other American choral work. It is an interesting fact that this work was unsuccessfully proposed for the prize offered by the National Conservatory, and which was won by the same composer with a smaller work called "The Dream King and His Love." "Hora Novissima" was first performed in New York at a concert of the Church Choral Society, and soon after at the Springfield Festival of 1894. Thence it rapidly made its way to performances by the principal choral societies of the country, crossed to England, where it made an unequivocal success at the Festival of The Three Choirs in Worcester.

In 1893 Parker removed to Boston, whither he had been called as organist of Trinity Church. Many of his smaller works date from this period. The two most important, "Cahal Mor" and "A Northern Ballad" (the former a very picturesque ballad for barytone solo and orchestration), were performed by the Symphony Orchestra in 1895. In the "Cahal Mor" he evinces a command of modern orchestral resources which he has seldom surpassed in his later works. In 1894 Parker was appointed to his present position, professor of music, at Yale, receiving at the same time the honorary degree of Master of Arts from the University. He removed to New Haven, but still continued as organist in Boston. In 1901 he resigned this position and went to Europe for a Sabbatical year. While there he received the honorary degree of Doctor of Music from Cambridge (England) University, probably the first instance in which it has been bestowed on an American musician.

His friend and comrade, Arthur Whiting, had also received good training under Boston teachers, and even at that time had given indication of possessing an interesting individuality of style in his compositions. The somewhat pedantic methods of the Munich School were hardly calculated to encourage this, but he persevered and, working much by himself, produced an overture which was played at a concert of the Music School in Munich in 1885.

Returning to America he settled in Boston as pianist and teacher, and made frequent public appearances at the Symphony Concerts, and at the chamber concerts of the Kneisel Quartet, and others. Several of his compositions were performed by this organization and by the Symphony Orchestra, the most important of which perhaps is Fantasie in B flat minor for piano and orchestra, a very poetic and effective work, showing much individuality of style and a mastery of modern piano writing not equaled by many.

Whiting is not a voluminous writer. To him the piano seems to be the most sympathetic medium of expression, but all his compositions show a refined poetic sense, often with a touch of sardonic humor, combined with a singular knowledge of the technical possibilities of the instrument, especially in the matter of tone tints.

Edward MacDowell resided in Boston from 1888 to 1897. His first piano concerto and some of his earlier piano music had already been played there and his reputation in Europe had already begun to grow. He was warmly welcomed by the Boston musicians, and at once took his place among them as a leading virtuoso and teacher. In the latter capacity his influence is felt to this day, and though his sojourn was not long, it will always be a grateful memory to those who came to know him intimately and enjoyed the privilege of his friendship. From this period date some of his finest and most characteristic works. The poetic "Sonata Tragica," the "Indian Suite," and some of his most beautiful songs were composed at this time. The second concerto, and that bijou masterpiece, the Suite in A minor Opus 42, belong to a somewhat earlier period.

The latter composition was first performed at the Worcester Festival of 1891, under the direction of Carl Zerrahn, and the writer still remembers the delight of the musicians and the audience which was created by its striking rhythmical vitality and unique instrumentation. The "Indian Suite" was first performed by the Boston Symphony Orchestra, under the direction of Emil Paur, to whom it was dedicated. Many repeated hearings have only confirmed the impression then made of its power, beauty and originality. For this is no mere piece of shopworn ballet music, torturing the noble red man's simple melodies into a sophisticated contrapuntal fabric and decorated with orchestral spangles and tinsel; rather, it is organic, elemental, sane, pervaded by a large dignity and eloquence, by a noble melancholy — the melancholy of the woods and mountains at twilight — and yet in places is suggests with striking vividness the fury of the tempest and the ferocity of war. Many other performances of MacDowell's compositions took place during his residence in Boston, among which were his "Hamlet and Ophelia," "Launcelot and Elaine," and a memorable performance of the second concerto by Teresa Carreño.

MacDowell enjoyed one great advantage which was denied to most of the other American composers: He had acquired his technical education early in life. At the age of sixteen or seventeen he was in Paris, delving at counterpoint and fugues, and that, too, at six o'clock in the morning. His long residence in Europe, at that susceptible period of his life, tended to develop his individuality and he thus became a master of his own style while still a very young man. Unpatriotic as it may appear, America did not offer at that time a favorable environment for the student of musical composition, although it has since greatly improved in that respect. There were excellent teachers here, but none of the schools could then give students the opportunities we now have in some places in our own country to experiment with an orchestra, either as composer or conductor. Little wonder then that many of the young Americans went to Munich, Leipsic or Berlin, where they could at least have occasional opportunities for hearing their own works.

Fortunate, too, was MacDowell in his association with Raff. Although a strict disciplinarian (he adhered to the stronger Satz in his teaching) Raff was no pedant. His inclination toward the Romantic School, and his own consummate technique as a modern orchestral colorist, made him quick to recognize and encourage the poetic and imaginative side of his young pupil, and their relation to one another soon grew into a close and lasting friendship, which lasted until Raff's death. MacDowell always spoke of Raff with great enthusiasm, and it was evident that he loved him as a man as much as he respected him as a musician. MacDowell's removal to New York in 1896, when he was appointed to the Chair of Music at Columbia University, left a void which is still felt in Boston.

Although Charles Martin Loeffler was not born in America, his intimate connection with Boston's musical life. as well as his long and useful career as a virtuoso, composer and teacher, give America the right to claim him as her own. He joined the Boston Symphony Orchestra in 1883, the third year of its existence, and from then until 1903 occupied the chair of the second concertmaster, frequently appearing as soloist, when his remarkable abilities as a virtuoso were demonstrated. Trained in the best French School (he was a pupil of Leonard and Massart) his style combined a beautiful tone and immaculate intonation with brilliant technical ability. Some of the modern concertos, like Godard's "Concerto Romantique" and Lalo's "Sinfonie espagnole," he performed for the first time in Boston. His

EDWARD ALEXANDER MACDOWELL
1861-1908

Born in New York City, he holds the first place as an American composer and is the most gifted and characteristic representative of our national music.

Probably his best known work is "The Indian Suite," inspired by the American Indian Folk-song. It is one of the first American compositions for the orchestra and holds its own in comparison with the work of modern European composers.

In 1896 a chair of music was endowed at Columbia University and MacDowell was called to fill it. He resigned this position in 1904, and two years later was run over by a cab in New York City, receiving injuries resulting in incurable mental and nervous diseases which caused his death two years later.

EDWARD ALEXANDER MACDOWELL

1861-1908

Born in New York City, he holds the first place as an American composer and is the most gifted and characteristic representative of our national music.

Probably his best known work is "The Indian Suite," inspired by the American Indian Folk-song. It is one of the first American compositions for the orchestra and holds its own in comparison with the work of modern European composers.

In 1896 a chair of music was endowed at Columbia University and MacDowell was called to fill it. He resigned this position in 1904, and two years later was run over by a cab in New York City, receiving injuries resulting in incurable mental and nervous diseases which caused his death two years later.

first appearance as an orchestral composer was in 1891, when he performed his "Les Veilles de l'Uraine" for solo violin and orchestra. This was followed in 1894 by his concerto for the violoncello, which was played by Alwin Schroeder.

These early works show many traces of the harmonic individuality which is such a striking characteristic of his later compositions. They are, however, more conservative, in form and color and much less daring in treatment than his later works.

The first piece to give full expression to Loeffler's matured style was his Divertimento in A minor for violin and orchestra, which was first performed by him at a concert of the Boston Symphony Orchestra in 1897. It was received with such approval that a "round robin" request was made to the other composers for its repetition, which however was not complied with. In this Divertimento Loeffler gave very positive evidence of his consummate mastery of orchestral color, especially with simple means, and of his skilful rhythmical invention, and most of all his unique harmonic talent.

His symphonic poem, "The Death of Tintagile," which was performed by the Boston Symphony Orchestra in its original version in 1899, shows much dramatic power as well as a singular sympathy with the inner significance of the poem. Its atmosphere of evil augury is suggested with both power and subtlety by the strange harmonies and weird orchestration of Loeffler's music.

He has always been a relentless critic of his own works, most of them having been revised many times, and the "Mort de Tintagiles" which was originally scored with two obbligato parts for solo violi d'amore, was afterwards rewritten with one of them omitted, and with many other changes. His two short pieces, "La Bonne chanson" and "Villanelle du Diable," after poems by Varlaine and Rollinat, performed under Mr. Gericke in 1902, present the strongest possible contrast of style. The one placid, idyllic; the other an orgy of diabolism beside which the "Witches' Sabbath" of Berlioz seems like tawdry theatre music. In this latter work he has made use of some of the French revolutionary tunes, like "Ca Ira" and "La Carmagnole," and the sardonic humor of some of his contrapuntal devices is at times startling.

Loeffler has always shown a fondness for unusual combinations, and to this some of his characteristic tone coloring is due. Thus his psalm for female voices is accompanied by a harp, organ, two flutes, and a solo violoncello. Several pieces are for oboe, viola and piano, while his latest work is for piano, orchestra and trumpets behind the scenes. Apart from this it is not easy to sum up the elements of Loeffler's style. Showing a certain consanguinity with the Modern French School, in harmonic treatment his variety of resource saves him from mannerisms with which works of the latter sort are sometimes blemished. Although most of his works are conceived from the poetic point of view, they contain much skilful contrapuntal treatment in the modern sense, and show a respect for legitimate polyphony not much affected by some of the ultra modern writers.

As a colorist, Loeffler has few rivals. His long experience in playing in an orchestra where works of every school were continually being rehearsed, and that, too, with the most minute attention given to detail, has given him an advantage that has been enjoyed by few composers. This, combined with his own artistic discrimination, his fastidious avoidance of the commonplace and his rigorous self-criticism, have made him a composer of whom Boston and all America are justly proud. His music is his own, and although his works are comparatively few in number, their quality is of the rarest.

Frederick Shepard Converse belongs to an old family of Boston. While at Harvard he took all the courses under Professor Paine, and in 1892 graduated with "Honors in Music" and was elected an honorary member of the Phi Beta Kappa. A sonata for violin and piano, dating from his college days, shows graceful melodic invention and interesting thematic development. He continued to work for some time after graduation with Boston teachers, and in 1896 he went to Munich to study with Rheinberger. The result of his work in the Munich School was a symphony in D minor, which was performed at a school concert, and was favorably criticized by the German press.

On his return to Boston in 1898 this symphony was performed by the Boston Symphony Orchestra and also, in part, at the Worcester Festival in 1898, when the composer himself conducted the work. This symphony shows excellent academic training, a thorough command of form, and a facility in contrapuntal invention, but of tone-painting in the modern sense there is but little. It would have been hardly possible for any work which showed a radical departure from recognized forms and methods to be considered for performance in the Munich School, and this symphony is not the only American work which has been affected by such conservatism.

In the case of Converse, it was not long before a reaction took place. Endowed with an imaginative and poetic nature, a well trained and vigorous mind, and with great capacity for work, he became an art student of modern scores, with the result that his next work, "The Festival of Pan," showed a radical departure from the maxims and methods of his early training, for in this work he shows an imaginative power, a wealth of harmonic resource, and an opulence of orchestral color of which his early work gives few hints. The form is frankly suggested by the action of the poem, while the contents reflect its joyous idyllic spirit in a most picturesque way. These qualities were still further shown in his next orchestral work, "Endymion's Narrative," performed by the Boston Symphony Orchestra in 1903, and afterwards by several other organizations. Another and more recent orchestral work of great power and beauty is founded on Walt Whitman's poem, "The Mystic Trumpeter." This work has been performed by the principal orchestras of this country, and by several in Europe. It remained, however, for Converse's opera, "The Pipe of Desire," to establish his reputation on a firm and permanent basis. Though hampered by a rather ineffective libretto (by George Barton) he shows in this piece true dramatic fire, power of characterization and constructive skill, remarkably varied and interesting harmonic and rhythmic ideas, to which is added a flood of brilliant orchestral color. This opera was performed in Boston in 1906 by a company of singers specially organized for the purpose.

It would be an interesting experiment for some of the managers, who are bewailing the dearth of dramatic novelties, to give this opera a professional production.

Another work for the stage (from which has been arranged a Suite in concert form) is the incidental music to Percy MacKaye's "Jeanne d'Arc" which was played by Julia Marlowe and Sothern during the season of 1906 and 1907. Converse has succeeded in giving to this piece a romantic, old world atmosphere, quite unusual in incidental music for the stage. His latest work is a short oratorio, "Job," which he composed for the Worcester Festival of 1907, and to be first performed at that time. It is his first effort in the wielding of large choral masses, but the score shows that he can use this material with a firm hand.

It is fortunate, not only for Converse but for American Musical Art, that he is able to devote himself almost exclusively to composition, unhampered by more material considerations. He has, however, since 1901 held the position of assistant professor of music at Harvard, and during a part of that time also, has been an instructor in Harmony and Composition at the New England Conservatory of Music.

Converse is above all a worker, as is shown by the list of large works completed during his comparatively short musical career. Admirable as this is, it is of less importance than the promise of his future, for with such talent, such an equipment, and such tireless energy, it is safe to predict for Converse an eventual recognition as one of the leaders of Musical Art.

This group of men, most of whom belonged to the same generation, were all living in Boston between 1890 and 1897. They knew each other well, for most of them belonged to the same club, and many a night after a Symphony concert they might have been seen gathered about the same table in convivial intercourse, whetting each other's wits with thrust and parry — rejoicing in each other's successes, and working for them too, but ever ready with the cooling compress of gentle humor or sarcasm if perchance a head showed an undue tendency to enlarge. And in that invigorating atmosphere of mutual respect and honest criticism, they worked with joy and enthusiasm, knowing that if only their work was good enough it would be pretty sure of a hearing sooner or later.

And so, one by one they found their way to the programs of the Symphony concerts, of the Kneisel Quartet, of the Handel and Haydn Society, and thence to the other cities of America, as well as to those of Europe.

It was to this group of "boys," as he called them, that Theodore Thomas was introduced in 1892 while on his way to his summer home. After that he was often with them in the spring and autumn, to their great delight and edification. On one memorable occasion he sat with them until two in the morning, with the score of Beethoven's ninth symphony in front of him, pointing out with reverent care the details of orchestral nuance as he had worked them out, his eyes flashing with enthusiasm as he lived the music over in his mind. Beethoven was his god and it was easy to see that he loved him "with all his heart, and with all his soul, and with all his mind."

In October, 1904, he was with them for the last time. Yet once more he came, but it was to his last sleep in Mt. Auburn.

Of this circle of men, only a few now remain in Boston. Great institutions have claimed some of them, where they are wielding a powerful influence for the good of music in this country. Some are leading active musical lives as conductors and virtuosos, but Boston can no longer claim them for her own. One has passed on, and another, perhaps the most gifted of all, passed into the shadow where we mourned him as lost even while he was still with us.

But there are promising signs that the vacancies will soon be filled. Boston, with its splendid orchestra, its remarkable libraries, and its unrivaled advantages for musical education, is fertile soil for the young musician. She has produced poets, painters and philosophers. Why not a great composer also?

[Editor's Note.—Mr. Chadwick, with a modesty which is understandable and doubtless admirable but which, nevertheless, causes a distinct shortcoming in his interesting and authoritative article on the Boston group of American composers, has omitted mention of himself, and the prominent part he and his works have played in the development of our native school of creative music. He writes of the performing in the seventies of the first symphony of John K. Paine, and of the "Hiawatha" Overture and the "Redemption Hymn" of James C. D. Parker, and points to these as the significant beginnings of our present day development along creative musical lines, but he neglects to mention that his own "Rip Van Winkle" Overture which he had composed in Leipsic and which in 1879 received highly praised performance there, also had presentation by the Harvard Musical Association in Boston and proved such a decided success that a repetition at a subsequent concert was unavoidable. The following year it was accorded a third hearing, this time under his own direction at the festival of the Handel and Haydn Society. Surely if the works of Paine and Parker meant much for native music at this time — and they did —

the Chadwick overture was "not a whit less significant." That it was with Mr. Chadwick, that Horatio Parker, Arthur Whiting, Wallace Goodrich, F. S. Converse and Henry Hadley studied in the formative days of their creative activity, makes the influence he has exerted upon the music of the United States greater perhaps than has been that of any of his colleagues he has mentioned in his essay. He has produced not only music of worth but also musicians who stand for the best and ablest that the country can boast. His compositions include notable works in almost every department of music save possibly those of opera and oratorio, and his activities as conductor and as pedagogue have been both important and highly successful. He stands easily among the foremost musical talent the country has produced, and no essay on our native composers, no matter how brief, would be in anywise complete without mention of him and what he has achieved.—W. L. HUBBARD.]

MUSIC IN THE PUBLIC SCHOOLS

FRANK DAMROSCH.

In the march of progress which has carried American civilization to its present position of equality among the nations of the earth, there is no factor more interesting, more valuable or significant than the advance in the general culture of music through the medium of the public schools.

To appreciate properly the conditions under which this development has taken place, it will be desirable to compare them with those of Europe, or at least with those in two or three European countries holding the foremost position in musical culture.

We find in Germany, France and Italy the results of a gradual growth, beginning in the misty period of medieval minstrelsy, of bard and troubadour, of Meistersinger and Minnesinger, but above all in the natural effort of the people to find expression of their feelings in a more satisfactory medium than was afforded by their limited vocabulary—namely, in the Folk-song. Such songs can only be created under conditions which exist no longer in these modern days of railroads, telegraphs and other means of rapid intercommunication.

A people, homogeneous in race, language and custom, living for centuries without admixture of foreign elements, enjoying the same pleasures, suffering the same griefs, praying to the same God and loving the same measure of soil upon which they dwell and where have dwelt their fathers for generations, their fatherland,— such a people could and did create folk-songs.

These songs were transmitted from generation to generation, and became, so to speak, the soul language of the people. Upon these folk-songs was built the structure of musical art for which these nations are famous, but more than that, they are the cornerstones, nay, the very foundations for the musical life of these people today.

In America conditions are different. True, our population has sprung from the same roots as did these European nations, but it came here in small bodies, in isolated families, as individuals, not in the nature of a "Voelkerwanderung" or simultaneous migration of a whole people. While at times certain races predominated in certain portions of this continent, such as the French in the North, the Spaniards in the South, the Dutch on the Hudson and the English on Massachusetts Bay, there various elements became commingled and the heterogeneous mass which resulted not only could not create its own songs but could not even retain the old songs of the countries whence its component members had sprung. For there were different skies, different trees, different soil and altogther new conditions. This was no land of legend — of a golden past, but the land of the stern, exacting present with its problems and anxieties and, perhaps, its golden future. But, alas, the golden past was one of golden dreams, while the golden future which beckoned here was the hard, metallic one of real gold, and its chink drowned out the sweeter, fainter sounds of human sentiment all too quickly.

So it came that the American people, as a people, became practically songless. The few localities in which the people. being homogeneous, could and did sing their own songs, such as the Creoles and the Canadian French, could not affect the general condition. How then could music enter the life of the people and exert its benign, ameliorating and uplifting influence? Sporadic appearances of musical virtuosos, of Italian, French or German operatic performances, of symphonic productions before a limited contingent of music lovers, while delightful, interesting and instructive, cannot affect the people in general. That can be accomplished only by causing the people themselves to be musically active and, that once accomplished, music will become here, as it was in the old countries across the sea, part of the people's life and its best and truest means of expression.

The recognition of this fact by Lowell Mason led to the first efforts to popularize music by teaching large numbers of people, men, women and children, to sing from notes.

At the age of 20, Lowell Mason began to teach singing classes in his leisure hours. He was at that time, 1812, clerk in a bank in Savannah, Ga. After his return to Boston, in 1827, he became the most active influence in the musical development of that city. Together with some of the prominent musicians and music lovers he organized the Boston Academy of Music.

The plan of operation of this organization is stated in its first annual report as follows:

1. To establish schools of vocal music for juvenile classes.

2. To establish similar schools for adult classes.

3. To form a class for instruction in the methods of teaching music, which may be composed of teachers, parents, and all other persons desirous to qualify themselves for teaching vocal music.

4. To form an association of choristers, and leading members of choirs, for the purpose of improvement in conducting and performing sacred music in churches.

5. To establish a course of popular lectures on the nature and objects of church music and style of composition and execution appropriate to it, with experimental illustrations by the performance of a select choir. These lectures might be extended to a great variety of subjects, such as the style

of sacred poetry, the adaptation of music, the prevailing defects on this subject, and the means of remedying them.

6. To establish a course of scientific lectures, as soon as circumstances shall permit, for teachers, choristers, and others desirous of understanding the science of music.

7. To establish exhibitions or concerts.

(1) Of juvenile and adult classes, to show the results of instruction.

(2) Of select performers, as specimens of the best style in the performance of ordinary church music.

(3) Of large numbers collected semi-annually or annually, for the performance of social, moral, and sacred music of a simple kind.

8. To introduce vocal music into schools, by the aid of such teachers as the Academy may be able to employ, each of whom shall instruct classes alternately in a number of schools.

9. To publish circulars and essays, either in newspapers and periodicals, or in the form of tracts and books for instruction, adapted to the purposes of the Academy.

It will be seen from this, that a broad, thorough and comprehensive plan of musical education was undertaken by the Academy, a work which was destined to produce most beneficial results not only in Boston but throughout the length and breadth of this continent.

The moving spirit in these efforts was Lowell Mason. He wrote and compiled collections of sacred music and other choral works required as material for his classes. He organized singing schools for adults, for children, for choristers and for teachers and taught them to sing from notes according to a newly developed system, based on Pestalozzian ideas. He convinced people that music could become their common property by giving them the key which opened their minds to the understanding of its simple theory and their eyes, ears and throat to its practical manifestations.

In his day, in Europe as well as in America, it was the common belief that only those specially gifted by nature could ever learn to sing from notes at sight. It required not a little confidence and courage to combat this idea and to prove its fallacy.

The most important service rendered by the Boston Academy of Music was its effort to influence the school authorities to introduce the systematic instruction in singing in the public schools. After much discussion and strong opposition, the following resolution was adopted by the school committee of Boston on January 17, 1832:

" Resolved, That one school from each district be selected for the introduction of systematic instruction in vocal music, under the direction of a committee to consist of one from each district and two from the standing committee."

Although the recommendations of the Academy were not fully carried out, the results were sufficiently encouraging, and a second and stronger effort was made in 1836 in a memorial to the school committee.

In an interesting paper by A. W. Braxley in The Musician, entitled " The Inception of Public School Music in America," he refers to this memorial and to the report of the committee which took it under consideration, and this is such an excellent exposition of the subject that the excerpts quoted therein are herewith reproduced:

"After mature deliberation and a careful scrutiny of arguments and evidence, the committee are unanimously of opinion that it is expedient to comply with the request of the petitioners. They are well aware the cause which they support can find no favor from a board like this, except so far as it reaches the convictions through the doors, not of the fancy, but of the understanding.

"And in regarding the effect of vocal music, as a branch of popular instruction, in our public schools, there are some practical considerations, which in the opinion of your committee are deserving of particular attention.

"Good reading, we all know, is an important object in the present system of instruction in our schools. And on what does it depend? Apart from emphasis, on two things mainly; modulation and articulation. Now modulation comes from the vowel sounds, and articulation from the consonant sounds of the language chiefly. Dynamics, therefore, or that part of vocal music which is concerned with the force and delivery of sounds, has a direct rhetorical connection. In fact, the daily sounding of the consonant and vowel sounds, deliberately, distinctly, and by themselves, as the committee has heard them sounded in the music lessons given according to the Pestalozzian system of instruction, would, in their opinion, be as good an exercise in the elements of harmonious and correct speech as could be imagined. Roger Ascham, the famous schoolmaster and scholar of the Elizabethan age, and surely no mean judge, holds this language: 'All voices, great and small, base and shrill, weak and soft, may be helped and brought to a good point by learning to sing.' The committee, after attentive observation, confess themselves of this opinion.

"There is another consideration not unworthy of remark. 'Recreation,' says Locke, 'is not being idle, as any one may observe, but easing the weary part by change of business.' This reflection, in its application to the purposes of instruction, contains deep wisdom. An alternation is needed in our schools, which without being idleness shall yet give rest. Vocal music seems exactly fitted to afford that alternation. A recreation, yet not a dissipation of the mind — a respite, yet not a relaxation — its office would thus be to restore the jaded energies, and send back the scholars with invigorated powers to other more laborious duties.

"There is one other consideration to which the committee ask the serious attention of the board. It is this: By the regulations of the school committee it is provided that in all the public schools the day shall open with becoming exercises of devotion. How naturally and how beautifully vocal music would mingle with these exercises; and what unity, harmony and meaning might thus be given to that which, at present, it is feared, is too often found to be a lifeless or an unfruitful service, need only be suggested to be understood. The committee asks the board to pause, and consider whether the importance has been sufficiently looked to, of letting in a predominant religious sentiment, independently of all forms of faith, to preside over the destinies of our schools.

"And now, before proceeding further, let us consider briefly the objections which have been urged against the adoption of vocal music into our system of public education. It is then objected that we aim at that which is impracticable, that singing depends upon a natural ear for music, without which all instruction will be useless. If musical writers and teachers are to be believed, the fact is not so. Undoubtedly in this as in other branches, Nature bestows an aptitude to excel, on different individuals, in very different degrees. Still, what is called a musical ear is mainly the result of cultivation. The ear discriminates sounds as the eye colors. They may both be educated. Early impressions can create an ear for music. It is with learning to sing as with acquiring the pronunciation of a foreign language. Instruction, to be available, must be given while the organs have the flexibility of youth. To learn late in life is generally to learn not at all. There may be cases, it is true, of some who from their earliest years defy efforts of instruction, like those who come into the world maimed in other senses; they are, however, rare. They are the unfortunate exceptions to a general rule.

"But it is said, the time spent would be quite inadequate to the end proposed; that the labor of a life is needed to form the musician. The answer to this objection is, that it mistakes the end proposed, which is not to form the musician. Let vocal music, in this respect, be treated like the other regular branches of instruction. As many probably would be found to excel in music as in arithmetic, writing, or any of the required studies, and no more. All cannot be orators, nor all poets, but shall we not, therefore, teach the elements of grammar, which orators and poets in common with all others use? It should never be forgotten that the power of understanding and appreciating music may be acquired, where the power of excelling in it is found wanting.

"Again it is objected, if one accomplishment is introduced into the schools, why not another? If instruction is given in vocal music why should it not be given in dancing also? The answer simply is, because music is not dancing; because music has an intellectual character which dancing has not, and above all, because music has its moral purposes which dancing has not. Drawing stands upon a very different footing. Drawing, like music, is not an accomplishment merely; it has important uses, and if music be successfully introduced into our public schools, your committee express the hope and conviction that drawing sooner or later will follow."

The committee subjoined the following resolutions:

"Resolved, That in the opinion of the school committee it is expedient to try the experiment of introducing vocal music, by public authority, as part of the system of public instruction, into the public schools of this city.

"Resolved, That the experiment be tried in the four following schools: The Hancock School for girls, in Hanover Street; the Eliot School for boys, in North Bennet Street; the Johnson School for girls, in Washington Street, and the Hawes School for boys and girls, at South Boston.

"Resolved, That this experiment be given in charge to the Boston Academy of Music, under the direction of this board; and that a committee of five be appointed from this board to confer with the Academy, arrange all necessary details of the plan, oversee its operation, and make quarterly report thereof to this board.

"Resolved, That the experiment be commenced as soon as practicable after the passing of these resolutions, and be continued and extended as the board may thereafter determine.

"Resolved, That these resolutions be transmitted to the City Council, and that it be respectfully requested to make such appropriation as may be necessary to carry this plan into effect."

On the following 19th of September (1837) this report was considered and accepted by the school board, and the resolutions, as they came from the committee, passed. But failing to obtain from the City Council the appropriations necessary to enable them to carry their plans into effect, on the scale contemplated in the resolutions, the measure was for the time defeated. In the meantime, one of the professors, Mr. Lowell Mason of the Academy, offered to give instruction gratuitously in one of the schools, to test the experiment, and at the quarterly meeting of the board, held in November of the same year, 1837, resolutions upon this subject were passed as follows:

"Resolved, That in the opinion of the school committee, it is expedient that the experiment be tried of introducing instruction in vocal music, by public authority, as part of the system of public instruction, into the public schools of this city.

"Resolved, That the experiment be tried in the Hawes School in South Boston, under the direction of the subcommittee of that school and the committee on music, already appointed by this board."

The Musical Magazine, an excellent publication of that period, in its issue of July 6, 1839, p. 220, expresses its appreciation as follows:

"The introduction of vocal music in public schools when well conducted exerts a powerful influence towards rendering both the taste for and knowledge of music more general and more popular. It will teach people that it is not absolutely necessary to have a fine voice in order to be able to take part in a chorus or other concerted vocal piece. They will learn that almost every one, by being properly taught in early life, can acquire enough of skill and flexibility, to enable him not only to derive pleasure himself from engaging in a musical performance but to give pleasure to others. They will also find that something besides a voice is necessary to make a successful performance; that a fine voice is only a beautiful but dead instrument which must be vivified by soul and feeling, and cultivated and brought under command, in order that one may sing with feeling and expression. This will have the general tendency to introduce a more correct judgment in regard to music, and a purer delight in the enjoyment of it. In this way, it will not be long before instruments will be brought in requisition and amateurs will be more and more taking their attention to the study and practise of them. To the exertions of the Academy of Music, undoubtedly, we are chiefly indebted for the introduction of music in the schools. They have thus taken upon themselves the heavy responsibility of a most important experiment, the good or ill success of which must exert the strongest influence on the future destinies of the art among us."

Lowell Mason became Superintendent of Music of the Boston schools and not only systematized the instruction so that every child was taught to sing and read music suited to his comprehension, but also organized classes for the preparation of teachers.

The following extract from the advertisement of the Boston Academy of Music will show the scope and tendency towards general musical culture of these classes:

TEACHERS' CLASS FOR 1839.

A Course of Instruction to Teachers of Vocal Music will commence on Tuesday, August 20th, at 10 o'clock a. m., and will continue daily for ten days, as follows, viz.:

1. Lectures on the Elementary Principles of Music.

2. Exercises in Singing, designed to improve the taste and promote a correct manner of performance in sacred and secular music.

3. Rudiments of Harmony and Thoroughbass.

4. Meetings of the class for the discussion of musical subjects.

5. It is expected, also, that there will be public performances of music by the class.

The whole course will be adapted to the wants of teachers of Singing Schools, consisting of either adult or juvenile singing classes; or for such teachers of Common Schools, male or female, as are desirous of introducing music as a regular branch of instruction, etc.

Having now reviewed the early history of the introduction of the systematic study of vocal music in the schools of Boston, and noted the praiseworthy efforts of Lowell Mason and his colaborers of the Boston Academy of Music it will be proper to investigate the development of the methods which produced such remarkable results in the schools of Boston, Cincinnati and such other cities as patterned their instruction in music after similar models.

Mason announced that, by pursuing the Pestalozzian method, every child, not physically incapacitated, could learn to sing and to read from notes. This claim was received with general incredulity. The majority of persons, including professional musicians, believed that the musical ear, i. e., the appreciation of pitch relations, rhythm and harmony — was innate and could not be developed except when it was already strongly in evidence. The only way to combat this attitude was to demonstrate its falsity, and Mason lost no time in doing so in the Boston schools.

Appreciating that the most direct way to reach the comprehension of children was through the senses and faculties, rather than through their reasoning powers, he taught them by a series of concrete musical phenomena.

Taking the major scale as a whole, it presented to the child a tune easily sung and easily remembered. This tune or scale afforded a standard of measurement of the relations of the tones of the scale with each other. By means of daily exercise these relations or, as they are technically called, intervals, became thoroughly familiar. In other words, in place of the more or less correct guessing of the so-called "musical" person in singing intervals, there appeared a definite, concrete conception, based upon the never varying tone relationships of the scale. As an aid to the learner the Guidonian syllables do, re, mi, fa, sol, la, si were employed to facilitate the fixing of the position of each tone in the scale, do always representing the first tone, the key note or tonic.

Every elementary musical fact or phenomenon was first sung and listened to before it was discussed or expressed in symbols. The child learned by doing.

Since Mason's time innumerable "methods" of instruction in music for public schools have sprung up, but all, with scarcely an exception, are based on these same simple pedagogic principles, varying among themselves only in the diversity of their application, and in the musical and artistic value of the exercises and songs provided in the text-books.

They were prepared for the most part by colaborers and pupils of the great master spirit — Lowell Mason, prominent among them being such men as Luther W. Mason, who distinguished himself by his work in Japan as well as in Boston, where he directed for many years the music in the common schools; Julius Eichberg, a musician of German birth and training, who, in charge of the music in the high schools did much to elevate the taste and to cultivate the music of the great German composers; H. E. Holt, one of the most remarkable and inspiring teachers; Charles Aiken, a pioneer in school music teaching in Cincinnati, and many others, too numerous to mention.

These men, gifted with magnetic personality, great ability in teaching, enthusiastic and at the same time convincing in their logic, were able to vitalize the most inert bodies of adults or children into performances truly remarkable.

Not only did they organize and systematize the regular work of instruction, but they arranged great festivals in which as many as 1200 children would sing in chorus. The music at these occasions was usually of excellent quality and tended not a little to raise the standards not only of the children performing it but also of the parents and friends who were impressed and inspired by its stirring performance.

Without entering into the characteristics of the various "methods" employed at the present time, it may prove of interest to outline briefly the successive steps or course of study adopted by the majority of schools and the manner of presenting the subject generally used.

As a foundation for all musical study it is necessary to create the appreciation of the beautiful in sound and at the same time to make the child realize that music is intended as a vehicle for self-expression. The child learns these things by means of the rote song. This is a song learned by imitation. It is carefully selected with a view to melodic beauty and simple but well marked rhythm, a text which interests and stimulates the imagination and a tone compass which lies easily within the child's voice range. This was formerly placed too low in pitch, but now, in order to develop the softer, more flute-like tone registers and to avoid the harsher and throaty "chest tones," as they are often called, the range of pitch generally comprises the octave from E flat in the fourth space of the treble clef to E flat on the first line.

The child thus learns to sing songs with a soft, musical quality of tone and with animation and interest. He learns to discriminate between musical and harsh tones and, by becoming interested in the subject, tune and rhythm of the song, to express his own mood in it as though it were a spontaneous effort.

The song as such should be the beginning and end of all musical instruction in the school. All musical conceptions should be based on it, and all technical drill should directly apply to it, and songs should be the ever present manifestation of music in the school.

After six months or a year of this singing of rote songs the child is ready to begin the study of the elementary facts of music. The scale, introduced as a song, furnishes the materials as described above. Each tone of the scale is brought into relation with every other tone and thus grouped in intervals, as, for instance, the child will sing at the dictation of the teacher do, re, mi, fa, then do, fa, and, by frequent repetition, will soon be able to sing do, fa without first going up the steps of the scale.

When sufficient facility in singing these tone combinations at the teacher's dictation has been attained, the next step is to name and to represent them by their symbols, the notes. In the application of the absolute pitch names, namely the letter names, c, d, e, f, g, a, b and their modifications with sharp and flat which are applied to tones of definite pitch regardless of their position in a scale, as opposed to the singing syllables do, re, mi, etc., which are always applied to the successive steps of the scale, do always representing the key note, the child proceeds always from the sound itself — which by this time is a familiar object — to its attendant theoretic adjuncts. In this manner every technical term and every symbol is directly associated with a concrete musical conception.

The position of the notes on the staff, the clef, the character of the note in its representation of relative duration in time, such as whole, half, quarter and eighth notes, the meter signatures, etc., are now gradually introduced, synchronic with the pupil's apprehension of the facts of musical ideas which they represent.

Every new conception is exemplified by its practical application in exercises and songs and the pupil is stimulated to give his own effort and individuality to the greatest possible extent.

Taught in this manner, music becomes one of the most valuable physical, mental and spiritual exercises in the curriculum of the school.

Singing, when properly conducted, promotes deep and regular breathing, conducive to the better circulation and aëration of the blood. The singing from notes requires great concentration of mind, quickness of vision and activity of brain. The voice is attuned to musical vocalization; the enunciation of consonants is made clear and distinct, and thus is gained a refining influence on speech.

Finally, the child's imagination is kindled and developed. His æsthetic sense is quickened, and his power of self-expression is greatly increased. In addition to these advantages, class or choral singing inculcates subordination, discretion and the recognition of the value of co-operation for a good or beautiful purpose.

It will not be necessary to pursue the method of instruction in its more advanced forms, as it would lead too far for the present purpose. Suffice it to say that the same pedagogic principles are applied throughout and, whenever logically, systematically and faithfully carried out, the result is a school whose upper grade pupils are able to sing any song, duet or part-song of moderate difficulty at sight.

A very important item in the musical training of a child at school is the material used in instruction, for this must be provided in ample quantity, of good quality and should be thoroughly well adapted to the method pursued.

Since the day of Lowell Mason many text-books and series of text-books have been published, generally compiled, written and edited by supervisors of music to harmonize with their individual ideas and introduced into their own schools and those of their pupils or adherents. These publications show, on the whole, a high average of merit considering the fact that only a small percentage of their authors were really thoroughly trained musicians, but rather pedagogues with musical proclivities. Certain it is, that there has been constant improvement in musical contents and pedagogic value and in this respect America stands in the foremost rank today among the nations of the world.

The material usually employed in the schools consists of charts for use in the primary grades in order to insure better concentration than would be possible with individual text-books; primers or first readers, and successive volumes appropriate to the higher grades. Then there are collections of songs for the Kindergarten, for use as rote songs, for assembly, for use of the school glee clubs for high schools, etc.

This material is usually of excellent typography, substantially bound and often artistically illustrated. The strong competition among publishers, while it may have some objectionable features, has tended to a truly remarkable improvement in every detail of the musical text-book.

Having now reviewed cursorily the musical training of the child in the public schools it may not be amiss to glance at the immediate practical manifestations.

The first valuable result is that the child gains a large repertory of good songs which he can sing not only in school but at home or at play. His taste is improved, and his æsthetic sense generally placed on a higher plane.

His most enjoyable musical exercise, however, is the singing in chorus, both because of the stimulation which comes with the participation of large numbers, and because of the element of harmony which is thereby introduced.

This exercise usually forms a part of the morning assembly and to the visitor who knows its possibilities it will be as a barometer to the degree of discipline, thoroughness and refinement of the school, its principal, teachers and pupils.

When these qualities are present to a proper degree, the school assembly is one of the most beautiful and impressive manifestations of our educational system.

The orderly, symmetric marching into place, the soft and pure singing of the opening hymn, the short reading from the Scriptures, the musical response. Then the salute to the flag, spoken or sung, the patriotic song, not shouted, but sung with spirit and enthusiasm, a chorus or part-song for two or three part chorus, a brief address by the principal or a distinguished visitor, a closing song and the march back to the class rooms. This is an opening of the day which cannot but react favorably on the pupil and teacher.

Special programs are prepared for the national holidays and for special school events, such as closing or graduation exercises. In addition to these larger choral exercises, many schools organize glee clubs from the upper grades of the school, selecting the best voices and readers for this purpose. These clubs contribute greatly to the pleasure and entertainment of the school, its guests and themselves. But the most beautiful and effective employment of large numbers of children are the choruses used to celebrate great civic events or festivals. When Admiral Dewey was welcomed by New York a chorus of 3000 school children sang " See the Conquering Hero Comes " and other songs so beautifully that the Admiral was moved to tears by their sweet, pure, childish voices and their enthusiastic greeting.

Such participation of children in great civic functions should be encouraged, as it engenders that pride in citizenship which is so essential to the performance of its duties later on.

In schools where a sufficient number of pupils are able to play violin or other stringed or wind instruments, small orchestras are frequently organized which contribute not a little to the pleasure of the school. Such orchestras are more common in the high schools than in the elementary schools, and they often reach a high degree of proficiency.

It is of the utmost benefit to the children to hear as much good music, whether sung or played on the piano or any other instrument, as possible, and some principals, recognizing this, arrange recitals by good artists or amateurs who volunteer to perform for the children. Often, too, a short biographical sketch of a composer with a simple explanation of the contents of the composition to be performed precedes the recital. All such influences are of the greatest value and will go far towards making music part of the people's life.

Having now examined the methods employed and the results sought in the introduction of music in public education, it will be interesting to note by what agencies and what kind of organization this is carried into effect and how it is made to co-ordinate and articulate with the general school system.

These are two ways in which the instruction in music may be carried on in the schools: by a special music teacher, employed solely for this purpose, or by the regular class teacher. The former would, under favorable conditions, be preferable, as not every class teacher has that natural gift, taste and training which is desirable in the teaching of art subjects. But in actual practise the latter plan has proved itself to be not only more economical — a weighty consideration with those entrusted with the management of public schools — but the superior discipline and consequent concentration obtaining as a rule under the regular teacher to whose ways the pupils are accustomed, outweighs, or at least balances, the lack of thorough musical training.

The class teacher is usually trained to a more or less limited extent in the elementary science of music in the normal or teachers' training schools instituted by the different States of the Union. This is, however, rarely sufficient to fit the graduate of these schools for teaching the subject and it becomes necessary, therefore, to provide adequate special instruction and supervision. This is secured by most cities of 8000 inhabitants and over by the employment of one or more so-called "special teachers of music," or "supervisors or directors of music," whose duty it is to teach the class teachers in conferences, class lessons, model lessons, by lectures, etc.; to supervise their work by regular visits; to select the proper material for instruction and explain its proper use and to aid, advise, encourage and stimulate the teachers.

Under such guidance, the regular teacher often produces excellent results and indeed it may be said that generally those teachers who excel in ability in the other branches of the curriculum, also prove to be the best teachers in music.

It will easily be seen that this system of supervision can be made very effective and is, of course, most economical, as it would entail a heavy expense to provide a special teacher for each school.

As it is, cities of from 8000 to 200,000 inhabitants usually employ only one special teacher of music, the salary ranging from $300 to $2500 per annum. Cities of 200,000 to 1,000,000 employ from two to seventeen special teachers averaging from $600 to $2500 in salary and cities of over a million in population usually have one or more supervisors or directors of music with salaries of from $3000 to $5000, who direct and supervise the work of numerous assistant special teachers. New York, for example, has three such directors of music with a salary of $4000 each and 52 special teachers whose salaries range from $1000 to $2160. Inasmuch as these 52 teachers have to supervise the instruction in music given by over 11,000 regular teachers, it will be seen that over 200 teachers and about 10,000 children fall to the share of each, and consequently it is of the utmost importance that the work should be done with the greatest possible system and regularity. To insure this the directors of music are employed to unify, organize and systematize the work of their assistants.

The task of these directors and special teachers would be a comparatively easy one were it merely a question of teaching the children, for these are not merely willing but anxious to learn to sing and are quick to grasp and well able to do everything comprised in the course of study in music. The training of the class teachers — especially in a very large school system like that of New York, in which the systematic study of music was introduced only ten years ago — is a far more difficult matter. The graduates of the modern normal or training schools are fairly well prepared to teach music, but the majority of those who began to teach ten, twenty or thirty years ago generally know little or nothing of music and are often adverse to undertake to teach a subject with which they have been unfamiliar all their lives.

In spite of these conditions, the beneficent culture of music in the schools has made wonderful progress and there are few educators today who do not look upon it as one of the most valuable factors in the training of the child.

It is needless to say that the personality and equipment of the music teacher governs to a large extent the success of the work. The more magnetic the personality, the more courteous the manner and the more interesting and inspiring the instruction, the more willing and responsive will be those who are to be instructed. Probably no other class of teachers is so well qualified in these respects as the music teachers, for the reason, perhaps, that music itself tends to refine and inspire those who practise it. But in one respect there is still much to be desired. The majority of the special teachers of music spring from the ranks of the regular teachers; those who have more or less musical talent and therefore find this work congenial. Their training as musicians, however, is often very fragmentary and inadequate and, while their pedagogic training and knowledge are good and serve to make their work technically satisfactory, their influence in the direction of art culture is not what it might be. The welding of the thorough musician with the pedagogue and psychologist makes the ideal teacher of music in schools, and this ideal is as yet rare in this country.

But no matter how excellent the music teacher, how willing the class teacher or how apt the children, the best results cannot be obtained without the hearty support and co-operation of the principal, superintendent and school board.

If one or all of these authorities look upon music as a "special" subject, a fad, a luxury, the plant nurtured in such stony ground will not flourish. It can only grow to full maturity and beauty when it receives the same consideration and care as do the other elementary subjects with which it should rank as coequal. It should be an indispensable part of the life of the school, correlated to the other subjects of study and so planned as to aid and not retard them. The clever principal can make music the vitalizing agent of the school by whose aid all tasks are accomplished willingly.

The duty of the school board should be to encourage the work in music by appropriations sufficient to secure the best teachers and to provide the best text-books in ample quantities. This will be found to be true economy, for the community will be enriched by a higher type of citizens as a result of the influence which music directly and indirectly exerts upon the children.

America is in need of music in the daily life of its people. The hard worker needs relaxation by doing something which turns his brain into a different channel and which gently stimulates while it does not excite. Music supplies this need better than any other agent, and there is no reason why it should not enter every home. Especially should vocal music be cultivated, and, if the children learn to sing from notes in school, it would be easy for members of the family and their friends to unite in duets, trios or part songs to the delight of all who participate and listen.

And blessed the community in which exists a chorus capable of singing the great choral works of the great masters of music. The cheap and vulgar vaudeville shows and stupid plays would soon lose their attraction.

The American people have every resource required for artistic development. They have a large and beautiful country, rich in all natural products; free institutions tending towards the higher mental, moral and social development of the citizens; pride in their homes and their country; strong family affection and patriotism; keen appreciation of the beautiful when awakened to its realization and comprehension and ample natural gifts for its production.

It is the general belief that America will soon furnish the greatest number of singers of the highest order.

But in order to bring these resources into operation, in order to awaken the latent, dormant musical powers of this nation, the children must be taught to sing and this must, of necessity, be the province of the public school and will prove to be one of its most notable and beneficent achievements.

MUSIC OF NORTH AMERICAN INDIANS

In treating of the subject of the history and evolution of music in America it is but natural to turn first to the music of the aborigine. Strictly speaking, the music of the American Indian has played little or no part in the development of our art music, and is introduced here only because of its interest as belonging to the aboriginal inhabitants of the country. Crude and primitive it was and crude and primitive it remains. Where the Indian has taken up the arts and civilization of the white man he has left behind him the peculiar features of his own arts and ceremonies. Thus it is that the music of the aborigine still remains as it was before the people of Europe had dreamed of the existence of this continent.

Research on the subject of Indian music has been made during the past few years by several American ethnologists and musicians. From the results of their study much has been learned of its derivation and characteristics. Much has been lost beyond recovery, but, as time goes on, that which has been saved will become of great historical value as touching the life and musical efforts of the American Indian. Civilization is fast driving him either to accept the ways of the white man or to complete extinction. As he disappears his music goes with him, and what is left remains but as an echo of the days when he roamed unmolested over the continent which has been wrested from him.

From what has been saved of the Indian music it is to be seen that much use was made of it by the people who gave it birth. Such as it was, it accompanied them from cradle to grave and played a vital part in their life. To the Indian, music acted as a means of communication between himself and the unseen but all-powerful spirits. Superstition is always rife among primitive peoples, and in invoking the aid of the spirits inhabiting the earth — air, fire and water — speech was not sacred enough for the purpose, so untutored man broke into song. This universal use made of music in all religious rites and ceremonies has been noted among all peoples from the earliest times. Making practically no advancement over the customs and usages of his forefathers of centuries ago, the Indian has continued to adhere to his primitive songs and musical utterances and, as far as may be learned, the Indian music of today remains just what it was before it ever greeted the ears of the white man.

For purposes of comparison, this music may be likened to that heard in Europe in the early centuries of the Christian era, when all the arts were subservient to that of war. Rude cradle songs were sung, as were also love songs of a kind, but the main use made of music was as an adjunct to the religious ceremonies and to those dealing with fighting and battle. Where the emotions are crude the expression of them will necessarily be so, and any individual coming of a civilized race would, on hearing the musical efforts of the Indian, instantly recognize them as the product of an uncultured people.

With the Indian, music never assumed an objective plane; it was cultivated simply as a means of expressing his subjective mood. There never was any effort at producing music for its own sake, but did he wish to make more impressive his religious songs and war songs he gave them a musical utterance, his naturally guttural voice but adding a touch of barbarism to them. On account of the Indian custom of strapping the pappoose or infant to a cradle-board and leaving him to swing from a bough or pole, cradle songs are comparatively rare. Where at all in use, they exhibit the same characteristics found in such songs the world over — a low croon, often sung impromptu, and with the idea of lulling the child to rest. When able to run about and play their childish games, simple songs and rhymes came into common use. Following the custom of children everywhere, they invent such songs as are fitting for the game then taking their attention, and at night the children are often entertained by some old myth or tale sung in a monotonous chant by one of the older members of the tribe.

In his early youth music again is closely associated with the life of the Indian. When the time comes for him to be initiated into the religious rites and mysteries of his tribe, the ceremonies connected therewith are performed with the aid of music, both vocal and instrumental. The love song is another musical product of his early manhood, for when the Indian youth decides that it is time for him to set up his own wigwam his love song, addressed to the maiden of his choice, may be heard in the early dawn when the women go to the spring for water. Or, if the youth feels incapable of a vocal declaration of his passion, he has recourse to the mystery whistle or flageolet and plays thereon his love calls.

Such customs, though still in use to some extent, are, with the Indian himself, rapidly dying out and may be spoken of in the past tense. Where the Indian has accepted the ways of the white man he has largely dropped his own individuality. Where he had his own particular and individual songs they have been lost with his other heritages. Indian songs were not, however, drifting bits of music that could be picked up anywhere and everywhere among the tribes indiscriminately. On the contrary, each and every song had its particular owner, who could, if he so chose, sell it to the member of another tribe, the sale involving on the part of the original owner some instruction as to its rendition.

As a rule, however, these songs belonged to societies, secular or religious; the Indian having a most complicated and highly developed ritual. Many of these songs are found to be peculiar to particular tribes or political organizations, or to some rite or ceremony, the medicine men having a monopoly of the religious songs. Songs of mourning frequently were rendered by women alone, such ceremonials among the Indian women being reminiscent of the "mourning women" of the Scriptures, while the historic songs hold within their themes elements and facts which link the Indian to American prehistoric times. The antiquity of many of these songs is shown by their occasionally containing words the meaning of which is entirely lost.

War is not conducive to the development of the gentler arts of any nation, and research discloses that the Indian has been no exception to this rule, for the more warlike tribes had few if any songs. It has been found that the Ojibways, the Zuni, the Moquis and the Omahas had a fairly large number, but the more aggressive Iroquois, Apaches and Comanches possessed little of song except that of a more primitive character and of the kind dedicated to war.

In addition to the religious songs, war songs, love songs, and songs of mourning, there were the mystery songs, which belonged exclusively to the medicine men, and the convivial or social songs which accompanied the games and which were used as exorcisms to secure good luck. Festive and solemn events were marked by their individual, standard song, which consisted of a few short words or a phrase or two, repeated many times, the one theme of the composition being insistently emphasized with much force. The rendition was characterized by sincerity, and in particular songs with a marked degree of pathos. Many of these songs, devoid of measure and rhyme as they were, have come down to posterity in the form of picture-writing, while the music is simplicity itself.

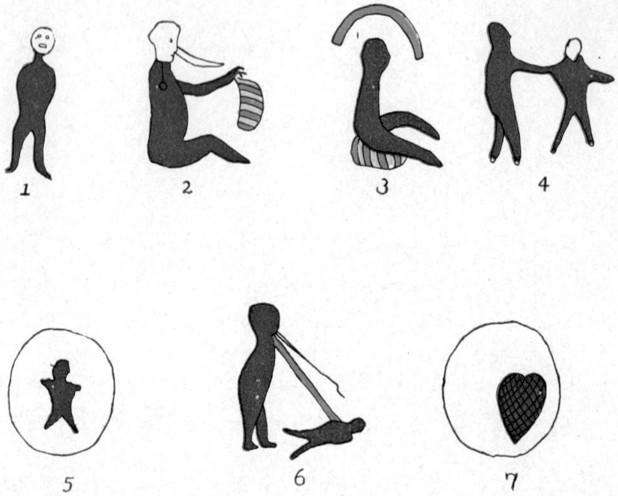

Fig. I

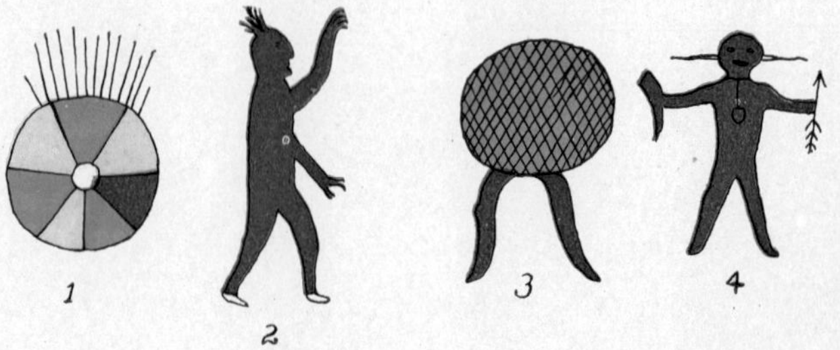

Fig. II

INDIAN SONG.

Figure I represents a love song, the free translation of which is:—

1. It is my form and person that makes me great.
2. Hear the voice of my song — it is my voice.
3. I shield myself in secret coverings.
4. All your thoughts are known to me — blush!
5. I could draw you hence, were you on a distant island;
6. Though you were on the other hemisphere.
7. I speak to your naked heart.

No. 1 represents one whose magic power charms the weaker sex. Hence this character instructs the singer to chant — It is my painting that makes me a god. No. 2, the charmer beating a magic drum, indicates — Hear the sounds of my voice, of my song; it is my voice. No. 3, showing him surrounded with a secret lodge — I cover myself in sitting down by her; No. 4, depicting the union of their affections, the two bodies being joined by one arm, represents the words — I can make her blush, because I hear all she says of me; No. 5, the girl upon an island — Were she on a distant island I could make her swim over; No. 6, his magic powers reaching her heart while she sleeps, is rudely translated — Though she was far off, even on the other hemisphere; No 7, a naked heart — I speak to your heart.

Figure II represents a war song Roughly translated the symbols mean:—

1. I am rising.
2. I take the sky, I take the earth.
3. I walk through the sky.
4. The Eastern Woman calls.

More freely it might read—

1. I am rising to seek the war-path.
2. The earth and the sky are before me.
3. I walk by day and by night.
4. And the evening star is my guide.

No. 1 represents the sun, the source of light and knowledge and a symbol of vigilance. No. 2 represents the warrior with one hand pointing to the heavens, the other to the earth, signifying his mighty power and dauntless prowess. No. 3 shows him stalking under the moon, during the hours best fit for secrecy and warlike achievements. No. 4, the warrior is personifying Venus, which is called the Eastern Woman or Evening Star, who is his guide and the witness of his heroic deeds.

Taken from Henry R. Schoolcraft's Information Respecting the History Condition and Prospects of the Indian Tribes of the United States, Vol. 1, pages 401-404.

The same chart is in Drake's Indian Tribes of the U. S. (a condensation of Schoolcraft's work), but without an explanation.

INDIAN SONG.

Figure I represents a love song, the free translation of which is:—

1. It is my form and person that makes me great.
2. Hear the voice of my song — it is my voice.
3. I shield myself in secret coverings.
4. All your thoughts are known to me — blush!
5. I could draw you hence, were you on a distant island;
6. Though you were on the other hemisphere.
7. I speak to your naked heart.

No. 1 represents one whose magic power charms the weaker sex. Hence this character instructs the singer to chant — It is my painting that makes me a god. No. 2, the charmer beating a magic drum, indicates — Hear the sounds of my voice, of my song; it is my voice. No. 3, showing him surrounded with a secret lodge — I cover myself in sitting down by her; No. 4, depicting the union of their affections, the two bodies being joined by one arm, represents the words — I can make her blush, because I hear all she says of me; No. 5, the girl upon an island — Were she on a distant island I could make her swim over; No. 6, his magic powers reaching her heart while she sleeps, is rudely translated — Though she was far off, even on the other hemisphere; No. 7, a naked heart — I speak to your heart.

Figure II represents a war song. Roughly translated the symbols mean:—

1. I am rising.
2. I take the sky, I take the earth.
3. I walk through the sky.
4. The Eastern Woman calls.

More freely it might read—

1. I am rising to seek the war-path.
2. The earth and the sky are before me.
3. I walk by day and by night.
4. And the evening star is my guide.

No. 1 represents the sun, the source of light and knowledge and a symbol of vigilance. No. 2 represents the warrior with one hand pointing to the heavens, the other to the earth, signifying his mighty power and dauntless prowess. No. 3 shows him stalking under the moon, during the hours best fit for secrecy and warlike achievements. No. 4, the warrior is personifying Venus, which is called the Eastern Woman or Evening Star, who is his guide and the witness of his heroic deeds.

Taken from Henry R. Schoolcraft's Information Respecting the History Condition and Prospects of the Indian Tribes of the United States, Vol. 1, pages 401-404.

The same chart is in Drake's Indian Tribes of the U. S. (a condensation of Schoolcraft's work), but without an explanation.

There is a certain consistency as well as import in these picture-songs. They inspire the singer to love, to adore the object of his affection or to perform deeds of combat and daring. These symbolic writings form the true key to the songs of the North American Indian, and show to what extent the neumic symbols were applied. It is one of the most primitive modes of annotation. The picture-writing was used only to recall to the reader ideas which already existed in his mind, and were well fitted for the Indian because of his disposition, which was pensive and reminiscent.

The Indian never devised any system of notation for expressing the melodies to his songs, these being carried in the memory and passed from one generation to the next by the medicine men or priests of the tribe, who frequently were chosen on account of their retentive memories and good voices. It is marvelous how so many songs could be retained through the passing years by this crude process of preservation.

Having little or nothing in the way of a fixed scale, the musical efforts of the Indian were rhythmical rather than melodic. In the rendition of his songs accompanied by the drum, voice and instrument were seldom in the same rhythm, this serving to create a peculiar effect. Although the difference is most pronounced, it does not impair the sense of symmetry. Where the melodies can be applied to our tonal system it is found that the majority are formed in the so-called pentatonic scale, a scale of five notes in which the fourth and seventh tones of our octave are missing. But in general the musical system of the Indian, if such it may be called, differs entirely from our own owing to the use of intervals less than the half tone, which is the smallest interval of which we take cognizance.

Some interesting experiments were conducted by Doctor Fewkes, who had Indians sing to piano acompaniment. It was found that very noticeable deflections in pitch were intentionally produced by the singers. In the rendition of his songs the Indian is guided entirely by his emotions, the effect of sentiment being to flatten the pitch, as seen in the love songs, while the emphasis used in the war songs called for a sharpening of the tone. The use of the falsetto voice also tended toward irregularities in this relation.

No harmonic efforts ever have been made by the Indian. Though it has been stated that he has an inherent feeling for harmony, it never has developed in any of his musical productions, for these are crudely melodious throughout, and though they may suggest harmonies to the cultured ear, there is no doubt that if the Indian had received the same suggestion he would have at least made some efforts in this direction. His songs are always rendered in unison and lose rather than gain by the process of harmonization.

With the Indian the dance was almost inseparable from his song. Religious songs and war songs invariably were accompanied by dancing, or the statement might be inverted and be equally correct, so close was the connection. Where the words of the song were improvised, interjections such as he, ha, heh, frequently were introduced, to better punctuate the rhythm. In fact some of the songs were sung throughout without words, or to words having no sense or meaning. In these wordless songs, the gentler emotions were sung to flowing vocables, while in the war songs they were aspirate and explosive.

Very crude were the instruments used by the Indians. The earliest explorers speak of the drum, and it is known that certain tribes used drums of two kinds. The mah-dwah-ke-quon, which was about two feet in length and made from a hollowed tree-trunk, had one end covered by a board, while over the other end was stretched an undressed deerskin on which to strike. This kind of drum, invariably met with among the Ojibways, was heard at sacred feasts only. The second kind, designated by the same tribe as ta-wae-gun, was made on the order of the common snare drum used by our military bands, and was the principal instrument at all festivals and on all amusement occasions.

Mr. Catlin, one of the first Americans to go to the far West for the purpose of studying the Indian in his native environment, gives a description of an instrument known as the mystery whistle. He speaks of it as being very ingeniously made, and says that the sound is produced on a principle entirely different from that employed in any wind instrument known among civilized inventions. He dwells particularly upon its peculiar sweetness of tone. He heard an Indian boy play it, and though making repeated efforts, he himself never succeeded in making a sound upon it. Miss Alice Fletcher, who spent some years studying the Indian in his native environment, probably had this instrument in mind when she wrote that "the native flageolet has proved a trusty friend to many a youth to whom nature had denied the power of expressing in vocal melody his fealty to the maiden of his choice."

The Indian also used another flute-like instrument, which was constructed of two pieces of cedar, each half round and then hollowed out until quite thin, and with four holes bored in it. The two parts were fastened together so as to form a tube, and sound being produced by blowing at the end. It is not known whether the design of this instrument was borrowed from that of the first white flute player who happened among the Indians, or whether it originated with the red man himself. Many of the tribes assert, however, that this instrument was "improved" after examples of like instruments used by the pale face. Another wind instrument is the war whistle, which was constructed of two clay pipes or tubes bound together side by side. It emitted two distinct sounds, one for battle and the other for retreat.

The rattle was also an instrument common among the Indians. By it they produced noise, if not music, to add to the enjoyment of their festivals. These rattles were of various kinds. The Algonquins used a gourd-shell in which a few dried beans were placed, while the turtle-shell was a favorite rattle among the Iroquois and other eastern tribes. This shell, with the skin attached was dried first, then a handful of flint corn was sewn up in the skin, and the skin of the neck stretched over a stick which served the purpose of a handle. The hoofs of animals, notably those of the deer, also were utilized by boring a hole in the narrow end of the hoofs and tying them to short sticks, which, being jerked up and down, produced a rattling sound.

For a long period, except from an ethnological point of view, research into the music of the North American Indian remained in abeyance. In the middle of the Seventeenth Century, the Jesuit missionaries, in their letters to the order in France, spoke of the native Indian music. They all speak of it as being somewhat heavy and grave in character, whether used in recreation or in devotion, yet they themselves made use of the Indian's song as a means of interesting him in their particular religious exercises.

These missionaries early discovered that the Indian was incapable of prolonged mental application, therefore they set all prayers to music, and succeeded most admirably by these means in interesting him in their form of worship. One of these missionaries, Father Mau, in writing to the Franciscan order in France, in 1735, says: "I often wish that the Rev. Father Landreau, who is so fond of well executed church music, could be present at our high mass; it would be a greater treat to him than anything to which he has yet listened. The men who lead off with the first verses he might take for a choir of cordeliers — Franciscan Friars — and the women for some great community of nuns. But what am I saying? Neither cordeliers nor nuns ever sang as do our Iroquois men and women. Their voices are both mellow and sonorous, and their ear is so correct that they do not miss a half tone in all their church hymns, which they know by heart."

Professor J. C. Fillmore and Mr. Edwin S. Tracy in later years have assisted Miss Alice C. Fletcher in her research in the domain of Indian song by harmonizing the melodies which she herself received from native sources. Mr. James R. Murie, an educated Pawnee, became her collaborator in recording the music of the rituals among the Omahas, the Dakotas, the Pawnees and other tribes. The songs belonging to the most important ceremonies were recorded by means of the graphophone, and then transcribed from the cylinders by Mr. Tracy, each transcription being verified by him from the singing of the Ku'rahus or medicine men.

During the past decade a few American composers have bestowed attention on the music of the aborigines with gratifying results. Among these the name of Edward MacDowell stands pre-eminent for his adaptation of the melodies of the American Indian to orchestral purposes. In the preface to his "Indian Suite" (Op. 48), Mr. MacDowell says:

"The thematic material of this work has been suggested for the most part by melodies of the North American Indians. Their occasional similarity to northern European themes seems to the author a direct testimony in corroboration of Thorfinnkarlsefin's saga. If separate titles for the different movements are desired, they should be arranged as follows: I, Legend; II, Love Song; III, In War-time; IV, Dirge; V, Village Festival."

In a quarterly published at Newton, Mass., in the interests of American compositions based on the folk-lore of the Indian, may be found a long list of more or less well-known writers who have made use of such material. Among the number may be mentioned Lawrence Gilman, Arthur Farwell, Campbell Tipton, Harvey W. Loomis and Edgar Stillman Kelley. None of these men, however, has won sufficient recognition as composers to attract unusual attention to their work in this field.

The most important work along lines suggestive of Indian music is Coleridge-Taylor's setting of Longfellow's "Hiawatha." In it the composer has made use of themes which, if not taken direct from Indian sources, are at least suggestive of such music. The text itself naturally would call for musical treatment after the manner of the music of the Indian.

NEGRO MUSIC AND NEGRO MINSTRELSY

While the songs of the American Indian are of questionable value musically, those of the negro, another peculiarly American song product, are of undoubted worth. The coming of the negro to America has served to introduce into our musical life features which are unique in the annals of history. From his advent may be traced influences which have had a marked effect in the production of music both of a popular and of a more pretentious character in this country.

America received its first importation of negro slaves in 1619 and these unfortunate people brought with them their own crude songs. Of all the undeveloped races the African negro seems to have been the most gifted musically, for his primitive melodies resemble those of the whites more closely than do those of any similar people. In his native home the negro made use of music in his incantations and religious observances much after the same manner as did the Indian in America. When first brought to this country it was but natural that he should cling to his Voodooism — the species of idolatry and superstition which constituted his religion. Connected with its rites were many weird chants which served to form the foundation of the music which developed under his new environment.

In spite of the continued contact with the whites, the negro melodies as we have them today still retain their exotic traits. In the older ones there is more of the barbaric character, while those of a later date show the influence of the music of the white masters. Again, in the dances of the negro are to be seen traces of their barbaric origin. The pantomime so generally associated with many songs points to derivation from the same sources. In common with those of all uncultured peoples, the negro melodies frequently are formed on the pentatonic scale, in which the fourth and seventh tones are omitted.

The first instruments used in this country by the negro slaves were patterned after those of the land from which they had come. Two kinds, or rather two sizes of drums were used, which were fashioned of hollowed logs, over one end of which was stretched a sheep or goat skin. These drums were not played in upright position but were laid on the ground and the player bestrode them, beating them with fists and feet, slowly on the large instrument and more rapidly on the smaller one. The small drum was often made from a section of the bamboo tree, hence the name bamboula, given to the dance which commonly was performed to the accompaniment of this drum.

Rattles similar to those of the Indian also were used. Another instrument, if such it may be called, was formed of the jawbone of some animal, such as the horse or mule, over the teeth of which a piece of metal was rattled. The morimbabrett was an instrument capable of producing something approaching melody. It was formed of a shallow box of thin wood about eight inches long by four or five wide, across which, under a single strand of wire, were placed several sections of reed of graduated lengths. The performer plucked the ends of the reeds with his thumb nails and so produced the music.

In Thomas Jefferson's Notes on Virginia (1784) he speaks of the negro as being naturally musical, and adds: "the instrument proper to them is the banjar, which they brought hither from Africa." This "banjar" or banjo was of four strings or possibly fewer in the earlier specimens; the head was covered with rattlesnake skin, the instrument in general being very similar to one in use by the Chinese. Late writers on the subject scout the idea of the banjo being the negroes' instrument, but there is no doubt that an instrument such as that described above was used by the slaves. Being of African origin it may naturally be supposed that it was tuned differently from our modern banjo and was played in the style of a melodic rather than of a harmonic instrument. The violin may be cited as a type of melodic instrument, as it is used principally to produce melody, while the banjo is commonly employed as a harmonic instrument, or one used in producing harmonies or chords. The musical efforts of the negro being essentially melodic, this may explain the stand taken by those who insist that the banjo was not devised by them.

Another instrument of the negro was a sort of Pan's pipe formed from two joints of the brake cane and designated quills. When he had become thoroughly familiar with the music of the whites, however, the negro seems to have found in the violin the instrument best suited to his needs. At the same time the triangle, bones, tambourine, jew's-harp, tin whistle, in fact all the "toy" instruments were brought into use.

It was not until about the middle of the Nineteenth Century that any effort was put forth in the direction of research regarding the music of the American negro. His songs had already become incorporated into the music of the whites and had been accepted as a part of our musical heritage. While not of strictly American origin they have undoubtedly gone to form the foundation of such folk-song literature as this country possesses.

The negro naturally is a care-free, happy, cheerful individual, but mirth and laughter find little expression in the song of a people long depressed with thoughts of exile, and unhappy under oppression with no promise of alleviation.

Songs born under such conditions naturally express, both in words and music, a spirit of resignation touched with yearnings to reach eventually the land of Canaan, which promised not so much a reward of virtue as freedom from bondage. That is why the great majority of slave songs are semi-religious in character. Where the negro did voice a happy mood his expression took the form of words conjured up by his ludicrous imagination and were humorous rather than witty.

In order to form a true conception of negro songs it is necessary to hear them sung by their creators, for the negro possesses a peculiar quality of voice which is next to impossible to imitate. He has, too, a manner of singing which is equally characteristic. Peculiar sounds are interjected, slurring from one note to another and swelling on emphatic words are common effects. When singing in chorus the leader starts the verse, the others joining in where fancy leads them, sometimes following the principal melody and again improvising parts, the general ensemble serving to produce unique harmony. It is strange how these untrained singers, in spite of their apparently haphazard manner of "joining in," will always keep the most perfect time and will rarely produce discords. In the matter of rhythm the negro seems to be more universally gifted than any other race.

The prevalent use of the minor mode is another characteristic of his music. It undoubtedly comes from two sources: first, from the fact that many of his melodies are formed in the pentatonic scale common to all uncultured peoples; second, on account of the sorrows and tribulations resultant from his particular environment, the minor key best expressing the feelings produced by such conditions. Triple time is rarely used, the large majority of songs having either two or four beats to the measure. Another feature of the rhythm is the common use of syncopations such as are found in the so-called "rag-time" music of today, which feature found its source in the negro melodies.

Song was to the negro the sole means of expressing his emotions and feelings, and from these songs may be formed the truest judgment of his character and disposition. In them is voiced the childlike simplicity and faith of a people as yet on the borderland of enlightenment. It is song which is intimately connected with the singer's work and his play, his joy and his sorrow, his expression of things temporal and things spiritual.

The Slave Songs edited by William Francis Allen, Charles Pickard Ware, and Lucy McKim Garrison, and published about 1867, represent, with a few exceptions, melodies taken from negro sources, although the direct connecting link between native African music and that of the American slave song itself is missing. The earlier songs seem to have preserved a kind of individuality, for while there was intercourse between the various plantations — slaves being sold from one to the other — the melodies seem to have been little affected by it, many of them retaining distinctly local features.

The "Sorrow Songs" of the negro, the oldest of the slave songs to survive, are permeated with a strain of suggestive sadness, and although few allusions are made to slavery itself, yet it requires no great mental acuteness to discover the yearning for relief from his surroundings, as well as the heart-throb when ties of home and family, no matter how simple nor how rude these may have been, were ruthlessly severed. Even the reading of the words of many of these songs, devoid of poetical treatment as they may appear, conveys to the mind a pathos, which regardless of the source from which they emanated, makes it appeal to humanity at large.

In many of these songs there may easily be detected the doctrine of the fatalist giving place to the yearning after things spiritual and the hope and faith of the life to come. At moments, even in the most despairing of the "Sorrow Songs," there floats out a triumphant note, as if the veil of darkness suddenly had been rent, and some fair world beyond had revealed itself to view. One of these inspirational moments is readily to be perceived in the following song, the first line of which is sung in slow recitative style, while the other lines, serving as a refrain and repeated several times, convey the mood characteristic of the plantation negro — the momentary drifting from sadness to joy:

Nobody knows who I am, who I will be till de comin' day,
O de heav'n-bells ringin'!
De sing-sol-singin'!
Heav'n-bells a-ringin' in mah soul.

Beside the "Slave Songs" there were "Sper'chels," which were sung under great religious excitement — death, the resurrection, and Satan, being the favorite themes. The negro utilized his satanic majesty in song much in the same way that he was introduced in the "miracle plays" of medieval Europe, as a source of amusement as well as of terror:

O, Satan comes, like a busy ole man,
Hal-ly, O hal-ly, O Hal-lelu!
He gets you down at the foot o' de hill,
Hal-ly, O hal-ly, O Hal-lelu!

Many of the early negro songs were extemporaneous outbursts of emotion while laboring under excitement, usually of a religious nature. One of their best known "Sper'chels" is said to have originated with an old negro slave, whose favorite subject was the final judgment. While at one of the cabin meetings he composed the following words, setting them to a tune of his own extemporizing:

I'm gwine to tell you 'bout de comin' ob de Savior,
Fare-you-well, Fare-you-well!
Dar's a better day a-comin', Fare-you-well, Fare-you-well!
Says Fader, I'm tired o' bearin', Fare-you-well, Fare-you-well!
Tired o' bearin' fo' po' sinners, Fare-you-well, Fare-you-well!
Oh, preachers fold your Bibles, Fare-you-well, Fare-you-well!
Prayer-makers pray no more, Fare-you-well, Fare-you-well!
For de last soul's converted, Fare-you-well, Fare-you-well!

In addition to the "Sper'chels" proper, which were sung sitting down, there were the "Running Sper'chels" or "Shout Songs" which were accompanied by all kinds of fantastic motions. Something of the primitive African dance is suggested by these "Shout Songs." They were only sung under stress of the greatest religious excitement and served as aids to the mourners who had not yet "got through." The "mourners" of these songs were not mourners in the general acceptation of the word, but were those who occupied the "mourners' bench" in the gospel meetings. Both words and music of these negro hymns are poetic, quaint, and plaintive and are often full of dramatic power, with marked contrasts of fear and bliss.

While religious emotions called into being the larger part of the songs, there are others which picture conditions in slave life. There were those sung at dusk when returning from work, and these plaintive songs show the dark side of slavery. There are again others which show the brighter side, when dancing was allowed in the evening, and unrestrained laughter resounded around the cabin fire. An interesting song of descriptive character is "Noble Skewball," which tells of a famous horse-race. This song more nearly approaches the epic character than does any other of the negro's efforts.

The love-songs of the negro with few exceptions, are trifling and perhaps frivolous. The negro sang not of the grande passion, his peculiar environment precluding even a thought of it. Yet in the following song there is a note of deep emotion and genuine feeling:

Poor Rosy, poor gal! Poor Rosy, poor gal!
Rosy break my poor heart! Heav'n shall-a-be my home.

One should read between the lines, perhaps, in order to realize the fate of "Poor Rosy" as bewailed by a lover, helpless to avert an impending catastrophe. A writer states: "There is a depth of history and meaning to the song," while an old negress avers that "it cannot be sung without a full heart and a troubled spirit."

Work on the plantations was often done to the accompaniment of songs whose rhythmic swing acted as an incentive to steadier and better labor; especially was this true with the mowers at harvest. Charles Peabody tells of a leader in a band of slaves who was besought by his companions not to sing a certain song because it made them work too hard. Again, on the boats plying between the West Indies and Baltimore and the southern ports, which were manned by the blacks, song was used for the same purpose. Later, on the southern river-boats the same method was utilized. These boat songs usually were constructed of a single line followed by an unmeaning chorus, the solo being sung by one of the leaders, and the rhythmical refrain repeated over and over by the workers.

During the war period negroes assisted in the construction of fortifications and earthworks. These bodies of laborers invariably kept pick and shovel going to the rhythmic, protracted chanting of words, original in thought and construction, and which were fashioned by one of their number who was looked upon as a leader. These songs became known generally throughout the South as "Railroad Songs," from the fact that tracks often were laid to the same long-drawn-out melody, and because the railroad itself made a profound impression upon the negro. They are of interest in the consideration of negro melodies since they were the last spontaneous outburst of the negro amid a rapidly changing environment.

The railroad idea was also utilized by the negro in his religious songs. He likened the Christian to a traveler on a train; the Lord was the conductor and the servants of the church were the brakemen. Stops were made at the gospel stations either to take up waiting converts or to replenish the engine with the water of life. This figure was carried out to its full extent and shows the tendency of the negro to fantastic imagery. Many of the "Railroad Songs" originated in the vigils of those who "sat up" with the dead, singing meanwhile to comfort the afflicted and mourning family. Such songs were sung in a low, monotonous croon and are irregular in everything excxept rhythm.

In Louisiana the music of the negro took on a special color owing to the influence of his Creole masters. This is noticeable not only in the French patois of his songs but in the character of the music of both his songs and his dances. The majority of songs were almost invariably accompanied by dancing, the singer being chosen not only for the quality of his voice but for his skill in improvisation, his words taking suggestion from the grace or pose of some danseuse or being in praise of some plantation hero. The dancers themselves did not sing, the musical accompaniment consisting of singing and rude instrumental efforts furnished by the onlookers. Such combination songs and dances were termed counjaille, name and dance being of African origin.

A distinctive feature of the early song of the Creole negro is its story of animal life. Many of these songs, which are of considerable length and invariably accompanied with a particular dance, refer to the elephant, the lion and the tiger. One of the most amusing tells of the entrance of a frog into a hornet's nest and of the unhappy results of his visit. Such a dancing song was designated a ronde. There is also found among these African Creole songs a few that are distinctively historical, and which seem to have been spontaneous effusions connected with some important episode relating to the community. Events such as the invasion of Louisiana by the British in 1814 and the capture and occupation of New Orleans by Commodore Farragut and General Butler in 1862 were chronicled in these songs.

The love songs of the negro of Louisiana, of which "Layotte" is a good example, are more distinctive than are those of the negro in general. Louis Moreau Gottschalk, a Creole of French and English parentage, born in New Orleans in 1829, and who won fame for himself as a pianist and composer, made use of "Layotte" and other Creole negro melodies in his piano pieces. His first important composition "Bananier," is founded on the melody

"En Avant Grenadier." It was Gottschalk who first made known to the world at large the peculiar charm of the Creole airs. One may judge of the interest attracted by both the music and its transcriber from an article appearing some sixty years ago in La France Musicale, relative to the appearance of Gottschalk in the Paris salons. A part of the article reads:

"Who does not know the 'Bamboula'? Who is there who has not read the description of that picturesque, exciting dance, which gives expression to the feelings of the negroes? Joyful or sad, plaintive, amorous, jealous, forsaken, solitary, fatigued, ennuied, or the heart filled with grief, the negro forgets all in dancing the 'Bamboula.' Look down there at those two black tinted women with short petticoats, their necks and ears ornamented with coral, le regard brulant, dancing under the banana tree; the whole of their bodies in the movement; further on are groups who excite and stimulate them to every excess of fancy; two negroes roll their active fingers over a noisy tambourine, accompanying it with a languishing chant, lively or impassioned, according to the pose of the dancers. Little negroes, like those on the canvas of Decamps, are jumping around the fiddlers; it is full of folly and delusion. The 'Bamboula' is at its height. This attractive dance has frequently furnished a theme for instrumental compositions which, however, have not obtained all the success that we expected from them. The Creole airs transported into our salons lose their character, at once wild, languishing, indescribable, and bear no resemblance to any other European music; some have thought that it was sufficient to have the chant written down, and to reproduce them with variations in order to obtain new effects. Not so; the effects have failed. One must have lived under the burning sky from whence the Creole draws his melodies; one must be impregnated with those eccentric chants, which are little dramas in action; in one word, one must be Creole, as composer and executant, in order to feel and make others understand the whole originality of the 'Bamboula.'"

The slave song is a music of the past, for these songs peculiar to plantation life in the South have faded away with the conditions that fostered them. Under the altered conditions the negro has undergone a marked change which has resulted in a dearth of song production. What he eventually will achieve musically remains for the years to tell. Orators, writers, thinkers and poets have come from the ranks of the American negro, but the composer is yet to arise who will take these bits of melody, typical of his race, and on them construct compositions of true artistic worth.

Though not of American birth, the name of Coleridge-Taylor may here be mentioned in this connection. Of African descent, Coleridge-Taylor has taken negro melodies as themes from which he has evolved many charming compositions. He is the first negro to win renown in the field of art music. His piano transcriptions of such songs as "Didn't my Lord deliver Daniel," "Steal Away," "Sometimes I feel like a Motherless Child." are really gems of their class.

Among the composers who have used negro themes as material in composition Antonin Dvořák ranks highest. His "New World" symphony is founded chiefly on such themes, and America owes much to him for showing the possibilities in the use of this material. Following his illustrious example other composers have come forward and scored successes in this line of endeavor. Among them may be mentioned G. W. Chadwick, who made use of such themes in his second symphony; Henry Schoenefeld with his "Sunny South" overture, "Rural" symphony, and sonata for piano and violin; and E. R. Kroeger in his "Ten American Sketches." From the efforts of these men it is to be seen that the negro melodies offer material capable of being developed with artistic results. Doubtless as America comes to produce something approaching nationalism in music more and more use will be made of this valuable thematic material.

At the close of the Civil War there were more than four million freed slaves reaching out for the promise of better conditions. An active, energetic endeavor was made therefore, toward the founding of schools for the negro, and from one of these institutions there developed a project which became of unique interest in the history of music in America. In 1865 measures were taken to found a university in the South for the benefit of the freed slaves, and against many discouraging odds, Fisk University was established at Nashville, Tennessee, in 1866.

Recalling the negro's innate love for song, the trustees resolved to make music a special feature of the instruction in the University. They therefore engaged George L. White, to give instruction in singing. His work with the pupils was productive of good results, for in the spring of 1867 he had them give a concert, and the following year they presented a program which included the cantata "Esther."

Mr. White now took part of his choir class to Memphis and again to Chattanooga, meeting in both cities with considerable success. About this time the National Teachers' Association of the United States held its annual convention at Nashville, and arrangements were made for the Fisk choir to sing at the opening exercises. This proved, in spite of prejudice on the part of certain people, to be so popular a feature that a demand was made on the singers for their services in every session until the close of the convention. It now was suggested that this choir might be made a means to an end and earn with its singing the funds needed to further the work of the University. With this object in view Mr. White started out with his choir of thirteen members, on Oct. 6, 1871.

The director had much to discourage him, but faith in the project lent courage to both singers and leader, and the first three months' work brought a considerable sum of money into the University treasury. An invitation to take part in the World's Peace Jubilee in Boston gave renewed encouragement. It was not altogether smooth sailing for the Fisk singers in Boston, however, for in the first concert there was abroad a spirit of antagonism which at one moment went beyond the bounds of civility and decorum. But the patient singers evinced neither disturbance nor resentment, and perhaps this forbearance on their part swung the balance of public opinion decidedly in their favor.

The supreme test came, however, when the singers were to take part in one of the Jubilee concerts. The "Battle Hymn of the Republic" was to be sung to the air of "John Brown," by some colored singers of Boston. Unfortunately, the key was pitched too high, and the first lines were voiced under obvious difficulties. The Fisk singers, owing to the good training they had received, found no difficulty with the high notes on which the others had failed, and when were reached the words "He hath sounded forth the trumpet that shall never call retreat," their cue for falling in, they took up the song as if swept by a wave of inspiration. At the chorus "Glory, glory, Hallelujah," the audience of twenty thousand people arose en masse, the women waving their handkerchiefs and the men throwing their hats high in the air, cheering and shouting "The Jubilees! The Jubilees forever!" And P. S. Gilmore, the originator and director of the Jubilee Concerts, motioned down to the dusky singers below, and massing them upon his own platform, from this position had them finish the remaining verses of the "Battle Hymn of the Republic."

The fame of the "Jubilee Singers" — for henceforth this was to be the designation of these vocalists from the South — having gone abroad, London expressed a desire to hear them. They therefore crossed the ocean, and with their simple and pathetic music won their way into the hearts of the British public. England, Scotland and Ireland received them graciously and bestowed upon them encouraging appreciation, for, from Queen Victoria to the humblest subject within her realm, the "peculiar minor" cadence in the simple song of an exiled people touched the heart as no other primitive music had done. A second tour was made later and concerts were given in Holland, Switzerland and Germany as well as in Great Britain.

Those who did not understand the language were moved to tears by the charm of the music. The older countries of Europe were quick to recognize the fact that in these negro songs America had a folk-music peculiarly and entirely its own — music which had sprung into being under specific historical conditions — and for two centuries had mellowed on the borders of civilization and culture and yet had no part in it. Strange enough too, a few English musicians as well as those from other European countries began to think that the negro had plagiarized the church music of the whites, so they set themselves the task of research into the old hymnology in order to prove that the "Slave Songs" were not as original as had been claimed. Their labors were of course in vain, for they found that such was not the case. On the contrary, England later borrowed one of her most popular Sunday School hymns from African music, the simple little melody to "There is a happy land, far, far away," belonging to the primitive music of the negro.

In Holland, there being no halls of suitable dimensions to accommodate the people desirous of hearing this unique band of singers, the Cathedrals were opened for concert purposes, and at The Hague the singers were received by the Queen and the nobility. After a sojourn of some two months in Holland, the Jubilee Singers passed on to Germany, where in Berlin, after being received by the Emperor, the Domkirche, in which the Imperial family worships, was placed at the disposal of the visitors for their concerts.

One of the most critical journals of the time, the Berliner Musik-Zeitung, in a lengthy article considered the program in detail and then summed up with the following: "What wealth of shading! What accuracy of declamation! Every musician felt that the performances of these singers are the result of high artistic talent, finely trained taste, and extraordinary diligence. Such a pianissimo, such a crescendo, such a decrescendo as those at the close of 'Steal Away' might raise envy in the soul of any choir-master!" The critique closes with: "Thus the balance turns decidedly in favor of the Jubilee Singers and we confess ourselves their debtors. Not only have we had a rare musical treat but our musical ideas have also received enlargement and we feel that something may be learned of these negro singers, if only we consent to break through the fetters of custom and of long usage."

Franz Abt, the composer and conductor, received the singers most cordially, bestowing upon them many attentions and in Brunswick placing at their disposal the hall in which he gave his own choral concerts. "We could not take even our German peasantry," he remarked, "and reach in generations of culture such results in art, conduct and character as appear in these freed slaves."

The career of the Jubilee Singers in unique in the music annals of the world. That these uncultured singers could bring all Europe to their feet by the inherent beauty of their song and by their charactertistic rendition of the same, demands for the negro a distinct place in the musical world. Funds to the amount of one hundred and fifty thousand dollars were earned by this band of singers and applied for the educational uplift of the race. It is a message of song that finds no parallel.

The negro has exerted an influence in the history of music in America not only by means of his own song but indirectly through the efforts of the negro minstrel, whose inspirations were derived from negro sources. Nationalities have each in turn had their minstrels, all closely allied by ties of resemblance in style and manner of performance; but America has had its own individual type. Unlike that of other nations, it made a specialty of framing the "mind to mirth and merriment" and developing among the people the desire for a humorous entertainment, simple and clean of character. This peculiar style of entertainment naturally called for music of a distinct type, and as a result of this demand there evolved a class of melodies which, together with the negro melodies themselves, eventually will be looked upon as our folk-song.

It is not a difficult matter to find the cause for the long continued popularity of negro minstrelsy, for it gave to the public an entertainment which was new and original and which at the same time made its appeal from many sides. In himself the negro was an interesting character, and when travestied, with all his peculiarities exaggerated, he became even more so. It was the droll humor of the southern darkey that first was fastened on as a feature suitable for stage presentation. The ludicrous side of the negro character, which showed itself in the performing of his songs by accompanying them with facial grimaces and contortions, made its appeal as did also the pathetic side which drew involuntary tears.

In all the efforts of the negro minstrel, it was song which served as the vehicle of expression, and the secret of his long continued success lay in the inherent appeal made by such songs. It was the song rather than the singer which first drew out and held the attention of the public. In addition to these songs the negro minstrel had a manner of performing instrumental music that was peculiarly his own. Trick music it might be termed, for the banjo and fiddle were played in all sorts of positions, under the leg, behind the back, and over the head. The fiddle was made to imitate almost all the sounds of nature, and even the tin whistle served to produce strange and peculiar imitations and inventions. And from such materials, with the song and dance, the ring of the tambourine and the clack of the bones — all given with the performers in black-face make-up — was the minstrel show fashioned.

There are many claimants to the origin of American minstrelsy, but it generally is conceded that W. D. Rice (born in New York in 1808, died in 1860) was really the father of this form of entertainment, if not its veritable

FISK JUBILEE SINGERS

A band of negro singers, organized in 1869 by George White to aid in securing funds for the Fisk University, Nashville, Tenn., a university for freedmen founded soon after the war.

They made their first great success in the Gilmore Jubilee Concerts in Boston and were known thereafter as the "Jubilee Singers;" made several concert tours in Europe, meeting everywhere with the most enthusiastic receptions, and attracting the attention of European composers to the negro melodies. These concerts gave the first intimation to many European composers that America had a folk-song of her own.

FISK JUBILEE SINGERS

A band of negro singers, organized in 1869 by George White to aid in securing funds for the Fisk University, Nashville, Tenn., a university for freedmen founded soon after the war.

They made their first great success in the Gilmore Jubilee Concerts in Boston and were known thereafter as the "Jubilee Singers;" made several concert tours in Europe, meeting everywhere with the most enthusiastic receptions, and attracting the attention of European composers to the negro melodies. These concerts gave the first intimation to many European composers that America had a folk-song of her own.

originator. Certain it is that Rice afterward became associated with the dandy darkey of the stage and that he had many followers, all more or less ingenious in their methods of presentation of this most exaggerated and grotesquely made-up character.

Rice's first negro impersonation was patterned after a song, with its accompanying dance, which he had heard sung by a negro in a stable in Cincinnati; but it was in Pittsburg in 1830 that the song first was given from the stage. While playing in the latter city, Rice induced a negro porter named Cuff to accompany him to the theatre and to loan him the clothes he was then wearing. When the time came therefore for Rice's specialty, he made his appearance arrayed in Cuff's garments, with face made up with burnt cork and with a black wig of matted moss on his head. Then followed the song which he had heard in Cincinnati:

O, Jim Crow's come to town, as you all must know,
An' he wheel' about, he turn about, he do jis so,
An' ebery time he wheel about, he jump Jim Crow.

Suiting the actions to the words, Mr. Rice emphasized his song by the movements of his body. He was greeted by tremendous applause, and when he proceeded to improvise, incorporating into the verses familiar local incidents, the house became uproarious.

Cuff, in the meantime, had received a call for his services, and after repeated though unsuccessful efforts to attract the actor's attention, he rushed on the stage regardless of appearances and demanded his clothes. The audience thought at first that his entrance and excited talk were a legitimate part of the show, but when it came to a realization of the true state of affairs the effect may be imagined. Thus the germ of the art of burnt cork minstrelsy was born, an art which afterward became a feature in the evolution of America's popular music.

"Jim Crow" in his grotesque make-up became a feature of the regular performances at the Fifth Street Theatre, and at the season's close, quarters known for a long time as "Beal's," were secured for entertainments exclusively Ethiopian in character. Song after song was added until there existed a good repertory from which to select an evening's entertainment. For two years Rice confined his Ethiopian specialties to Pittsburg, but afterward he went to Philadelphia, Boston and New York, and ultimately crossed to England. He opened at the Surrey Theatre, London, and after a prolonged engagement in the British metropolis made a tour of the other large cities of Great Britain, being most favorably received everywhere, and in the four years of his tour making a fortune. Rice died in 1860 after having given to the stage the first and best type of negro minstrelsy.

It is interesting to note that many actors who later became famous, in their early careers appeared first as negro minstrels, among the number being Forrest, Booth and Joe Jefferson. Forrest's appearance in such roles really antedates that of "Jim Crow" Rice by seven years, but as he did not long continue to play negro parts his influence was not felt in the development of negro minstrelsy. Jefferson made his stage debut in 1833, when only four years of age, being carried in a bag on the shoulders of W. D. Rice and turned out of it with the introduction:

Ladies and gentlemen,
I'd have you to know
I's got a little darkey here
To jump Jim Crow.

Other names connected with early American minstrelsy might be given more than passing mention. For three years Ralph Keeler was one of the most popular of the black-face brotherhood and made a tremendous hit with his negro impersonations. George Washington Dixon, who made his debut in 1830, accompanying his singing with a banjo, was one of the pioneers of this art. His "Zip Coon" was the original of what later were designated "Coon songs." Charles White and Daniel Emmett were general favorites in their day, Emmett being better known as the composer of the popular songs "Old Dan Tucker," "Early in the Morning" and "Dixie." There were many others who played their part well in the earlier as well as in the declining period of this phase of entertainment and whose names will always be associated with America's particular form of minstrelsy, that of the blackened face.

The name of Christy was for some years synonymous with negro minstrel specialties. Edwin P. Christy was the founder of the famous troupe which was organized in 1842, and its performances were given with uninterrupted regularity in New York for eight years. Under the management of E. P. Christy, George Harrington, his nephew (better known to the world as George W. Christy), made his debut at Buffalo, N. Y., and was really for some years the star of the troupe, being, it is said, the original "Lucy Long."

E. P. Christy had two sons, R. Byron and William A., who were also members of what was known as the "Christy's Minstrels." This troupe went to England and occupied St. James' Hall, London, night after night for many years, becoming one of the most popular forms of entertainment in the British metropolis.

To Christy is due the credit for so arranging the performance as to have it comprise the whole evening's entertainment rather than being an accessory to other features. The minstrel performance, under his management, was divided into three divisions, namely "first part," "olio," and "afterpiece."

In the "first part" the performers were seen seated in a single row, the number varying from four to twenty, the "Interlocutor" in the center, with "Bones" and "Tambo," the boneplayers and tambourine performers, respectively, as end men. The second part, "olio," was a variety entertainment made up of banjo-playing, clog-dancing and other specialties. It in no way partook of the representative features of plantation life as in the performances of the earlier Ethiopian minstrels, and the third part or "afterpiece" very rarely touched upon anything in connection with negro life. These innovations, in spite of the clever rendition of individual parts, were the beginning of the end of American minstrelsy. Edwin P. Christy and William A. Christy died in 1862; E. Byron Christy in 1866, and George W. Christy in 1868.

Many songs, mere echoes of the Southland, were given in these performances, and from the fervor with which they were received both in America and in England and their influence upon the people, they must, perforce, be classed with the popular music. The sentimental strain in these songs or ballads made its quick appeal to the heart. Thackeray, who had witnessed one of the performances, writes in one of his "Roundabout" sketches: "I heard a humorous balladist not long since, a minstrel with wool on his head, and an ultra-Ethiopian complexion, who performed a negro ballad that I confess moistened these spectacles in a most unexpected manner. I have gazed at thousands of tragedy queens dying on the stage and expiring in appropriate blank verse, and I never wanted to wipe them. They have looked up, be it said, at many scores of clergymen without being dimmed, and behold! a vagabond with a corked face and a banjo sings a little song, strikes a wild note which sets the heart thrilling with happy pity."

Among many minstrel organizations contemporary with the Christies were Buckley's "New Orleans Serenaders," which was organized in 1843, White's "Serenaders," Bryant's Minstrels, Wood's Minstrels, and Sharpley's Minstrels. Kelly and Leon introduced "Africanized opéra bouffe" to New York in 1867. At a somewhat later period came Cotton and Reed, Haverley, Thatcher, Pelham, Primrose and West, Billy Van, Dockstader and others. Haverley's "Mastodon Minstrels" first appeared before the public about the year 1882.

In the earlier minstrel shows and indeed for many years following, the stage negro was patterned after the plantation "darkey," but in the organizations of a later date he assumed a distinct character of his own. The Haverley troupe was among the first to make a lavish display. They created somewhat of a sensation at the time, both in America and in England, by the dazzling stage spectacle they presented. From this time on there was little in the minstrel show to suggest the plantation "nigger" other than the ultra-blackened faces. The "darkey" song became the "coon" song and assumed a new and different character. There was very little suggestion left of the music of the negro himself on which the early minstrel songs were founded.

It is impossible to class the coon songs of the last twenty years apart from popular music in general, for they have been given to the public much more frequently without the accompaniment of the burnt cork make-up than with it. From the time the negro minstrel ceased to travesty the real article the minstrel show has steadily dropped in public favor until at the present time there are but few troupes in existence. Lew Dockstader still holds the board, but his only by ceaseless endeavor. The black-face comedian seems doomed to extinction, but he will leave behind him the characteristic type of popular music developed through his efforts. He served his purpose, and the legacy he left behind him in the "darkey" and "coon" songs has done much in adding variety to the literature of popular music.

America owes much to the negro in the creation and development of its popular music, for a large part of such music is due either directly or indirectly to negro sources. He gave to us, first of all, of his own peculiarly characteristic melodies which, as time goes on, are tending more and more to form the foundation of our folk-song literature. Had it not been for the negro there would never have come into existence the early minstrel songs which were patterned after those of the negro himself. From the demand of the minstrels for songs of a suitable style there developed the ever popular compositions of Stephen C. Foster and others of like character.

At a later date there have followed the multitudinous "coon songs" as the natural outcome of the "darkey songs," and in all of them, both in words and music, may be traced the influence of the negro. The words are still in the quasi-negro dialect, and the music abounds in the peculiar syncopations found in the true negro melodies. From all of these facts the conclusion that the negro has played a most pronounced part in the development of our popular music is naturally and easily reached. There is no doubt that America has proved to be the gainer musically from the unconscious influence of the unfortunate people first brought to the country as slaves.

POPULAR MUSIC

The considering of popular music naturally follows a review of negro minstrelsy because the minstrel show so long served as the medium by which such music was given to the public. Popular music always has had and always will have its place in the lives of the people. Interest in it therefore is general.

In early times among the nations of Europe the folk-songs and dance tunes were the music of the people. These old melodies, handed down from generation to generation, still form the nucleus of the popular music of the various European countries. To them have been added from time to time songs written in a simple style and dance music, marches, and airs from the operas. Here in America, where, on account of our youth as a nation we can have no true folk-songs, we must of necessity begin to build on a different foundation.

In a broad sense, popular music may be defined, as its name implies, as that of the populace — that is, of people who have made no special study of the art of music. It must be of a kind that can be easily learned and readily recalled. This music need not be trifling or trivial, but it must be simple. If it be a song the words must contain some sentiment common in appeal to all, sentiment touching the home, love, joy or sorrow; or the theme may be some subject which at the time is agitating the public mind. The melody must be singable and the rhythm infectious. If the composition be purely instrumental, such as a march or waltz, the same musical characteristics must be in evidence.

In order to attain popularity this music need not be trashy, but may be and in fact often is of true musical worth. Witness for instance the "Largo" of Handel, Rubinstein's "Melody in F," the "Toreador's Song" from Carmen or the "Soldiers' Chorus" from Faust, all of which belong to art music but which nevertheless are distinctly and undeniably popular. Popular music becomes such because it requires for its enjoyment neither special musical training nor serious mental effort on the part of the listener. The difference between popular and so-called classical music really rests with the hearer rather than with the music itself. For, speaking in general, classical music calls for those very elements of musical culture and mental effort for its appreciation which popular music does not require.

After a hard day in shop or factory, after strenuous hours in the commercial world or at the desk, physical and mental relaxation are absolutely necessary to the enjoyment of any entertainment, not excepting music — even by one who thoroughly appreciates the art. No pleasure, either of a physical or mental nature, can be enjoyed where weary body and mind have to make effort for the occasion. Therefore the music of the people must be such that the hearer catches it almost unconsciously.

In treating of the subject of popular music the words as well as the music of the songs necessarily must be discussed, for very often it is the words rather than the music which win success for a popular song. Either the subject must make its appeal, or the words must have a jingle which carries them along. It is very doubtful whether the melody of "Home, Sweet Home" would have obtained such lasting popularity were it not for the words. On the other hand the tune of "Dixie" simply goes of itself, irrespective of the words used.

The earliest type of purely American popular song was called into existence by political excitement. In every particular the "Liberty Song" was our first possession of this kind, although adapted to a foreign air. This song found its origin in the refusal of the Massachusetts Legislature to rescind the "Circular Letter" of Feb. 11, 1768, relating to the imposition of duties and taxes upon the American colonies. A short time after this incident, John Dickinson of Delaware forwarded to James Otis of Massachusetts, with permission to publish it, a song appealing to Americans to unite for liberty. The words were first published in the Boston Gazette of July 18, 1768, and in September of the same year it appeared in printed form on a single sheet, along with its musical setting. This song was sung with enthusiasm throughout the colonies and retained its popularity for many years. The text of the poem runs:

Come join hand in hand, brave Americans all,
And rouse your bold hearts at fair Liberty's call;
No tyrannous acts shall suppress your just claim,
Or stain with dishonor America's name.
In freedom we're born, and in freedom we'll live;
Our purses are ready,
Steady, Friends, steady,
Not as slaves but as freemen our money we'll give.

All ages shall speak with amaze and applause,
Of the courage we'll show in support of our laws;
To die we can bear, but to serve we disdain,
For shame is to freemen more dreadful than pain.
In freedom we're born, etc.

The tune to which it was adapted was composed for David Garrick's celebrated "Hearts of Oak," by Dr. Boyce of England, and was first sung at Drury Lane Theatre, London, at Christmastide, 1759. It is a spirited air, and as the colonists were familiar with it, the song, consisting of nine stanzas, became exceedingly popular. It was America's first popular song in the fullest sense of that which constitutes such music, that which "arrests people's attention, and when heard again, compels recognition."

It is but natural that tea, the subject of much animated political discussion at this time, should form the subject matter of many similar songs. One of them, written between the battles of Lexington and Concord and that of Bunker Hill, was sung to the tune of "Derry Down" and became a great favorite at all political gatherings as well as on the street, ultimately finding its way into camp with the Revolutionary army:

What a court hath Old England of folly and sin,
Spite of Chatham, and Camden, Barre, Burke, Wilkes and Glynne.
Not content with the game act, they tax fish and sea,
And Americans drench with hot water and tea,
Derry down, down, hey derry down.

Then freedom's the word, both at home and abroad,
And for every scabbard that hides a good sword!
Our forefathers gave us this freedom in hand,
And we'll die in defense of the rights of our land.
Derry down, down, hey derry down.

Another song on the same subject was sung to a sacred air. The verses first appeared in print, July 22, 1774, afterwards being published in single sheet form or broadside. It is attributed to Meshech Weare, who became president of the State of New Hampshire, in 1776.

Rouse every generous thoughtful mind,
The rising danger flee,
If you would lasting freedom find,
Now then abandon tea!

Since we so great a plenty have
Of all that's for our health;
Shall we that blasted herb receive
Impoverishing our wealth?

Adieu! away, oh tea! begone!
Salute our taste no more!
Though thou are coveted by some
Who're destined to be poor!

The first popular sentimental song printed in America appeared in the Philadelphia Ledger in 1775, and was known as the "Banks of the Dee." It is a tender little love song, adapted to the old Irish air of "Langolee" and tells of a young Scotchman who left his native land for the purpose of joining the British forces in America, having bade his fiancée adieu on the banks of the Dee. The song-writer, John Tait, pictures the girl's sadness and despair, as well as her admiration for her brave lover.

> But now he's gone from me, and left me thus mourning,
> To quell the proud rebels, for valiant is he.
> But ah! there's no hope for his speedy returning,
> To wander again on the banks of the Dee.
> He's gone, hapless youth, o'er the rude, roaring billows,
> The kindest, the sweetest of all his brave fellows;
> And left me to stray 'mongst these once loved willows,
> The loneliest lass on the banks of the Dee.

Its great popularity rested, perhaps, in the fact that it resolved itself into a direct appeal to many a colonial maiden's heart, for lovers marched to the field in the Revolutionary forces and bravely and valiantly performed their part, while the girls they loved, like the Scottish maiden, remained at home to wait, and, perchance, to weep.

With few exceptions, the popular music of the colonial and Revolutionary period, whether vocal or instrumental, was adapted from other countries, chiefly from Great Britain. It has been customary to date the evolution of America's popular music from the period of the Civil War and the decades that followed, but song-music by this time already had become familiar to the people by way of the minstrels, while banjo, flute, violin, melodion and piano had come into common use in the home.

Few popular songs survive, however, beyond the particular period for which they are written. Many of them are as evanescent as thistle-down, wafted hither and yon by a gentle zephyr of sentiment, and then banished by the stronger under-current of popular opinion. As a rule, songs involving home sentiments, domestic affections, emotions that play on the heartstrings of the people, these are they which neither time nor constant repetition consign quickly to oblivion. In periods of great political disturbance this feeling resolves itself into a fervor of patriotism, and the war song is the result. This is the music of the people, for it becomes the popular music of the period and invariably is in the form of song. Then follows an aftermath, in which longings and yearnings for the home life are more deeply expressed, when the word "mother" becomes the dominant note, and her joy or her sorrow, her sense of loss or bereavement, forms the chord around which the song is built.

And yet certain of these songs of sentiment outlive those of more artistic composition simply because they touch the hearts of the people. Each and every word is understood because it has been written for them, and the music usually is simple enough to be readily grasped. America has produced much music of this kind, songs that will never die because they essentially vibrate in the home-life of the nation. Such a song is "Home, Sweet Home," which for three-quarters of a century has held its popularity and promises to continue to do so indefinitely. From minstrel performance to opera this charming song has held its own on the stage; from street singer to prima donna the public has received it with applause; from farmhouse to palace it has ingratiated its universal sentiment until it belongs to the whole world. Yet it is a rather ironical fact that the writer of the words, all his life was a wanderer, and died in a foreign land.

A few miles from Tunis, in Northern Africa, is a monument bearing the following inscription:

"In memory of Honorable John Howard Payne, twice Consul of the United States of America for the city and kingdom of Tunis, this stone is here placed by a grateful country. He died at the American Consulate in this city, after a tedious illness, April 1, 1852. He was born at the city of Boston, state of Massachusetts. His fame as a Poet and Dramatist is well known wherever the English language is understood through his celebrated ballad of 'Home, Sweet Home,' and his popular tragedy of 'Brutus' and other similar productions." Around the tomb are engraved the following lines:

> Sure, when thy gentle spirit fled
> To realms beyond the azure dome,
> With arms outstretched, God's angel said;
> Welcome to Heaven's Home, Sweet Home!

Here the remains of the poet rested until, in 1883, W. W. Corcoran, who cherished some remembrances of Payne as a youth, transferred them to Washington, where the Corcoran Art Gallery received the casket until its reinterment in Oak Hill Cemetery. The President of the United States with his Cabinet and a military escort, together with many sympathizers in the movement, formed a distinguished cortège to the cemetery, and Payne, in body and in spirit, was no longer "an exile from home."

Payne was not a Bostonian, however. He was born in New York, the greater part of his childhood being spent in East Hampton, where his father was principal of the Clinton Academy. After spending some years in business and at college, Payne eventually turned to the stage. His career was full of ups and downs until finally he landed in the debtors' prison in London. While in confinement he made an adaptation of a French play which he sent to the management of Drury Lane Theatre, London. It was accepted and staged within a fortnight, and the remuneration for his work freed its adapter of debt.

Drury Lane's rival, Covent Garden Theatre, now sent him to Paris to look out for successful plays and to make adaptations of the same. One of these plays, from which Payne used little other than the plot, was advertised at Covent Garden as an "opera." It was for this "opera" of "Clari" that Payne wrote the now world-famous song, "Home, Sweet Home." The heroine, Clari, elopes with a nobleman, but is brought to see the error of her ways by hearing a band of strolling players sing the verses which Payne had introduced.

The words were adapted to a tune by Henry Rowley Bishop, which he had designated "Sicilian Air," and which had been familiar in London to words by Thomas Haynes Bayly, beginning "To the home of my childhood in sorrow I came." This was essentially a home song, yet when Payne's verses were set to the same tune London soon forgot that it ever had sung this air to anything but "Home, Sweet Home!"

Another song that became exceedingly popular, and after having been almost forgotten received a revived popularity through its introduction into the plot of a popular novel, is "Ben Bolt." The author of the words was Thomas Dunn English, a physician of New Jersey who also was a writer of distinction. The words of "Ben Bolt" first appeared in the New York Mirror of Sept. 2, 1843. They received several musical settings, but the air by which they gained popularity was adapted to them by an actor named Nelson Kneass.

While Kneass was playing in Pittsburg, the manager of a theatre was preparing to stage a new play and was anxious to have an original song introduced in it. A friend gave Kneass the words of "Ben Bolt;" a German air was adapted to them, and being sung in the play, the song won an immediate favor which it held for many a day.

The name of George F. Root for many years was prominent in the field of popular song. Mr. Root was born in Sheffield, Massachusetts, on Aug. 13, 1820. While a child he was extremely fond of music and attempted to play every musical instrument that came within his reach. He went to Boston while still young and began the study of music in real earnest. Instruction was received in singing, piano and organ, with a flute as a recreation. After some years spent in study, Mr. Root became organist and choirmaster and for five years was one of Lowell Mason's assistants in teaching music in the Boston public schools. In 1844 a position was offered him in New York, and here for many years he lived and worked. It was while in New York that he first gained fame as a writer of popular music. "Hazel Dell" was his first successful popular song. Others were "Rosalie, the Prairie Flower" and "The Vacant Chair."

George F. Root was one of the first musicians in America to realize the opening in the field of popular music. In writing for the people he would invariably consider the difficulty of the intervals and the intricacy of the accompaniments. That is why there is always found such simplicity in all his harmonies. He was a born composer in this field and he reaped a well deserved success. The degree of Doctor of Music was conferred upon him by Chicago University. He died in 1895.

Among the many names associated with popular song in America that of Stephen C. Foster stands pre-eminent. Stephen Foster was born at Lawrenceville, Pennsylvania, on July 4, 1826. Shortly after his birth the family moved to Allegheny, where Stephen attended school and continued his studies until, at the age of thirteen, he was sent to Athens Academy at Towanda, Pennsylvania. After a year spent at Towanda he returned to his home in Allegheny, later attending Jefferson College at Canonsburg. As a boy he had shown remarkable precocity in music and at seventeen he was the leader of a small club which met at his home for the purpose of learning to sing in parts. When the club had exhausted the repertory of such songs as were in favor at the time, Stephen Foster resolved to try the writing of songs himself. "Louisiana Belle" was the result of his first effort, and in a week "Old Uncle Ned" followed. The style and text of these songs evidently was patterned after those used in the minstrel shows which were so popular at the time.

Mr. Foster's brother Dunning was then in business in Cincinnati, and thither Stephen now went to act as bookkeeper for him. It was while interested in mercantile pursuits that his leisure moments developed "Oh, Susanna." Little dreaming that his compositions were worth anything from a financial point of view, he made a present of "Uncle Ned" and "Oh, Susanna" to W. C. Peters, who was then in the music publishing business in Cincinnati. The publisher made ten thousand dollars out of these two songs, each of which gained world-wide popularity.

When in his twenty-second year Stephen Foster concluded that he was not adapted to a commercial life, and he now turned to music in earnest. He seemed unable to abandon altogether the negro dialect in the words of his songs, but they are characterized by a certain refinement in marked contrast to the grotesque and clownish effects produced by previous writers in the same field, and there is an expression of tender sentiment pervading each song. Foster laid bare the heart-life of the negro, and ridicule found no place in his song-texts. When his "Nelly Was a Lady" was published and grew into popularity Foster received commissions for future songs. This song has a certain rhythmic charm; the tune is easily learned, and the note of pathos incorporated in the chorus, "Toll de bell for lubbly Nell" lays hold of the feelings.

> Down on de Mississippi floating,
> Long time I trabble on de way,
> All night de cottonwood a toting,
> Sing for my true lub all de day.
> Nelly was a lady,
> Last night she died,
> Toll de bell for lubbly Nell,
> My dark Virginny bride.

Other songs beside those designated as plantation melodies, but all more or less impregnated with sentiment, now came rapidly from his pen and obtained a wide popularity not only in America but in Europe as well. Such songs as "Old Folks at Home," "Come Where My Love Lies Dreaming," "Gentle Annie," "Hard Times Come Again No More," "Massa's in the Cold, Cold Ground," "My Old Kentucky Home," "Nelly Bly," "Old Dog Tray" and "Old Black Joe," have become familiar to many nationalities.

When Christy, the famous minstrel, with his company was making a decided hit in New York City, he wrote to

Stephen Foster asking for a song, with permission to sing it before publication, desiring also to have at least one edition with his own name appended thereto as author and composer, agreeing to pay five hundred dollars for the privilege. This accounts for Christy's name, instead of Foster's, appearing on the title-page of the first edition of "Old Folks at Home," as well as for the mistaken idea that Christy, and not Foster, was the author and composer. This is essentially a home song, a song in which the yearnings for associations of home and kindred are strongly defined. In spite of the fact that Foster wrote it in the negro dialect, it is more often sung in language with no suggestion of dialect whatever. Memories rise unbidden at the words:

> All the world is sad and dreary,
> Everywhere I roam,
> Oh! darkies, how my heart grows weary,
> Far from the old folks at home.

Stephen Foster with his sister visited a relative, John Rowan, who was a judge as well as a United States Senator, at the latter's plantation home at Bardstown, Kentucky. Seated one morning in the garden, Foster and his sister heard the notes of a mocking-bird in a tree overhead, and the song of the thrush in a nearby bush, while the slaves were at work and their children at play. Inspiration was upon the poet-composer, and he jotted down what had come to him. Then, when sufficient of it was written from which to obtain an idea of song, he handed the manuscript to his sister, who sang:

> The sun shines bright in the old Kentucky home;
> 'Tis summer; the darkies are gay;
> The corn top's ripe and the meadow's in bloom,
> While the birds make music all the day.

A simple song of Foster's that always will retain a large degree of popularity is "Old Black Joe." It has, with its harmonious chorus, been more frequently sung and has had a greater variety of instrumental settings than has any other song by the same composer. The reminiscent mood of this song gives it a peculiar attraction. All the world loves memories, be they sweet or sad, and Foster understood the sentimental side of human nature and how he might appeal to its tenderest emotions. We not only picture the old negro bereft of home ties and looking forward to a reunion in the mystic Beyond, but the heart-yearnings of "Old Black Joe" become more general and touch a responsive chord in each of us.

Stephen Foster was the most successful popular song-writer which America has yet produced. His success, however, was not a financial one, for he died in extreme poverty in New York in 1864; but he is judged successful in that his songs have obtained a wider and more lasting popularity than have those of any other native writer in the same field. In their general appeal his songs most nearly approach the requirements of what popular song should be, and he justly has been termed the American people's composer par excellence.

Henry Clay Work (1832-1884) won considerable fame as a writer of popular songs. "We are coming, Sister Mary" first brought him into prominence, and E. P. Christy sang it at all his concerts. In 1865, Mr. Work went to Europe and on his return wrote several popular songs relating to the temperance question, the one known as "Come Home, Father" having a wide popularity on both sides of the Atlantic. He wrote about eighty compositions in all, among them being the well-known "Grandfather's Clock."

Will S. Hayes was another writer who had remarkable success with his songs for the people. His "Write me a Letter from Home" had a sale of three hundred and fifty thousand copies, while "Parted by the River" and some others reached the three hundred thousand mark. Mr. Hayes wrote altogether some three hundred songs, in all of which there is charming sentiment, flowing melody, and very effective accompaniments.

There were at this period many other popular song writers who had wide success. T. F. Seward's "Rally Round the Flag, Boys" and "The Shining Shore" became great favorites. "Listen to the Mocking Bird," a song by Alice Hawthorne, who wrote under the nom de plume of Sep. Winner, is still much admired by the amateur whistlers. H. P. Danks wrote many songs which had a large sale, among them being "Anna Lee," "Don't be angry with me darling" and "Silver Threads Among the Gold." Among other successful writers in the same field were J. R. Thomas, William B. Bradbury, Chas. Carrol Sawyer, Henry Tucker, Daniel Emmett and C. A. White.

Popular music in America has obtained an ever-increasing vogue during the last quarter century owing to the growth of what was first termed the variety, and later, the vaudeville show. Previous to this time the negro minstrel troupe had served as the leading factor in introducing this class of music to the public at large. Now it is in the vaudeville houses that popular songs first are heard. If a hit is made the song almost immediately has a large sale. Another mode of introduction is by way of the light opera or musical comedy; in fact many of these musical plays are made up almost entirely of songs and instrumental pieces of a popular style. Whether such music finds wide favor depends to a certain extent on the manner of its first introduction, and it is for this reason that writers of popular music make strenuous effort to become associated with successful players.

And yet, with a few notable exceptions, America's popular song writers are unknown, for we as a public give little heed as to who writes the song so long as words and music are pleasing. Such songs are almost impersonal. They do not bear the stamp of the composer's individuality so much as they reflect the taste of the day. When a song attains genuine and wide popularity it usually contains a sentiment which appeals to the heart of a whole people. Among the song hits of the present era "Comrades" was one of the first. While the melody was pretty and catchy it was the spirit of fellowship suggested in the words which won for it its popularity. "Annie Rooney" was another song of the same period which gained success through its appeal to the remembrance of sweetheart days.

In all of the popular songs of the early part of the present era there is to be noted a very general similarity of construction and treatment; the melodies, harmonies and rhythms are simple, though not to the same extent as those of an earlier time. But our typical popular songs of the present day are far more complicated harmonically and rhythmically, if not in melody, than those of a decade ago. It is pleasing to note that the most popular songs of the closing years of the Nineteenth Century were songs of home, honor and pure love. Among them may be cited "Sweet Marie," "Sweetest Story Every Told," "Sunshine of Paradise Alley," "On the Banks of the Wabash," "She was bred in Old Kentucky." There also were many coon songs of the period which exhibited a refinement not seen in those of the present day. Such songs were "Little Alabama Coon," "Kentucky Babe," "My Gal's a High Born Lady," "Stay in your own back yard."

Just why one song will make a hit, while another of equal merit will not, is a problem which writers and publishers never have been able to solve. In some cases a catch phrase will do the trick; witness for instance "Ta-ra-ra boom de ay," "There'll be a Hot Time," and the rather vulgar "Lemon" song. It is rather pleasing to learn that such hits are growing shorter lived from year to year. The test of time is the surest proof of the real worth of any song. "After the Ball," "Daisy Bell," "Mr. Dooley," "Hiawatha" and "Bedelia" each in turn have had enormous sales, but they are now completely forgotten, while "Oh, Promise Me," "The Holy City" and "The Rosary," all songs of comparative intrinsic merit, still are heard.

Among the popular song writers of recent years the name of Chas. K. Harris of Milwaukee has become best known, owing perhaps first of all, to the fact that he has more surely gauged the public taste than has any contemporary writer in the same field, and also because he is his own publisher. Mr. Harris was born in Poughkeepsie, New York, in 1865. He early began his career as a popular song writer, composing songs to order for professional people. "After the Ball" was the song which first brought him into prominence. Indeed it may be said that it was this song which really started the popular song craze as we know it today. Over $100,000 was realized by the composer from the sale of this one song alone. As will be remembered, "After the Ball" is a song of the ballad character and tells a complete story. It was first presented to the public by May Irwin in New York City, afterward being introduced in Hoyt's "A Trip to Chinatown."

Mr. Harris has stated that he received many suggestions from the stage for the subjects of popular songs. He writes: "For example, about twelve years ago such plays as 'The Second Mrs. Tanqueray' and 'The Crust of Society' were in vogue. I then wrote 'Cast Aside,' 'Fallen by the Wayside' and 'There'll Come a Time Someday.' Over 300,000 copies were sold of each. Then came the era of society dramas such as Belasco's 'Charity Ball' and 'The Wife.' I wrote and published 'While the Dance Goes On,' 'Hearts,' 'You'll Never Know' and 'Can Hearts So Soon Forget;' which had enormous sales." Military dramas such as "Held by the Enemy" and "Secret Service" called out such songs as "Just Break the News to Mother" and "Tell Her that I Loved Her, Too."

Among the many successful popular song-writers of today are William B. Gray, who made a small fortune by his "Volunteer Organist;" H. W. Petrie, whose name is associated with the child song "I Don't Want to Play in Your Yard;" Charles Graham, who wrote "Two Little Girls in Blue." Other familiar names are those of Raymon Moore, Paul Dresser, Felix McGlennon, Mabel McKinley, Edward B. Marks, Gus Edwards, Egbert Van Alstyne, Harry Von Tilzer and Neil Moret.

Modern popular songs have been classified as follows: Coon Songs (rough, comic, refined, love or serenade); Comic Songs (topical, character or dialect); March Songs (patriotic, war, girl or character); Waltz Songs; Home or Mother Songs; Descriptive or Story Ballads; Child Songs; Love Ballads; Ballads of a Higher Class; Sacred Songs; Production Songs (for interpolation in big musical productions, entailing use of chorus, costumes, and stage business).

In the popular song of today the chorus is of most importance, for upon this part of the song usually rests its ultimate success or failure. The words of the chorus usually are applicable to every verse. In the descriptive song, the writer aims to tell a complete story in as few words and as graphically as possible. The success of the comic or topical song rests on the "gag" introduced into each verse and made apparent by the first or last line of the chorus. In the several classes or divisions of popular songs those of more serious character strive to make their appeal equally through both words and music; in the march song the music is of most account, while the comic song depends largely on the words.

Many reasons may be given for the ever-increasing vogue of popular music. Not the least of these is to be found in the presence of a piano or some musical instrument in nearly every home. Such was not the case a quarter century ago. The advent of the pianola and other mechanical players, together with the phonograph and gramophone also have tended to create a demand for popular music. Again, the teaching of the rudiments of music in the public schools has served to bring the art more closely before the public, with the result that nearly every girl in the country, whose parents can afford it, is receiving music lessons as a part of her general education. In homes where very little music of any kind previously had been heard it is but natural that music of a popular style at first would be most acceptable, this serving to satisfy until the taste be elevated so as to desire something of a better nature.

The appearance of singers of the first rank in musical comedy and in vaudeville undoubtedly has become a factor in forwarding the cause of popular music. While the presence of such singers in the vaudeville ranks has been deplored, the fact that they have made their appearance there has to some extent raised the standard of popular music in this country; for the class of music which they have sung has been in advance of that generally produced. There is no question but what the purveyors of popular music have shown more enterprise in the production of music that will please their patrons than have those who cater to a class with higher artistic perceptions.

Of the quantities of popular songs published in the last thirty years but few have attained any lasting popularity. Songs of which hundreds of thousands of copies have been sold now are completely forgotten. The reason for this is hard to ascertain. It is not because the later songs are of inferior merit, for a steady advance has been made in all popular music. The public now readily accepts harmonies which but a few years ago would have been looked upon as too difficult and complicated.

In the matter of the text of our present day popular songs, however, the same advancement has not been made. There rarely is shown the same simplicity and wholesome sentiment seen in our earlier songs, such as "Home, Sweet Home" and "Old Black Joe." Popular taste now looks for words touching on the events of the moment rather than those dealing with emotions and feeling which are common to all and which always are in evidence.

For short periods the majority of compositions written in popular style will be very similar. Take, for instance, the introduction of ragtime melodies. At first the words of such songs dealt almost exclusively with negro characterizations. Later came songs in a quasi-Indian manner. Mexico, Japan, China were all used as ragtime suggestions. Ragtime has been much abused and its incessant use decried by many people, yet it has done much in educating the public to an appreciation of the more complicated rhythms used in music of a higher grade. The tendencies all are favorable for the production of popular music of an even better character. What would have been listened to with delight by the public a generation ago now would be looked upon as decidedly flat and uninteresting. In the light operas and musical comedies of such composers as Victor Herbert and Reginald De Koven many numbers will be found which are of real musical worth. And yet they rarely last beyond two or three years at the most. As before suggested, the inanition of the text probably is responsible for the short life of the songs, while the nervous desire of the public for something new gives to the best of the popular instrumental music of today but an ephemeral existence. Doubtless as time goes on we shall revert to the ever passing stream of popular songs and the best will be saved, until finally they become incorporated into our folk-song literature. It is only in rare cases that a tune has any lengthy existence when separated from words of universal context.

Two special classes of songs, which, in a way, may be termed popular, are college songs and gospel hymns. Of the two, the hymns more properly may be classified as popular music, insomuch as they are sung by all sorts and conditions of people, while the college songs are somewhat limited in their employment, although some of them have come into general use. Many of the latter did not originate as student songs but have been appropriated from various sources until now they are conceded to be the especial property of the undergraduate.

The college glee club, for which many of these songs originally were indited, is patterned after the German Männerchor, though the singing and the selections hardly attain to the dignity of those of the Teutonic choruses. Nevertheless excellent musical and dramatic effects, though often of an exaggerated order, are obtained by the college men. The songs themselves, with which most of us are familiar, contain as their most salient feature a sharply marked rhythm, thus making them especially effective when given in chorus. The melodies and harmonies are pleasing and catchy, while the words usually are sentimental or humorous, certain of them being elaborations of Mother Goose rhymes. All of the larger and older institutions have their own individual songs which are looked upon as the special property of the student body, both graduate and undergraduate.

Among the songs most popular with all the colleges are "Gaudeamus," "Integer Vitæ," "Vive l'Amour," "Bingo," "Mary had a little Lamb," "Tarpaulin Jacket," "The Dutch Company," "Spanish Cavalier," "Good-night, Ladies," "Soldier's Farewell," "Nelly was a Lady," "Old Cabin Home" and scores of others. It will be seen that many of these have been appropriated from the repertory of popular music in general, until they have become recognized by the public as essentially "college" songs. A special feature of student life which has given rise to many songs has been the amateur theatricals conducted by the various societies and fraternities; for in many of these productions, which often are written by the students themselves, and given elaborate presentations, songs and instrumental numbers figure prominently.

The growth of the gospel and Sunday-school hymn is the outcome of the revival and Sunday-school movements, added to the trend of popular music in general. In the early days of these two religious factors use was made of the ordinary hymns and chorals of the church, but as popular secular music assumed a new form the demand for sacred music of a similar nature had to be met. Consequently a number of writers came forward with simple melodies, arranged with fundamental harmonies, which they set to suitable words. Here then was the counterpart of the popular secular song. There has been much outcry among church musicians against the continued use of this too often trashy music and there is no question that its spirit is far from religious; but it is music which satisfies the uncultured taste and as such is necessary in the less formal services of the church. The idea of adapting secular airs and those of a secular character to church uses is not new, for in the time of Luther, and even earlier, similar practises were common. In the matter of the words of the gospel hymns the same spirit is seen, for literary culture is as necessary for the appreciation of verse of a high character as is musical culture for true enjoyment of music of the better class. There is as great a chance for improvement in the text of both sacred and secular popular songs as there is in the musical settings.

Many of the gospel hymns have become extremely popular and are known the world over. Such a hymn as " Sweet Bye and Bye," by J. P. Webster, is sung wherever the English language is heard. There are many Americans, writers of gospel hymns, whose names have been associated almost exclusively with this branch of popular music. Among them are Lowell Mason, P. P. Bliss, Ira D. Sankey, Phillipp Phillipps, L. O. Emerson and Horatio R. Palmer. George F. Root wrote many popular hymns such as " Hold the Fort," " Pull for the Shore " and " Rescue the Perishing." " What a Friend we have in Jesus " was written by Charles C. Converse, while Lowell Mason's best known hymn is " Blest be the tie that binds."

Popular instrumental music in America dates practically from the period following the Civil War. True, the dance tunes of England, Ireland and Scotland previously had been used to display the musical attainments of the maiden of the period, but it was not until recent years that any effort was made to satisfy the growing demand for instrumental music of a popular style. As piano playing became more general (for the piano is the true " home " instrument, following the cabinet organ, which was not adapted to music of a showy character) several writers came forward with compositions gauged to appeal to the average musical intelligence. This music usually is formed of a simple and pleasing melody set to elemental harmony and brightened with arpeggios and similar stock passages, the whole capable of being performed, or executed, by players of small attainment.

The variation pieces by A. P. Wyman, T. P. Ryder, and Chas. L. Blake, together with the operatic arrangements of James Bellak and others, are representative of this class of music. Well-known melodies such as "Old Oaken Bucket," "Nearer My God to Thee," "Old Black Joe," "Suwanee River," "Sweet Bye and Bye" and others of like character were arranged with variations. There were again other pieces, of which "Silvery Waves" and "Maiden's Prayer" are typical of the class, which had an immense sale and which went to form the repertory of many an amateur pianist. At a later date came the various waltzes and marches and still later the two-step and pieces of the intermezzo character.

Foremost among the successful American writers of popular instrumental music stands the name of John Philip Sousa, the "March King." It has been said that Sousa writes with the metronome at his elbow running at one hundred and twenty clicks to the minute. Sousa's marches never have been surpassed and rarely equaled. They are without doubt the most typical music which this country has yet produced, for they are indeed deeply imbued with the American spirit. Sousa above all others has caught the true martial swing; his music also has the stamp of his own distinct individuality and he practically has revolutionized march music. No other composer, not even Johann Strauss, has attained such world-wide popularity as has Sousa. His music has been sold to thousands of bands in the United States alone and has been heard in all parts of the civilized world. It has been very aptly stated that Sousa's marches contain all the nuances of military psychology, the long unisonal stride, the grip on the musket, the pride in the regiment and the esprit de corps. They also have served as dance music, and the two-step was directly borne into vogue by them.

John Philip Sousa was born in Washington, D. C., on Nov. 6, 1859, his mother being a German and his father a Spanish political exile. At eight years of age Sousa was playing the fiddle in a dancing school and at sixteen led an orchestra in a variety theatre. Two years later he became director of a traveling theatrical troupe, composing music for the members and also appearing in negro minstrel roles. At nineteen he toured the country as a member of Offenbach's Orchestra, and shortly after he became director of the Pinafore Opera Company. For some years after this he directed the United States Marine Band and in 1892 formed his own Concert Band. His career from this time on is familiar to the American public. Sousa's chief claim to fame lies in his marches, from which he has derived a princely income. The most popular of these are "Washington Post," "Liberty Bell," "High School Cadets," "King Cotton," "Manhattan Beach," "El Capitan" and "Stars and Stripes Forever." As will be seen, the titles are derived either from patriotic subjects or from some subject-matter of national import or interest. Sousa's efforts in the comic opera field receive mention elsewhere in this chapter.

Marked advancement in the public taste for instrumental music has been shown in recent years and many compositions of an artistic nature have been adopted into the repertory of popular music. Pieces such as Handel's "Largo," Rubinstein's "Melody in F," Nevin's "Narcissus" and even Schumann's "Träumerei" may now be classed as popular music. The concert bands have done much in familiarizing the public with music of this character, and it is no uncommon thing to find the public making special requests for the works of Wagner and Liszt. Another feature which has tended to elevate the popular taste for instrumental rather than for vocal music is the general study of the piano by the young. The teaching material of necessity is of higher grade than the songs commonly sung and America has gained much from the general introduction of the piano into the home.

In light opera and musical comedy is seen the most elaborate phase which popular music has assumed. Of late years the country has been deluged with musical plays until their effect has been felt on the legitimate drama. These productions are the natural sequence of the decadent minstrel show, and while they lack the dignity, if such a word may here be used, of the comic operas of the European peoples, the American public has wafted them into favor until they have become the most popular form of entertainment presented on the stage.

The better class of American light operas is built somewhat after the style of those of Gilbert and Sullivan, while the "near" operas or musical comedies are simply a series of solos, concerted pieces and choruses held together by a mere thread of a plot. Several of the better sort have become standards and bid fair to remain for some years to come; but the vogue of the vast majority is fleeting, lasting at the best but for a few years.

Light opera first sprang into favor with the American public in 1878, in which year James C. Duff, a brother-in-law of Augustin Daly, brought from England Gilbert and Sullivan's "H. M. S. Pinafore" and produced it at the Standard Theatre (now the Manhattan) in New York. The success of the charming opera was remarkable, and as there was no copyright on the work different managers at once took it up and within a short time five theatres in New York alone were playing it to full houses. Such was the furore which "Pinafore" created that soon it was being produced in all parts of the country and by all sorts of companies — children's, church-choir, and even negro.

When the "Pinafore" craze struck Boston a Miss Ober decided to form a company composed of the best church and concert singers of the city in order to produce the popular operetta in the most adequate manner possible. She was successful in bringing together an excellent organization which took the name of the Boston Ideal Pinafore Company. The outcome of this was the famous Bostonians, which survived the "Pinafore" craze and which for so many years maintained undiminished popularity. From this company came many of the best light opera singers which this country has produced, among them being Jessie Bartlett Davis, Adelaide Phillips, Marie Stone, H. C. Barnabee, Myron W.

Whitney, Eugene Cowles and Tom Karl. No other company of American singers ever has achieved such lasting success as did the Bostonians. For twelve years they toured the country, season after season, until they became a national institution. Their repertory included all the popular light operas of their day, but DeKoven's "Robin Hood" became the especial favorite, this opera receiving over a thousand performances at their hands.

The name of John A. McCaull for many years was associated with the production of light opera in New York. When, in 1880, "Pirates of Penzance" was brought out by Gilbert and Sullivan, precautionary measures were taken to prevent American pirates from appropriating the score and an alliance with Mr. McCaull was formed to produce the new work at the Fifth Avenue Theatre. About this time Rudolph Aronson instituted the Casino, and for several seasons McCaull supplied the company in which Francis Wilson was the principal comedian. Mr. McCaull then took charge of Wallack's Theatre, and it was in this house that he made his best productions. The stock company which he formed was of unusual excellence and included De Wolfe Hopper, Jefferson de Angelis, Digby Bell, Laura Joyce, Marion Manola and Eugene Ondine. So successful did the company become that its very success led to its downfall, for the best talent too soon followed Francis Wilson into the world of star productions, and as a result the organization suffered a decline.

The "star" system largely was responsible for the decadence of light opera of the better class, for good general ensemble was allowed to suffer in order to exploit the "star" or "stars." Instead of the opera being written as an exposition of suitable music and libretto, such as contained in the Gilbert and Sullivan and earlier DeKoven operas, it became merely a vehicle to bring forward this or that "star" with his or her peculiar limitations, vocally or histrionically skilfully concealed. Thus it was that light opera degenerated into musical comedy, for undoubtedly it is a degeneration, and the productions of recent years are no longer properly to be classed with light opera.

The musical comedy of today partakes of the character of the old German singspiel or song-play, in which the spoken dialogue was interspersed with musical numbers. As before stated, it is a decadent form of comic or light opera and its forte is dramatic rather than musical, for the music is brought in rather as incidental than as an integral part of the performance. Many of the popular musical comedies were first brought out by organizations or clubs connected with well-known societies and colleges prominent among which are the "Cadets of Boston," the "Hasty Pudding Club" at Harvard, "Monk and Wig" at University of Pennsylvania, and "The Strollers" at Columbia. The Boston "Cadets" particularly have placed many hits to their credit, "1492" and "Jack and the Beanstock" being especially successful.

Among all the American light operas those of DeKoven and Herbert are intrinsically the best, for they are cleverly put together and show the evidence of musicianly treatment. America, however, has never produced a writer of librettos to at all compare with W. S. Gilbert of Gilbert and Sullivan fame, and without the requisite of a good libretto no opera, no matter what its musical value, can attain to lasting popularity. The operas of Reginald DeKoven, of which he has written fifteen, have achieved wide popularity. "Robin Hood" alone has been enacted more than three thousand times, while "The Fencing Master," "The Highwayman" (which is considered his best work), "Foxy Quiller," "Red Feather," "Maid Marion," "The Little Duchess," "Rob Roy," and others have all had successful runs. Mr. DeKoven also has written two ballets "The Man in the Moon" and "The Man in the Moon, Jr.," as well as many songs which have had a large sale. More than a million copies of "Oh, Promise Me" alone have been sold. DeKoven now stands at the head of our writers of popular music of the better class. He was born in Middletown, Connecticut, in 1859, and now is a resident of New York.

Victor Herbert, an American by adoption, is another writer who has made a reputation for himself in the light opera field. Although he has composed more serious works and has been associated with musical matters of a higher order he is best known by his lighter creations. Mr. Herbert is a native of Ireland and first came to this country in 1886, when he joined the Metropolitan Opera Company in New York. He for several seasons was first cellist of the Theodore Thomas Orchestra, later became the conductor of the Symphony Orchestra in Pittsburg, Pennsylvania, which position he held for a number of years, and then formed an orchestra of his own in New York. His operas and musical comedies, while possibly not of quite as high an order as those of DeKoven, are extremely tuneful and pleasing and always show the touch of the musician. Among the most popular are "The Wizard of the Nile," "Serenade," "The Idol's Eye," "The Fortune Teller," "Babes in Toyland," "Babette," "It Happened in Nordland," "The Red Mill," "Mdlle. Modiste," which latter has served to perfect the establishing of Fritzi Scheff as a light opera singer.

Three American teams of light opera and musical comedy writers, Smith & DeKoven, Barnet & Stone, and Pixley & Luders, have become well known; for the joint works which they have produced have been among the best of their class. With the work of the librettists we are not especially concerned, notwithstanding the fact that on the libretto depends to a large extent the success of an opera. The music of DeKoven as well as that of Victor Herbert, who perhaps is his nearest competitor, already has been noted. R. A. Barnet's best works undoubtedly are "1492" and "Jack and the Beanstock," which latter work developed into one of the best extravaganzas ever produced on the American stage. Gustave Luders has many successes placed to his credit, such as "Prince of Pilsen," "King Dodo" and Grand Mogul."

Edgar Stillman Kelley wrote a comic opera "Puritania," which was excellent musically, but which suffered through the libretto. Sousa has brought out several operas, "El

Capitan," "The Charlatan," "The Bride Elect" and "The Free Lance," as well as an extravaganza, "Chris and the Wonderful Lamp," each of which had some success. The youngest and one of the most typical of musical comedy writers is Geo. M. Cohan. Mr. Cohan was born at Providence, Rhode Island, on July 4, 1878, and it is most fitting that his contributions to popular music should catch the American spirit. The "Yankee Doodle Boy," as he has been called, very aptly describes both him and his music. "Little Johnny Jones," "Forty-five Minutes from Broadway," "George Washington, Jr." and "Fifty Miles from Boston" have won fame and fortune for him while he is still under thirty.

It is almost impossible to judge of the composer of our current musical comedies, for so many songs by writers other than the originator are interpolated that the name of the initiatory writer becomes lost in the hodge-podge finally produced. The musical comedies of today recall the "Ballad Operas" of more than a century ago, and it is seen that we thus have reverted to the tastes of our forefathers. Truly, there is nothing new under the sun. The only difference to be seen is in the character and make-up of the music itself, for the structure of musical comedy is very similar to that of the "Beggar's Opera."

In the true comic or light opera the librettist aims to form either a consistent farcical story or a clever satire, but in musical comedy this unfortunately is hardly considered necessary. So long as there are two or three acts of more or less amusing dialogue, striking stage pictures and taking music, nothing more is regarded as of importance. Although not an American production Franz Lehar's "Merry Widow," which has taken the world by storm, may be cited as a typical light opera of today, while Victor Herbert's "Red Mill" is characteristic of musical comedy. The difference in general make-up easily may be noted and compared.

The enumeration of the musical comedies, writers of such works, and singers and players appearing in the same within recent years, is out of the question, for new writers and performers are continually coming forward and the existence of the works themselves at the best is but a matter of a few years. As representative writers of musical comedy, beside those already spoken of may be cited Richard Carle, Gus Edwards, Raymond Hubbell, Joe Howard, A. B. Sloane, Jean Schwartz, Alfred Robyn and M. Klein. Numbers of adaptations of English, French and German musical comedies and extravaganzas as well as our own products have been successfully exploited in this country within the last few years. From the time when Francis Wilson first was brought forward as a star there has been a steady stream of singers of the lighter musical works who have won fame for themselves in this field. Some, such as Alice Nielsen, have used the light opera roles as stepping stones to more ambitious achievements, while there are again others who have reversed the process. There are many names beside those already enumerated which have become closely associated with the more popular musical productions of the American stage. It will suffice to mention the following as representative of their class: Lillian Russell, Virginia Earle, Fay Templeton, Madge Lessing, Marie Cahill, Camille D'Arville, Marie Tempest, Edna Wallace Hopper, Lulu Glaser, Edna May, Jeff De Angelis, De Wolfe Hopper, Richard Carle and Frank Daniels. It will be seen that the laurels in its field rest with the fair sex. Williams and Walker occupy a unique place through their excellent presentation of musical plays by a company composed wholly of negroes.

What will be the next phase to be assumed by popular music in this country is impossible to state. However, it appears highly probable that within a few years there will come a revulsion of feeling against the inanities of musical comedy, and the more legitimate forms of light opera again will assume their place in public favor. Despite the outcry heard in some quarters against the popular music of the day, it is serving its purpose in educating the public to desire something better. Popular music in its various forms always will have a place, for it is music which the musically uncultured can enjoy. Just as art music continually is changing its character and structure, so is popular music undergoing the same evolution, and the last word has not been said in either field. From the fact that musical culture ever is becoming more general, it is but natural to assume that the increased familiarity of the public with music of the better class must have its effect on the popular productions. An unbiased investigator will find marked improvement in the general trend of popular music produced in the last twenty-five years, and we still are advancing.

PATRIOTIC AND NATIONAL MUSIC

While all patriotic and national music is to a greater or less extent popular music, it may be classed apart in that its growth largely is due to the circumstance of war and is the specific outcome of such conditions. America's war songs and sea songs have played their part as incentives to patriotism, to enlistment in the ranks, to valor in the field and on the sea, and have served to inspire and cheer the fighting forces of the Republic. They thus have become national both in scope and in character.

People of every nationality are moved to speech or to song by that which permeates the thoughts or appeals to the emotions in times of political excitement. Love of country, together with a pride in its institutions, be the latter of a primitive or more cultured form, smolders in the breast of all mankind. This latent spark when fanned into a blaze of fervor finds vent in speech and in song, which in turn inspires to action.

Such is the birth of patriotic music. No country, as history proves, can afford to ignore the patriotic force capable of being brought into play through the power of music, either in song or in instrumental form, both of which performed their part in inciting to action. It is said that the songs written by Charles Dibdin had so potent an influence in war, that, in 1803, the British government engaged him to write a series of them "to keep alive the national feelings against the French," and his biographer relates the pertinent fact that "his engagement ceased with the war he thus assisted in bringing to a glorious close."

The repertory of popular music in America is especially rich in patriotic and national songs, in fact so much so that it is hard to fix on any one and term it our national anthem. These songs have been called into existence chiefly at the various times that the country has been at war, either international or civil. The first incentive to patriotic vocal utterance was the Revolution, later followed by the War of 1812 and still later by the Civil War. The songs brought out at these three periods were typical of the individual times at which they were written and many of them were colored by particular incidents. Thus in them there is a graphic history of the American Republic.

The colonists of America, who had been schooled to hardship and privation, finding little time for the cultivation of the arts, were not found wanting when the critical moment presented itself. True, there was little of secular music at the period immediately preceding the Revolution. Psalm-singing was at this time the only music tolerated by the Puritan element. Thus it happens that the early musical efforts of a patriotic nature were semi-religious in character.

The first war song in America originated with William Billings, of whom further mention is made in a later chapter of this volume. In his Singing Master's Assistant, one of the most important musical publications of its time, are found, among other of his original compositions, two that became exceedingly popular with the Revolutionary troops. The significance of the political agitation at this time presented opportunity for Billings to display his aptitude in verse. He possessed a keen intuition of the temper of the times, and his compositions are an outburst of the patriotic fervor that had been awaiting just such opportunity for development. So to his favorite tune of Chester he set the following text:

Let tyrants shake their iron rod,
And slavery clank her galling chains,
We'll fear them not, we'll trust in God;
New England's God forever reigns.

The foe comes on with haughty stride,
Our troops advance with martial noise;
Their veterans flee before our arms.
And generals yield to beardless boys.

Naturally enough, these words, set to a familiar tune and so thoroughly characteristic of the spirit of the hour, caught the taste of the people. Indeed, these half sacred, half secular ebullitions may be classed as our pioneer patriotic and popular music. The enthusiasm with which Billings sang and taught these songs communicated itself to the people, even to those who in the prejudice of their time had strenuously opposed singing in the churches, for no one could doubt the composer's sincere patriotism.

Billings' songs, anthems, hymns, or whatever we may please to call them, their nature almost defying accuracy of definition though the use to which they were put, went with the soldiers into camp and on the field; they were sung with enthusiasm, and served to cheer the drooping spirit and nerve the arm to strike. These songs cannot be separated from the annals of our country, as they proved an incentive to that which made history. There is an impressive simplicity in the two following stanzas forming part of the text which has been quoted above:

When God inspir'd us for the fight,
Their ranks were broken, their lines were forc'd,
Their ships were shattered in our sight,
Or swiftly driven from the coast.

What grateful offering shall we bring?
What shall we render to the Lord?
Loud hallelujahs let us sing,
And praise his name on every cord.

The following stanza is taken from a song, set to an old Scotch tune, which was sung by the Pennsylvania regiments. It was first heard in 1775, but there is no record of its author:

We are the troops that ne'er will stoop
 To wretched slavery,
Nor shall our seed by our base deed
 Despised vassals be!
Freedom we will bequeath to them,
 Or we will bravely die;
Our greatest foe ere long shall know
 How much did Sandwich lie.
And all the world shall know
 Americans are free;
Nor slaves nor cowards will we prove
 Great Britain soon shall see.

In 1778, an Englishman, Henry Archer, who had been educated at a military school in his native land, renounced a handsome inheritance, left England, and became through his sympathy in the cause a volunteer in the American army. Archer composed a song which was sung with much enthusiasm by the soldiers. It is rather in the nature of a convivial than of a war song, although it was a particular favorite in camp, and is as follows:

THE VOLUNTEER BOYS.

Hence with the lover who sighs o'er his wine,
 Chloes and Phillises toasting,
Hence with the slave who will whimper and whine,
 Of ardor and constancy boasting.
  Hence with love's joys,
  Follies and noise,
 The toast that I give is the Volunteer Boys.

Here's to the squire who goes to parade,
 Here's to the citizen soldier;
Here's to the merchant who fights for his trade,
 Whom danger increasing makes bolder.
  Let mirth appear
  Union is here,
 The toast that I give is the brave Volunteer.

Then follows the health of the "law" volunteer; the "veteran chiefs who become volunteers," referring to those who have served before and are ready to serve again; and to the farmer or ploughman, who is toasted as the "stout volunteer." One can readily understand with what vim this song would be sung in a day when there was so little music of a martial nature.

It was a period when writers of verse were more active than composers of music. This resulted in the former adapting their songs to music already written and with which the people were familiar. Such was the origin of "Rise Columbia," which, in 1794, was set to the tune of "Rule Britannia" by Robert Treat Paine, the sentiment of the words being somewhat plagiarized in doing duty as an American song of patriotism. In order that the reader may better comprehend this, a reprint of the original first stanza of the American and the British song is here given:

RISE COLUMBIA.

When first the sun o'er ocean glow'd,
And earth unveiled her virgin breast,
Supreme mid Nature's, mid Nature's vast abode,
Was heard th' Almighty's dread behest:
    Rise Columbia, Columbia brave and free,
    Poise the globe and bound the sea.

RULE BRITANNIA.

When Britain first at Heav'n's command,
Arose from out the azure main,
This was the charter, the charter of the land,
And guardian angels sang this strain:
    "Rule Britannia! Britannia rules the waves;
    Britons never shall be slaves."

Among other names distinguished for their contributions to the military songs of this period may be mentioned Benjamin Young Prime, and James McClurg, both of whom were physicians; Rednap Howell, who was a schoolmaster at Deep River, North Carolina; David Humphreys, who became a captain on the staff of General Putnam; Joel Barlow, and Timothy Dwight; all of whom wrote songs for the soldiers.

Barlow, on entering the army as chaplain, is recorded as expressing himself as "not knowing whether he could do more for the cause in the capacity of chaplain or in that of poet," adding, "I have great faith in the influence of songs — one good song is worth a dozen addresses or proclamations."

One of the best contributions to the song lore of the Revolutionary period is "Columbia," by Timothy Dwight, afterward president of Yale College. In 1777 the classes of Yale were scattered on account of the war, and in the month of May of that year Mr. Dwight with a number of students repaired to Wethersfield, Connecticut, remaining until the autumn, when he received his license as a minister of the Congregational Church. He now joined the army as chaplain, and while serving he wrote several patriotic songs as inspiration to the troops composing his brigade, which was made up principally of farmers who were more or less serious-minded men. These songs were also sung with zest throughout the New England communities. "Columbia," which must be considered in the light of the period in which it was written, is permeated by a strong, hopeful, prophetic spirit.

Columbia, Columbia, to glory arise,
The queen of the world and the child of the skies;
Thy genius commands thee; with rapture behold,
While ages on ages thy splendors unfold,
Thy reign is the last and the noblest of time,
Most fruitful thy soil, most inviting thy clime;
Let the crimes of the east ne'er encrimson thy name;
Be freedom and science, and virtue and fame.

Thus, as down a lone valley, with cedars o'erspread,
From war's dread confusion I pensively strayed —
The gloom from the face of fair heaven retired,
The winds ceased to murmur, the thunders expired;

Perfumes as of Eden, flowed sweetly along,
And a voice, as of angels, enchantingly sang—
Columbia, Columbia, to glory arise,
The queen of the world and the child of the skies.

Not a song of boast, nor of warlike trend, yet one momentarily to lift the heart, and to impart a clear insight into the issue at stake, when from the struggle and strife of combat with all its attendant sufferings, there would arise a nation purified by its trials, and upon whose altar should be laid, not alone the laurels of conquest, but the gifts of liberty and fraternity, justice, science, art and genius.

There were many songs written in which the war-spirit prevailed. There were also the semi-religious songs, sung both at the hearthstone and around the camp-fire. The more spirited songs were used in the weary marches or on the field of combat, while in the churches were found those in which serenity of thought, peace of mind, patience and fortitude were incorporated, with an appeal to a Higher Power for help and sustenance. Perhaps the most notable lyric of this kind came from the pen of Nathaniel Niles.

Mr. Niles was graduated from Princeton in 1766. He was a man of remarkable versatility, having studied both medicine and law, taught school for a time in New York City, was a member of the Vermont legislature and a judge of the supreme court, as well as a representative to Congress. When the news of the battle of Bunker Hill reached him he was at his home in Norwich, Connecticut, and being deeply moved he wrote "The American Hero," which was immediately set to music and sung in all the churches during the troubled years that followed. Space cannot here be given to the whole of this ode of some fifteen stanzas, but a few verses will illustrate its depth of feeling as well as its incentive to strike for the cause of freedom:

Infinite wisdom teacheth us submission;
Bids us be quiet under all His dealings;
Never repining, but forever praising
God our Creator.

Then to the goodness of my Lord and Master,
I will commit all that I have or wish for;
Sweetly as babes sleep, will I give my life up
When called to yield it.

Fame and dear Freedom, lure me on to battle;
While a fell despot, grimmer than a death's head
Stings me with serpents fiercer than Medusa's,
To the encounter.

Life for my country and the cause of freedom,
Is but a cheap price for a worm to part with;
And if preserved in so great a contest,
Life is redoubled.

Such songs are typical of those of the Revolutionary period and serve to give an idea of the patriotic songs of that day. They are all more or less touched with the religious spirit and in their musical settings show the same tendencies. It was a time when piety and seriousness were more in evidence than they have been during the later wars waged by the American Republic, and such characteristics are faithfully portrayed in these martial songs.

It also was during the Revolutionary period that "Yankee Doodle" was bestowed upon us. It has clung to us with unshaken tenacity ever since and is ours by right of adoption. The tune has been pronounced frivolous and lacking in dignity, yet England, Holland, Turkey, Persia and Spain have laid claim to its origin. The more one tries to ascertain from whence it came the more one finds himself floundering amid an overwhelming mass of incident and anecdote connecting the original with the version first heard in our Revolutionary period. The Englishman will tell you that "Yankee Doodle" originated in a derisive song directed against Cromwell, while the Dutchman persists that the same melody has been a favorite song of the harvesters of the Netherlands for centuries.

"Yankee Doodle" began its career in America as a song of exasperation. It was an ever ready weapon by which the British troops sought to ridicule the American soldiery; but when the keen-witted "Yankee" turned its edge by adopting the air and using it as a means of retort upon the British royalists its popularity became unbounded. It was played at the battle of Lexington when repelling the foe; at the surrender of Burgoyne, and finally at the surrender of Yorktown, where Lafayette in a spirit of pleasantry ordered the tune played. It thus became our first triumphant melody.

That "Yankee Doodle" was an English song at the beginning of the Revolution and an American song at its close, later becoming incorporated in our national song, there is no reason to doubt. Most authorities on the subject have now conceded that Richard Shuckburgh, a surgeon with the English troops, was the writer of the satirical verses which he adapted to a familiar air — an old English dance tune dating back to the reign of Charles I. From the New York Journal bearing date Oct. 13, 1768, is taken the following paragraph which connects the song with the British troops:

"The British fleet was bro't to anchor near Castle William, in Boston Harbor, and the opinion of the visitors to the ships was that the 'Yankee Doodle Song' was the capital piece in the band of their musicians."

The treaty of peace between Great Britain and America was signed on Dec. 24, 1814, at Ghent, where Henry Clay and John Quincy Adams met the British ambassador. Here it was that the burghers, to show their satisfaction at the treaty being signed within their domain, resolved upon serenading the two embassies. The national song of England was familiar enough to them, but they were not sure as to the national hymn of America. They sought the band-master for enlightenment and he referred the matter to Mr. Clay.

"Yankee Doodle," responded the American commissioner. The band-master, not being familiar with the melody requested Mr. Clay to hum it so that he might note it down. Mr. Clay tried but failed. Then the secretary of the legation made a futile attempt to voice the melody.

Finally Mr. Clay called in his servant, saying: "Bob, whistle 'Yankee Doodle' for this gentleman." Thus Europe received its transcription of our first truly national song from the puckered lips of an American negro. It was harmonized and copied, and became known in Europe as the "National Anthem of America." While "Yankee Doodle" has been looked upon as a national song, it is the tune rather than the words which makes its appeal, for the melody is everything and the words are nothing; and although forming a stirring instrumental piece it is not adapted to vocal harmonization.

Of all the songs of national import which America claims, "Hail Columbia!" is particularly her own — words and music both emanating from a deep spirit of patriotism and both finding birth at a critical moment in our national life. There has been a difference of opinion among our music historians as to its author, and although all agree as to its claim of American origin, they disagree as to who was its composer. The music, in the first place, was not written for the words. The former had become familiar in the nature of a march, while the words were written afterward to fit the tune. During the Revolutionary War much march music sprang into existence. It was one of these marches that was selected to do duty to words composed expressly to meet a certain need. Joseph Hopkinson, its author, states that the words of "Hail Columbia!" were written in the summer of 1798 when war with France was thought to be inevitable. The contest between England and France was raging and the people of the United States were divided as to the cause of which nation it was better to espouse.

At this time Gilbert Fox, a young actor, was to be given a benefit performance at a theatre in Philadelphia. Fox requested Mr. Hopkinson to write some patriotic words for use as a closing number, and "Hail Columbia!" was the result of his endeavor. Mr. Hopkinson had been careful to make no allusion to either England or France, particularly as to the quarrel between them; on the contrary he had struck the happy suggestion to American patriotism, love of country, especially emphasizing the idea of independence, which was uppermost in the minds of all. This was the touch of the diplomat, for the song was taken into the favor of both parties, for all were Americans.

The words were adapted without loss of time to the music of the "President's March," and on the morning of April 25, 1798, the morning papers of Philadelphia announced Gilbert Fox's benefit, in which an "entire new song (written by a citizen of Philadelphia), to the tune of 'The President's March' will be sung, accompanied by a full band and a grand chorus."

Hail Columbia, happy land!
Hail ye heroes! heaven-born band,
Who fought and bled in freedom's cause,
Who fought and bled in freedom's cause!
And when the storm of war had gone,
Enjoy'd the peace your valor won;
Let Independence be your boast,
Ever mindful what it cost!
Ever grateful for the prize,
Let its altar reach the skies.
    Firm united let us be,
    Rallying round our liberty;
    As a band of brothers joined,
    Peace and safety we shall find.

The audience being in a condition both politically and emotionally to receive such a song, and the tune being already familiar, it caught the words of the refrain without difficulty. By the time the last verse was sung the people stood up, and joining the chorus heartily voiced this plea for unity and their thankfulness for independence.

The "President's March," the music to which the words were set, is said to have been composed by a German named Fyles, who, being leader of the orchestra in the John Street Theatre, New York, in 1789, and desiring to compliment the President, composed this march in his honor, playing it on the occasion of General Washington's attendance at the theatre. The son of Fyles claimed later, however, that his father first played this march on Trenton bridge as Washington rode over on his way to the New York inauguration. Claims have also been made for a musician by the name of Roth, at that time resident in Philadelphia, in which city "Feyles" or "Fyles" is said to have lived.

It is also stated by more modern commentators that Francis Hopkinson, father of Joseph Hopkinson, the author of the song, wrote a march — the original "Washington's March" it is claimed — which later became known as "Washington's March at the Battle of Trenton," and ultimately as "The President's March." Whether this is the "President's March" to which the words of "Hail Columbia" were adapted is uncertain.

On June 1, 1798, the Massachusetts Charitable Fire Society of Boston was about to celebrate its anniversary with a meeting and a banquet, and commissioned Robert Paine to write the text of a song for the occasion. "Adams and Liberty," or what was later known as "The Sons of Columbia," was the poem in question. Paine received seven hundred and fifty dollars from its sale, and after its publication, forwarded a copy to General Washington, who replied by letter:

"You will be sure that I am never more gratified than when I see the effusion of genius from some of the rising generation, which promises to secure our national rank in the literary world: as I trust their firm, manly, patriotic conduct will ever maintain it with dignity in the political."

There seems to have been no composer at hand to endow the words with an original musical setting, and Paine, who had been successful in adapting various texts to familiar tunes, now turned again to English melodies for a selection, finally fixing on the air "To Anacreon in Heaven." This air had been used by the Anacreontic Society, a famous London organization of the latter half of the Eighteenth Century, as their club song.

It was in the atmosphere of this society that the music set first to the words of "Adams and Liberty" and now doing duty as the tune to the "Star-Spangled Banner" was born. It has been said that this music did not originate with the Anacreontic Society; that it was adapted from an old French air. But it is now generally conceded that the music and words known as the song "To Anacreon in Heaven" sprang into being at one and the same moment, as the Anacreontic club song — the words being written by Ralph Tomlinson while presiding officer of the society, and the music by Dr. Samuel Arnold, composer and organist of the Chapel Royal.

This tune for nearly a century has been associated with the words of the "Star-Spangled Banner," and the fact that it originated with the London organization is almost forgotten. The poem itself is a beautiful one, full of incentive to patriotism, and is one of the finest tributes to a national flag that has emanated from any nation. The story of the author's inspiration also serves to endear the words, for they were not born of a flight of imagination but from actual incident.

Francis Scott Key, whose fame is associated with this poem, was a lawyer by profession, a graduate of St. John's College, Annapolis, and practised law both in Frederick City, Maryland, and in Washington, D. C. The second war between England and the United States was being waged on land and sea, when Dr. Beanes, an old resident of Maryland and a warm personal friend of the young lawyer, was being held a prisoner on the British frigate "Surprise." Key determined to seek his release, and providing himself with the necessary credentials, as well as proofs of the non-combatant status of the physician, set out on his errand of kindness.

With John S. Skinner, who had been appointed by President Madison to conduct negotiations with the British forces relative to the exchange of prisoners, he was subsequently taken on board the "Surprise." From this point, on the thirteenth of September, 1814, he witnessed the bombardment of Fort McHenry, and under the inspiration of the moment he penned the words of the "Star-Spangled Banner." Eight days after the bombardment the song appeared in the Baltimore American under the title "Defence of Fort McHenry, Tune — Anacreon in Heaven," and with the following notice:

"The annexed song was composed under the following circumstances: A gentleman had left Baltimore with a flag of truce, for the purpose of getting released from the British fleet a friend of his who had been captured at Marlborough. He went as far as the mouth of the Patuxent, and was not permitted to return lest the intended attack on Baltimore should be disclosed. He was therefore brought up the Bay to the mouth of the Patapsco, where the flag vessel was kept under the guns of a frigate, and he was compelled to witness the bombardment of Ft. McHenry, which the Admiral had boasted that he would carry in a few hours, and that the city must fall. He watched the flag at the fort through the whole day with an anxiety that can better be felt than described, until the night prevented him from seeing it. In the night he watched the bomb shells, and at early dawn his eye was again greeted by the proudly waving flag of his country."

Being born under such auspicious circumstances it is very fitting that the "Star-Spangled Banner" should have become the authorized music at the salute of the colors both in the army and navy. At the time in which the words of this song were written there was located in the vicinity of the Holliday Street Theatre, Baltimore, a small one-story frame house which was occupied as a tavern. It was here that Captain Benjamin Edes of the Twenty-seventh Regiment first introduced the song to a group of volunteers who had assembled for drill. The patriotic words, read by the captain, were received with shouts and cheers, and when the singing of the words was suggested, Ferdinand Durang, an actor, who was one of the group, rendered it to the tune of

"Anacreon in Heaven" as adapted by Key himself. It is said that Durang "mounted an old rush-bottomed chair, singing the song with admirable effect" and that "the chorus of each verse was re-echoed by those present with infinite harmony of voices."

Honor has been shown to the memory of Francis Scott Key by the erection of several monuments to his memory, notably one in California by James Lick, who in 1874 gave one hundred and fifty thousand dollars for the erection and maintenance of such a monument in San Francisco; and that at Frederick, Maryland, which was unveiled in August, 1898.

A patriotic song which has long retained its popularity is "Columbia, the Gem of the Ocean." The history of this song begins in 1843, in which year Thomas à Becket, an English actor, was playing an engagement at the Chestnut Street Theatre, Philadelphia. David T. Shaw, who was at this time singing at the Museum, called on Mr. à Becket with some patriotic verses he had written. Mr. à Becket, not finding them satisfactory, rewrote them and composed a musical setting for them.

A few weeks afterward, while playing in New Orleans, he was somewhat astonished to find a published copy of "Columbia, the Pride of the Ocean," in which David T. Shaw was credited with the authorship of both words and music, and Thos. à Becket with the arrangement of the same. Upon his return to Philadelphia he called upon the publisher and convinced him of his claim to the copyright. Negotiations with another publisher were at once begun and the song appeared a short time afterward under its proper title, with T. à Becket as author and composer, and with the additional information "Sung by D. T. Shaw." Mr. à Becket stated that when he visited London in 1847 he found this song claimed as an English composition, it being known there as "Britannia, the Pride of the Ocean." Though of undoubted American origin this song became so well liked in England that, by a slight alteration of the words, the "Red, White and Blue" became a favorite army and navy song.

So profound its import, historians declare that the shot at Fort Sumter reverberated around the world, and it may be added that the songs it inspired also have re-echoed around the globe. When the Civil War really became a fact our soldiers felt the need of martial music. This need first was met by an ineffectual attempt to revive the old Revolutionary songs and naval tunes of England, and also by adapting verses to any tune so long as its strains were inspiriting and one to which the troops could readily and easily march. Every officer bears testimony to the fact that songs and march music are essential to the campaign and field equipment of the general soldier. They inspire him with the necessary courage; danger is forgotten, and until shot and shell create a pandemonium of wild and harsh strains amid which men fight to kill, music is necessary to cheer the soldier, be he of the regular troops or of the volunteer forces made up from all ranks of the people.

"If we had had your war songs you would never have beaten us," said a Confederate officer to his brother of the Federal army. There is more in this statement than one may at first suppose. But the war songs, the kind that penetrate the heart of the soldier and that are caught up by the people in a frenzy of patriotism, are never coolly and deliberately made, but are born of circumstance. Such are the songs that were the outgrowth of our four years of strife, and numbers of them live and will live so long as there remains a flag to be protected and a country to be cherished.

One of the earlier, and perhaps the earliest of our Civil War songs, and one which seems never to lose its popularity, had its origin as a negro camp-meeting song. That is, the tune itself was originally sung to the words:

Say, brothers, will you meet us,
Say, brothers, will you meet us,
Say, brothers, will you meet us,
On Canaan's happy shore?
By the grace of God we'll meet you,
By the grace of God we'll meet you,
By the grace of God we'll meet you,
Where parting is no more.

The song in question is "Glory Hallelujah!" or "John Brown's Body." Lieutenant Chandler, in writing of Sherman's March to the Sea, tells that when the troops were halted at Shady Dale, Georgia, the regimental band played "John Brown's Body," whereupon a number of negro girls coming from houses supposed to have been deserted, formed a circle around the band, and in a solemn and dignified manner danced to the tune. The negro girls, with faces grave and demeanor characteristic of having performed a ceremony of religious tenor, retired to their cabins. It was learned from the older negroes that this air, without any particular words to it, had long been known among them as the "wedding tune." They considered it a sort of voodoo air, which held within its strains a mysterious hold upon the young colored women, who had been taught that unless they danced when they heard it played they would be doomed to a life of spinsterhood. This air, with the words quoted above, had been familiar in many church hymnals, notably the "Plymouth Collection," compiled by Henry Ward Beecher, and published about 1852.

Let there be conceded then to the war song of the Rebellion known as "John Brown's Body" a mysterious origin and admit its mystic spell. Its swing is such that any one, even a child, can grasp its subtle suggestion to the foot-beats and heart-throbs of moving and excited masses of humanity. As a war song or as a folk-lore song, if you will, it has scarcely an equal.

As a war song it was born in a locality where our heroes of the Revolution made famous that equally trifling melody "Yankee Doodle." At the outbreak of the war, the Second Battalion of Massachusetts Infantry was stationed at Fort Warren in Boston Harbor. The men forming this battalion were a jolly set of fellows and were familiarly designated "The Tigers." They had a glee club among the members, and the old camp-meeting tune was familiar to them. Among the singers in the glee club was a Scotchman by the name of John Brown, and the analogy in the name to that of the hero of Harper's Ferry made him the butt of many good-natured jokes among the soldiers. Thus it was that his name became the original suggestion to the "John Brown" song.

Some time later the Second was merged into the Twelfth Massachusetts Regiment under command of Colonel Fletcher Webster, and it was Webster's men who sung the song into general popularity. On July 18, 1861, in Boston, the Hon. Edward Everett presented a flag to the Twelfth Massachusetts a few days previous to its onward movement to the front. Over a thousand voices now took up the chorus of this song that had already taken its place as a favorite not only with the soldiers themselves but with the public. Reaching New York City, the regiment there sang the song and here also it was appropriated without delay. Three days later it electrified Baltimore, and on the first of March, 1862, the "Websters," as the soldiers of the Twelfth Massachusetts were designated, sang it in Charlestown, Virginia, when they were assembled in hollow square around the site on which the execution of John Brown had taken place three years previously.

When, in 1864, Sherman began his famous March to the Sea, with an army of over fifty-five thousand, at the moment when the Fourteenth Corps swung into column, one of the bands struck up the never-to-be-forgotten tune, and under the inspiration of the movement the men caught up the refrain — "Glory, Glory, Hallelujah!" It was a sea of sound, a great wave of melody by which a daring resolve was formed, and officers and men alike were affected by its significance.

Many attempts have been made to dignify the words. An effort was made by the officers to substitute the name of Ellsworth for that of John Brown — Ellsworth being the first Federal officer to yield his life in battle — but the men still persisted in keeping to their old favorite.

In December, 1861, Julia Ward Howe visited the Army of the Potomac. Mrs. Howe here conceived the idea of writing words that might be sung to the favorite tune of

"John Brown." The thought remained with her, and in the night she arose from her bed and wrote this poem, one of the gems of the Nineteenth Century American verse. When she returned to Boston she submitted it to James T. Fields, then editor of the Atlantic Monthly. It was he who suggested the title, "Battle Hymn of the Republic," and it was published in the February number of the magazine, the name of the author not being mentioned.

BATTLE HYMN OF THE REPUBLIC.

Mine eyes have seen the glory of the coming of the Lord;
He is tramping out the vintage where the grapes of wrath are stored;
He hath loosed the fateful lightning of his terrible swift sword;
His truth is marching on.

I have read a fiery gospel, writ in burnished rows of steel;
"As ye deal with my contemners, so with you my grace shall deal;
Let the Hero, born of woman, crush the serpent with his heel,
Since God is marching on."

He has sounded forth the trumpet that shall never call retreat;
He is sifting out the hearts of men before his judgment-seat;
O, be swift, my soul, to answer him! be jubilant, my feet!
Our God is marching on.

In the beauty of the lilies Christ was born across the sea,
With a glory in his bosom that transfigures you and me;
As he died to make men holy, let us die to make men free,
While God is marching on.

Grander words never were incorporated in any battle hymn. The call came for the poet; it was answered by a gentle woman. And though soldiers and the people will continue to sing the simpler words to the tune of "John Brown's Body," the two being amalgamated, so to speak, the composer has yet to hearken to the call of the Muse ere America shall receive for her most famous battle lyric a musical setting worthy of the theme.

In the summer of 1861, President Lincoln issued his second call for troops. There was living in Chicago at this time, George F. Root, who had come to the city the previous year, and had entered the music publishing business with his brother, E. T. Root. Deeply interested in church music and popular song, he bent all his energies in this direction. His whole sympathies were aroused by the President's proclamation, and he felt that there was a pressing need for a rallying song, one which would quicken the patriotism of the hour. The result of his endeavor was the "Battle Cry of Freedom." This song was first given to the public by the well-known Lumbard brothers, Jules and Frank, in the Chicago Court House Square. Over the heads of the crowd rang the voices of the brothers: "The Union forever! Hurrah, boys, hurrah!" The crowd soon caught the refrain, and like a mighty ocean wave whose power no man can arrest, the music welled upward and onward until the whole of the North caught the inspiration, and the "boys" responding, and "springing to the call," carried their rallying song to camp and field, many of them yielding their lives while still "Shouting the battle cry of Freedom."

George F. Root, more than any other song-writer during the period of the Civil War, possessed a keen understanding of the variety of songs needed, and his compositions became famous incentives to enlistment, messengers of cheer and hope in camp, as well as bracing the men to withstand the shock of battle. Such a song was the "Battle Cry of Freedom." But there is another phase of war which often is dreaded by the fighter: that of being taken prisoner by the enemy. So, early in the war, Dr. Root brought out the song of hope and encouragement, "Trapm, tramp, tramp, the boys are marching." It has been designated by a distinguished officer as the "song of hope." For this was its mission, and well did it accomplish its errand as one particular incident will prove.

In the autumn of 1864, several hundred of the northern soldiers were herded in a prison in Charleston. One afternoon they were marched out of the pen, for release as they had hoped. But it was only for making an exchange of one prisoner for another. The exchange being made, the remainder, who still hoped for release, burst forth in chorus:

Tramp, tramp, tramp, the boys are marching,
Cheer up, comrades, they will come,
And beneath the starry flag, we shall breathe the air again
Of the freeland in our own beloved home.

The song became one of assurance and uplift, and in a few months they realized that the boys had at length come marching, and were now throwing wide the prison doors for their release.

Another war song of extraordinary power and lasting popularity is Work's "Marching Through Georgia." It also is a war song of intrinsic merit and forms an appropriate commemoration of one of the most striking episodes in the Civil War. Henry Clay Work, encouraged by Dr. Root, had written many songs which had become popular during the war, but "Marching Through Georgia" is his best effort. It is a song of triumph, and its retrospective character will endear it to the army for all time.

The humorous aspect of the following stanza certainly places this song as peculiarly individual to the nation from which it originated:

How the darkies shouted
When they heard the joyful sound,
How the turkeys gobbled
Which our commissary found,
How the sweet potatoes
Even started from the ground,
While we were marching through Georgia.

It is during the period of strife and combat, when feeling runs high, and when the fighting spirit needs either encouragement or an outlet, that martial songs are born rather than made. Each combatant force had unbounded faith in its own strength, and each believes its own cause a just one. Such were the conditions of North and South during the Civil War, and war songs were heard on both sides. A few of these songs will never die, for the Blue and the Gray have since fought shoulder to shoulder, under one flag and for one cause, and the war songs of each have become common property.

But in the dark days of the Civil War, when the South fought under its newly adopted banner, its brave sons were singing a new song — singing it with the same hopeful outlook as the northern boys their "Star-Spangled Banner," and, rallying round their "Bonnie Blue Flag," ardently they voiced their sentiments as follows:

We are a band of brothers, and native to the soil,
Fighting for our liberty, with treasure, blood, and toil;
And when our rights were threatened, the cry rose near and far
Hurrah for the Bonnie Blue Flag that bears a single star.
Hurrah! Hurrah! For Southern Rights Hurrah!
Hurrah for the Bonnie Blue Flag, that bears a single star.

These words of Henry McCarthy, an actor, were adapted to an old Irish air reminiscent of that known as the "Irish Jaunting Car." The public heard it for the first time in the Variety Theatre, New Orleans, in the latter part of 1861, when it was taken up with wild enthusiasm.

One of the most beautiful lyrical poems of the war emanated from the South, but, unfortunately, there was no native composer to give it a musical setting, and an old German student tune, "O Tannenbaum," was appropriated. This song is a passionate appeal to defend, to uphold — a true war song. Its author, James Ryder Randall, was born in Baltimore in 1839. About two years before the war broke out he went to New Orleans to serve on the staff of the Daily Delta. Soon afterward he was appointed professor of English literature at Pointe Coupée College, situate about one hundred miles from New Orleans.

It was while engaged in his professional duties, in April, 1861, that he read of the attack on the Sixth Massachusetts Infantry while marching through Baltimore on their way south. Mr. Randall became greatly excited over the news and at night, after retiring, found it impossible to sleep. So at midnight he left his bed, and under the excitement wrote the words of "My Maryland." In the morning he read the poem to the college boys and they suggested that it be published in the Delta. From here it was copied into every southern journal, and in less than two months it really became what Alexander H. Stephens designated it, "the Marseillaise of the Confederacy."

The words were adapted to the music of which mention has been made, by Miss Jennie Cary of Baltimore, and the song was sung for the first time in the Cary home, when a meeting was held for the purpose of considering ways and means of assisting the Confederacy. The sisters, Jenny and Hetty Cary, then carried the words and the tune to which they had wedded it to the army when they went to visit the headquarters of General Beauregard at Manassas. The artillery band from New Orleans played a serenade in their honor, and on request of one of the officers Miss Jenny Cary sang "My Maryland!" There could be but one result. The refrain was taken up by the southern soldiers, the chorus growing in power as it was wafted onward and onward, until it became the fervent battle-song of the Southrons.

The air of "John Brown," as has been seen, originated in the South long before the war and, to other words, grew to be the most popular war song of the North. The North returned the compliment by giving to the South not only the music but the title also of the famous song known as "Dixie."

The author of "Dixie" was Daniel D. Emmett, of Mount Vernon, Ohio. In 1859 Emmett was a member of the Bryant Minstrel troupe, then having its headquarters in New York City. He already had won fame as a writer of minstrel songs, and when he engaged with the Bryant troupe it was with the understanding that he should hold himself in readiness to compose a "walk-around" whenever desirable. On a certain Saturday Mr. Emmett was on his way homeward when Bryant overtook him and asked him for a new song for Monday rehearsal. On the morning of that day words and music were both ready, and the new "walk-around" which had been named "Dixie's Land," won its way into immediate popularity. The original first stanza was as follows:

I wish I was in the land of cotton, old times dar are not forgotten;
Look away, look away, look away, Dixie land!
In Dixie land whar I was born in, early on one frosty mornin',
Look away, look away, look away, Dixie land!

Chorus:
Den I wish I was in Dixie, hooray! hooray!
In Dixie land I'll took my stand, to lib and die in Dixie.
Away, away, away down south in Dixie!
Away, away, away down south in Dixie!

It will be seen that this was essentially a stage negro song and it soon became a favorite with all the minstrel troupes throughout the United States. In the autumn of 1860, in the city of New Orleans, "Dixie" was first used as a march. The tune was infectious, and from that moment became popular on the street, in the home, and in all the concert halls. From here it was taken to the battlefields and became the most popular war song of the Confederate army.

It is said that the name and words of "Dixie" were suggested to Mr. Emmett by a saying common among the minstrels. On a cold day in the North it would be remarked, "I wish I were in Dixie's land," meaning that they would rather be in the more congenial climate of the South. Bryant, in his "Songs from Dixie's Land," claims that Dixie was the "negro's paradise on earth," in times when slavery and the slave trade were flourishing, and that the word "Dixie" to the negro "became synonymous with an ideal locality combining ineffable happiness and every imaginable requisite of earthly beatitude."

Many attempts were made during the war to dignify the tune by other words. The most successful of these were the verses by General Albert Pike, first published in the Natchez Courier, on May 30, 1861, and which became popular with the southern army:

Southrons, hear your country call you!
Up, lest worse than death befall you!
  To arms! To arms! To arms! in Dixie!
Lo! all the beacon fires are lighted—
Let all your hearts be now united!
  To arms! To arms! To arms! in Dixie!
    Advance the flag of Dixie!
      Hurrah! Hurrah!
For Dixie's land we take our stand
And live or die for Dixie!
      To arms! To arms!
And conquer peace for Dixie!

The next song to claim our attention is the one known as "America," and which as a national expression, breathing deep love and devotion to country as well as a religious spirit of hope and faith, is far superior in every way to any of our other national songs. Its writer, Rev. Samuel Smith, showed his keen understanding of the simple chant-like grandeur of an air which should constitute a setting for a national song, when he selected that used by the British people as their national anthem. Of all our national songs "America" is the most satisfactory in that it is suitable for all times and occasions.

Rev. Samuel Smith was born in Boston, October 21, 1808, and was graduated at Harvard in the class of '29. In 1831 Lowell Mason placed in his hands some books of music which he had received from Europe, asking him to select anything which he considered of value. In looking them over Dr. Smith came upon the anthem known as "God Save the King." The dignity of both words and music appealed to him and he subsequently wrote the words of "My Country 'Tis of Thee," setting them to the above named hymn. This hymn which afterward was to become the most popular national song of America, was given in public for the first time at a children's celebration of Independence Day, July 4, 1832, at the Park Street Theatre, Boston. Until the commencement of the Civil War "My Country 'Tis of Thee" had not acquired any particular popularity, but from the moment of the assault on the flag at Fort Sumter it was sung and played with devotional earnestness in church, in public halls, in the home and on the street, and has ever since received recognition as America's national anthem. Its author, Dr. Smith, died in 1895.

The history of the origin of the air, known in this country as "America" and in England as "God Save the King," had been the subject of much controversy, but it is now generally understood to be the work of the English composer, Henry Carey, both words and music being ascribed to him and claimed for him by his son. The song is said to have been sung first by Carey at a meeting held at a tavern in London to celebrate the capture of Porto Bello, at which time Carey acknowledged it as his own composition. Others again insist that it was heard in the time of James I. It may be that there was at that time an air which may have borne a resemblance to the present national anthem of England, but in spite of the claims made to place it earlier than the Eighteenth Century, the tune now known to the Twentieth Century undoubtedly had its origin with Carey.

At the close of the Eighteenth Century no less than five nations, Prussia, Russia, Switzerland, England and America, were using the same air to express their individual patriotic sentiments in verse. What greater proof can one have of its peculiar and wonderful adaptability as a national air? It has existed for more than a century, and it is likely to live in the affections of the nations which have adopted it for centuries to come. Its simplicity is a guarantee of its lasting popularity, as it is easily learned and readily recalled. Haydn, on a visit to England, was so favorably impressed by the simplicity of both music and words, that he considered it an ideal national anthem, and on returning to his own country composed after the same style the song known as the "Austrian Hymn."

The next song is so well known that it really has rank among our popular music, but as it was a product of wartimes it is included in this chapter. The infectious rhythm of the music, together with the unusual accentuation on certain words, give it a unique charm and make it of lasting value:

When Johnnie comes marching home again,
    Hurrah! Hurrah!
We'll give them hearty welcome then,
    Hurrah! Hurrah!
The men will cheer, the boys will shout,
The ladies they will all turn out,
And we'll feel gay
When Johnnie comes marching home.

This very characteristic song which strangely enough is in a minor key, is the work of "Louis Lambert," better known as Patrick S. Gilmore, one of America's notable band-masters and the projector of the Peace Jubilee Concerts given at Boston in 1869 and 1872. Mr. Gilmore wrote the song in 1863 and published it under a nom de plume. It became a popular marching tune for the troops, and many a heart has been cheered by the thought of the happy home-coming even while marching to the front.

In the Spanish-American War these battle songs of the Civil War were in favor, and frequently words were improvised to the old tunes, to fit the need. The war was too short, however, to develop anything new in the way of war songs.

America's war songs were heard on the battlefields of the Franco-Prussian War, and they were carried by the British troops to the Soudan and to Africa, "Dixie" and "When Johnnie comes Marching Home" being the favorites.

No matter how adversely some of this music may be criticized, it has had its influence; it has proven itself a power while that of a more artistic nature has failed of recognition. America has reason to be proud of its war songs, for they have served, as have perhaps no other means, as incentives to a fighting spirit in time of war and in instilling a love of the country and its institutions in time of peace.

In the preceding part of this chapter reference has been made almost entirely to the songs of the soldier. It is these songs which have gone to form our patriotic and national music, for the songs of the sailor never have left their naval environment. He had, nevertheless, a class of songs peculiarly his own. As a rule such songs embody a bit of history or delineate some emotion. Again, the song may be but a collection of words strung together in some rhythmic fashion that adds zest to his labor. These latter generally are called chants, or chanties and, originating with the sailing vessels, are becoming more and more scarce since steam has superseded wind as a motive power.

During the period of the Revolution and the War of 1812, England had a fine repertory of sea songs. Her sailor poets had given to the British some good, stirring verses. The themes were characteristic of undaunted courage, bravery and heroism on the part of the seamen, and were familiar not only on the men-of-war but on the merchant vessels. At this time the American sailor poet found himself in much the same predicament as his brother "lubber" on land. He could string together verses and possibly give them poetical finish, but he lacked ability in giving them a musical setting; so he simply followed the example of the soldier-poets and adapted his words to the tunes sung by the enemy.

One of the earliest of these sea songs is that designated "The Yankee Man-of-War." It is not known who was the author of the words. The tune to which it was sung has appeared in English editions of naval songs and is also of unknown origin. It commemorates John Paul Jones' cruise in "The Ranger" in 1778. A typical verse is here quoted:

'Tis of a gallant ship that flew the stripes and stars,
And the whistling wind from the west-nor'-west blew through the pitch-pine spars,
With her starboard backs aboard, my boys, she hung above the gale;
On an autumn night we raised the light on the Head of old Kinsale.

Another of the exploits of John Paul Jones is immortalized in the sea song known as "Paul Jones' Victory." He was then in command of the "Bonhomme Richard," with a fleet of sailing vessels. While off Flamborough Head on Sept. 23, 1799, he fell in with the English ship "Serapis" and a desperate fight ensued, the latter ship being compelled to strike its colors. This song is a capital illustration of the manner in which sea songs were made to serve the exploitation of deeds of daring, coupled with a pardonable boast of victory over the enemy. It was sung to an English air, but the authorship of the words is lost in oblivion.

In the War of 1812 America had not a single line of battleships, and her petty fleet of cruisers had inveigled the enemy into the belief that the latter was invincible to any attack from that quarter. But this same small fleet of cruisers rendered the more powerful ships of the foe inactive by a clever blockade, while the single ship fights have become historical in song. Of these songs that known as "The Constitution and Guerriere," and also as "Hull's Victory," became the most famous. This song, of which a verse is given below, was sung to the tune of an old English song known as "The Landlady's Daughter of France":

It ofttimes has been told
That the British sailors bold
Could flog the tars of France so neat and handy, O.
And they never found their match
Till the Yankees did them catch.
Oh, the Yankee boys for fighting are the dandy, O.

Another song of the period tells of the fight between the American sloop-of-war "Wasp," and the English sloop "Frolic," in which the "Wasp" came off victorious. Still another tells of the victory of the frigate "United States" over the "Macedonian."

Other victories during this period of warfare were celebrated in song which of necessity had ships and sailors and the sea for inspiration. But as has been seen, while the verses were original, most of the music to which they were sung was borrowed. One of these songs, known as "The Hornet, or Victory No. 5," and which was sung by our sailors to the tune of an old British naval song, not only tells of the victory won by the "Hornet" on Feb. 24, 1813, when she sunk the British sloop-of-war "Peacock" at the mouth of the Demarara River, but enumerates previous victories by other vessels and gives due meed of praise to their individual commanders. There is a ring of triumph in the opening words of each verse, the first of which runs:

> Rejoice, Rejoice! Fredonia's sons rejoice,
> And swell the loud trumpet in patriotic strain;
> Your choice, your choice, fair freedom is your choice,
> Then celebrate her triumphs on the main.

The Civil War, while it added somewhat to the repertory of American sea songs, did not bring forth many original tunes. This war's specialty in music was the songs composed especially for the army, and which incidentally became the songs of the people. There was heroism enough displayed in naval warfare by both North and South to have originated sea songs which, like the army songs, would have survived, but unfortunately no composer came forward at the time to do them justice. All the sea songs of this period naturally center around the names of Farragut and Winslow on one side and Semmes on the other. "The Cumberland's Crew" commemorates in plaintive words and music the sinking of the frigate "Cumberland" by the "Merrimac," on March 8, 1862:

> She struck us amidship, our planks did they sever,
> Her sharp iron-prow pierced our noble ship through;
> And they cried, as they sank in that dark rolling river
> We'll die at our guns! cried the Cumberland's crew.

It will be recalled that the Merrimac was an iron-clad, and here we have the first naval song born of this circumstance.

The history of the "Alabama" is familiar to all, for an important international question was involved in her origin and in her depredations upon the seas for a period of nearly two years. This particular song was written by E. King, author of Naval Songs of the South, and was dedicated to "gallant Captain Semmes, his officers and crew, and to the officers and seamen of the C. S. Navy." The air, by F. W. Rosier, is simple in character and readily learned and became a favorite with the southern seamen.

The wind blows off yon rocky shore,
  Boys, set your sails all free;
And soon the booming cannon's roar
  Shall ring out merrily.
Run up your bunting taut a peak,
  And swear, lads, to defend her
'Gainst every foe, where-e'er we go,
  Our motto "No Surrender."

On June 19, 1864, the "Kearsarge," commanded by Captain J. A. Winslow, U. S. Navy, fought and sunk the "Alabama" off the coast of Cherbourg, France. This naval duel fought in the presence, one might almost say, of two powerful and non-combatant nations, has been commemorated in one or two songs. The best perhaps, is the following, which has a certain sailor-like freedom of theme and music:

It was early Sunday morning in the year of sixty-four,
The Alabama she steamed out along the Frenchman's shore,
Long time she cruised about, long time she held her sway;
But now beneath the Frenchman's shore, she lies off Cherbourg Bay.

There are six stanzas to this song, reminding one of the style of sea songs during the time of Hull, but the first will suffice to show how well the story of the engagement is incorporated in the words:

A challenge unto Captain Semmes bold Winslow he did send;
"Bring on your 'Alabama' and to her we will attend,
For we think your boasting privateer is not so hard to whip,
And we'll show you that the 'Kearsarge' is not a merchant ship."

The Spanish-American war developed little in original sea songs. The movement of our forces as an invading power was swift, and the conflict too short for the development of song akin to that which had followed earlier naval victories. Newspapers and magazines were rich in poems and lyrics, but the composer was not at hand to give them a setting worthy of the theme. Yet our fleet was not without its incidents of courage, heroism, and level-headedness at critical moments — virtues that might have called forth inspiration from our song-writers and composers. But our sailors made good use of all of the songs, patriotic, national and popular, even to "rag-time," with which they were familiar.

The following description, from the pen of Richard Harding Davis, will give a general idea of the trend of musical thought on the part of our navy in the Spanish-American war. In speaking of the landing of the troops at Baiquiri, Cuba, this gifted war correspondent says: "While our troops were landing, the big warships were thundering away and playing havoc along the shore. The men still on the transports were cheering, and every band on troop-ship and man-of-war was playing 'Yankee Doodle' as hard as they could, while way back on the hills above the barred red and yellow of the Spanish flag fluttered against the sky. Up the San Juan steeps went the men of Wheeler, singing the 'Star-Spangled Banner' as they rushed forward with swinging steps."

The writer, in telling of the exchange of Hobson and his seven "immortals," says: "The trail up which they came was a broad one between the high banks with the great trees above meeting in an arch overhead. For hours before they came, officers and men who were not on duty in the rifle-pits, had been awaiting on these banks, sprawling in the sun and crowded together as close as men on the bleaching-boards of a baseball field. Hobson's coming was one dramatic picture of the war. The sun was setting behind the trail, and as he came up over the crest he was outlined against it. Under the triumphal arch of palms the soldiers saw a young man in the uniform of the navy, his face white with the prison pallor as his white duck and strangely in contrast with the fierce mien of their own, with serious eyes looking down on them with a steady gaze. For a moment he seemed to stand motionless and then the waiting band struck up 'Star-Spangled Banner.' No one cheered, no one shouted." So in the Spanish-American War army and navy alike recognized the value of these two time-tried melodies, "Yankee Doodle" and "Star-Spangled Banner," as an inspiration towards deeds of valor and glory for the honor of the flag for which they were first indited and sung.

Though not properly coming under the heading of patriotic and national music, a word relative to American sea songs in general may here be appended. These songs are an essential feature toward the performance of good concerted work, and they are common to the sailors of all maritime nations. Although they may vary with individual characteristics of nationality, the theme is much the same and they are all sung to the accompaniment of the "thrilling shrouds, the booming doublebass of the hollow topsails, and the multitudinous chorus of ocean."

Most of the songs or chanties — the name being derived from a corruption of the French chansons or chantees — of the American sailor of today are of negro origin, and were undoubtedly heard first in southern ports while the negroes were in engaged in stowing the holds of the vessels with bales of cotton, while some few of them may be traced back to old English tunes. They were of two kinds — pulling songs and windlass songs. The pulling songs were used as an incentive to the men to pull together. One can better understand this from the rhythmic flow of the following stanza, which has its counterpart in the sailor songs of varied nationalities:

> Haul on the bowlin', the fore and maintop bowlin',
> Haul on the bowlin', the bowlin', Haul!

At the close of each stanza the word "Haul" is given with marked emphasis, and the tug on the rope necessarily becomes stronger. The song imparts a unity of spirit and purpose to the work at hand.

The windlass songs beguile the men into temporary forgetfulness while working the pumps or weighing the anchor. One man, from his power of voice and ingenuity at improvisation, is looked upon as the leader. He begins by singing the chorus, as an intimation to the men of the manner in which it is to be sung; then he sings his solo, very seldom more than one line, and the men, from his musical intonation of the last word, catch the words and pitch with the inspiration intended. One of the best of windlass songs, in which the melody rises and falls in a manner suggestive of the swell of the ocean, runs:

I'm bound away this very day,
(Chorus) Oh, you Rio!
I'm bound away this very day,
(Chorus) I'm bound for the Rio Grande!
And away, you Rio, oh, you Rio!
I'm bound away this very day,
(Chorus) I'm bound for the Rio Grande!

A favorite windlass song is that known as "Shanandore," the title being a corruption of Shenandoah, upon which river the song undoubtedly originated with the negroes:

You, Shanandore, I long to hear you;
(Chorus) Hurrah, hurrah you rollin' river!
You Shanandore, I long to hear you,
(Chorus) Ah, ha, you Shanandore.

In the West and South the chanties still may be heard. You may catch their strains upon the sweeping Mississippi, whose forest environment first caught the chansons of the French voyageurs. Even now the boat songs and working songs of the sailors in the neighborhood of St. Louis and New Orleans are suggestive of French influence. Along the Ohio, too, and other water-ways, these melodies in form of a low, hoarse chant, are still reminiscent of the old chanties.

On the Atlantic coast the fisher fleets are perhaps the only vessels which still make use of these almost forgotten melodies, for the steam-worked windlass, the pumps, the clatter of the cog-wheels, the shrieking whistles and hissing steam are not conducive to song, and the sailor of the Twentieth Century, like the landsman, has caught the spirit of rush and speed, and no one dare attempt to revive the old chanty songs on board the steamships of today. But our fighting ships and our merchantmen of yore each had their repertory of sea songs — the music that was an incentive to do and to dare. This music made easier the coarsest and hardest kind of labor, and the work was performed in an atmosphere of pleasurable emotion. The complete change wrought in seafaring life by modern conditions has made of the chanties a music of the past. They served their purpose, and they will be of value in future years as being descriptive of their time.

PSALMODY AND CHURCH MUSIC

The preceding chapters have dealt with music native to the soil, with negro music, and with popular music in general. These several phases assumed by music in America are something quite apart from our progress in the production and appreciation of art music.

It will be remembered that at the period when America received its first settlers England was undergoing a fierce struggle between the Royalists and the Puritans. The point of contention largely was religious, the Royalists upholding the Established Church and "Merrie" England, while the Puritans battled for the simplest form of worship and the most austere piety. Macaulay sums up the Puritanical views in the following paragraph:

"The dress, the deportment, the language, the studies, the amusements of this rigid sect were regulated on principles resembling those of the Pharisees, who, proud of their washed hands and broad phylacteries, taunted the Redeemer as a Sabbath-breaker and a wine-bibber. It was a sin to hang garlands on the May-pole, to drink a friend's health, to fly a hawk, to hunt a stag, to play at chess, to wear lovelocks, to put starch into a ruff, to touch the virginals, to read the Faerie Queene."

As a result of their success in the struggle the Puritans were enabled to place the ban on all matters appertaining to the arts and amusements of their time. Consequently it is seen that, as music was in ill repute in the mother country, conditions were not favorable for its growth in the colonies. True, the Virginian settlers were of Royalist stock, but the colonists in the northern part of the country were deeply imbued with the Puritan spirit. On account of the different views held in the two colonies, secular music came to have its place in the South while the North frowned on music of any description excepting the few psalm-tunes allowed by the sect. Indeed many in the North even held that it was sinful to sing at all, while instrumental music was looked upon as an invention of the devil. Art music in America, as in other countries, owes its development to the church; and although the religious element for a long period was detrimental to the growth of art, the triumph which eventually was brought about came through the same medium.

It now is the purpose to discuss the various stages through which we have passed such as touch on our musical development from the artistic and æsthetic side. Each branch of the art — church music, oratorio, opera, orchestral music, etc. — will be taken up separately and its growth traced from its beginning to the present time.

It is a matter of interest to note that, so far as may be learned, the southern colonies played little or no part in our early struggle for music. This may be accounted for, however, by the more liberal views held in the South, which precluded any cause for strife in reference to the matter. It was because of the seriousness of just such a struggle that the outcome meant more to the New Englanders than to their southern brethren. So, in tracing our musical development one must turn first to the Pilgrim and Puritan settlements of New England.

It was to a church reared in the wilderness that the Puritans, some eight years after the landing of the Pilgrims, carried their psalmody. The Puritans were not willing exiles from their native land, but left only under stress of circumstances. They were not influenced by commercial

LOWELL MASON. 1792-1872

Born at Medfield, Mass., he has been called the "Father of American Church Music." He labored for many years collecting church music, teaching and directing the music in different churches, but he believed that the knowledge of music could best be given to the American people through the public schools and labored unceasingly to that end.

Although Lowell Mason does not stand in the front rank of American composers, his ability as a teacher and his energy in advancing the cause of music has won him the highest regard of his countrymen.

enterprise or ambition, but from the desire to make a home in a new country in which they would be free to worship God after their own manner. Milton designates these Puritan fathers "faithful and freeborn Englishmen and good Christians constrained to forsake their dearest home, their friends and kindred, whom nothing but the wide ocean and the savage deserts of America could hide and shelter from the fury of the bishops."

The music of the Puritans was entirely religious in character, and it is their psalmody which marks the commencement of our music development. There has been much controversy among music historians as to which psalm-books first were used by the early Puritans. From the data available it appears probable that both Ainsworth's and Sternhold and Hopkins' versions of the psalms were used. The tunes sung were taken from a collection published in England by Thos. Ravenscroft in 1621. It was the best book of its kind at that period and held its popularity for more than a hundred and fifty years. The notation in this book was arranged in four parts, each part written by itself and with the words beneath so that the same words actually were printed four times. There were twenty-three English, six Northern, seven Scottish, and five Welsh tunes. Most of the names, such as York, Durham, and Chester; Duke Street, Dundee, Glasgow and Martyrs; Landoff, Bangor, St. David's, St. Asaph, Wrixham and Ludlow, were familiar tunes in church choirs for many years, and are still found, although in somewhat altered form, in the hymn-books used in our churches today. The excellent harmonizations in the Ravenscroft Psalter however were of little consequence to the early Puritans, for they made use only of the melodies.

In the preface to the Ravenscroft Psalter the author formulates the following instructions:

(I) That psalms of tribulation be sung with a low voice and in long measure:

(II) That psalms of Thanksgiving be sung with an indifferent voice, neither too loud nor too slow:

(III) That psalms of rejoicing be sung with a loud voice, and in a swift and jocund measure.

It is interesting to note that in this edition the tune familiarly known as "Old Hundred," and set to the One Hundredth Psalm, was designated "French Tune" and credited to J. Dowland, Doctor of Music. In most hymn-books this tune is ascribed to Martin Luther. While the latter may have originated the melody others, among them Dr. Dowland, harmonized it. Most authorities agree that "Old Hundred" was originally composed for the One Hundred and Thirty-fourth Psalm in the Geneva Psalter and adapted by English Protestants to the One Hundredth Psalm about the year 1562. This tune was ascribed by Handel to Luther and by others to Claude Goudimel, a composer who met his death by assassination during the massacre of St. Bartholomew. Others attribute it to La Franc, a musician of Rouen, who is said to have compiled it from the Roman chants, while still others as persistently hark back to an old French love song for its origin. We probably shall never learn its true origin: it is sufficient here to know that it was sung in England, and that the Puritans brought it with them to America.

The few psalm-tunes used by the Puritans were of the simplest character, for they had been stripped of everything that might suggest the design of the devil in entrapping the godly Puritan into worldly thoughts — otherwise, a love of music for its own sake. So he naturally shrank from any attempt to render the psalm-tune after any scientific fashion, preferring to sing the same according to his individual idea of propriety. It must have been a strange conglomeration of sound, this Puritan psalmody that first came to our shores. As Puritan influence had proven itself a stumbling-block to musical culture in England, so for many years it threatened the same disastrous effect upon the evolution of musical art in New England. From the older country there was the inherited mandate: "We allow the people to join in one voice in a psalm-tune, but not in tossing the psalm from one side to the other, with intermingling of organs." In other words there was to be no attempt at polyphonic or harmonic psalmody, nor any use of instruments.

The same prejudices inculcated under Puritan influence in England were cherished with deeper bitterness in the colonies, with the result that many sincere and worthy Christians maintained that it was wrong to sing at all, declaring that a Christian should make melody only in his heart. There were not a few who, while raising no objection to singing itself, really suffered from qualms of conscience regarding the setting of the psalms to music, and what is more, were brave enough to give expression to their convictions. How deeply rooted was this prejudice against the singing of psalms is shown in the following incident:

In 1656 the First Baptist Church of Newport, R. I., suffered a division: twenty-one members seceded and organized an anti-singing church. They gave as a reason for their secession that they "disapproved of psalmody." For more than one hundred years no singing was permitted in this church. It was not until 1765, after a long struggle, that by the vote of a small majority permission was obtained to sing one psalm at the commencement of each service, and even then many of the members remained outside until the offensive exercise was ended.

It is not clear just what brought about the first changes made in the versions of the psalms used in the New England colonies. The alterations probably were due to the strong desire to be rid of everything in any way appertaining to the Established Church in England. The New England Puritans wished to pattern their church and religious observances after the simplest and purest forms. With this end in view a committee of clergymen was appointed to prepare a version of the psalms suitable for public and private worship. This attempted reform was almost entirely literary in its aspect and barely touched on the musical side of the matter. It must not be supposed, however, that it was accomplished without opposition, for there were many who were opposed to any "meddling" with the psalms whatever.

The Bay Psalm Book — so named from its origin in the colony of Massachusetts Bay — afterward known as the New England Psalm Book and later as the New England Version of the Psalms, was the outcome of the work of the Rev. Thomas Welde, the Rev. John Eliot and the Rev. Richard Mather, the latter setting forth in the preface: "If therefore the verfes are not always fo fmooth and elegant as fome may defire or expect; let them confider that Gods Altar needs no pollifshings: (Ex. 20.) for wee have respected rather a plaine tranflation, than to fmooth our verfes with the fweetnes of any paraphrafe, and foe have attended Confcience rather than Elegance, fidelity rather than poetry, in tranflating the Hebrew words into englifh language, and Davids poetry into englifh meetre; that foe wee may fing in Sion the Lords fongs of prayfe ascending to his owne will; until hee take us from hence, and wipe away all our teares, and bid us enter into our mafters joye to fing eternall Halleluiahs."

The Bay Psalm Book is on record as the first book of importance published in the colonies, and in spite of its many typographical errors its publication meant much in the early days. Nevertheless, this psalter did not receive the spontaneous welcome it merited. Prejudice always is difficult to overcome, and the Psalms of David, according to the metrical version prepared by the New England clergy in 1640, set the churches in a state of dissension. This without doubt was the first of the congregational turmoils which since have beset the churches of all denominations in America when innovations arising from a spirit of progression have been suggested in regard to religious matters. The churches in Salem and its vicinity still clung to the Ainsworth Psalter, while the Plymouth Church, in which it first had been used, gave it preference for over fifty years after its competitor appeared.

In the Bay Psalm Book there were appended the few psalm-tunes then in use, but little employment was made of the music itself, for all singing at that time was done by rote. So great was the reverence in which the psalms were held that hats were doffed during the rendition as they would be during prayer. The early Puritans considered their few psalm-tunes to be as sacred as the words themselves, and they were as little disposed in any way to alter or add to them as they were to make any change in the text. Singing in parts scarcely was known, and their ability to sing the eight or ten known tunes constituted their entire knowledge of music. The psalms were sung in rotation, and with the limited number of tunes in use (most of these being in common meter) the same ones often were heard several times during the day or even in the same service. It was similarly the case in family worship, at which it also was customary to sing the psalms.

In 1648 a new edition of the Bay Psalm Book was printed, and a few hymns or spiritual songs, as they were designated, were added. Many of the typographical errors appearing in the first edition were corrected, but the revised edition had to pass through the same wave of dissension as did its predecessor. In order to prepare the people for this edition the Reverend John Cotton, a man of progressive spirit, issued a treatise on the singing of the psalms, discussing the subject most ably and with considerable earnestness under the following significant headings:

I. Touching the duty itself.
II. Touching the matter to be sung.
III. Touching the singers.
IV. Touching the manner of singing.

The doubts and fears which pressed upon the Puritan conscience at this time regarding the propriety of particular methods of singing in church were of no small consideration. How the psalms should be sung became a vital question, and Mr. Cotton now endeavored to elucidate many points touching on the matter which had led the churches to question:

(1) Whether it was proper for one to sing while others joined in spirit only, uniting in an audible Amen at the close of the tune: (2) whether women as well as

men, or men alone should sing: (3) whether the unconverted — (pagans they designated them) — should join in the psalm tune: (4) whether it was lawful to sing psalms at all in tunes devised by man: (5) whether it was proper to learn new tunes which were uninspired.

In the treatise, published in tract form, which was distributed throughout the churches, Mr. Cotton set forth that the singing of psalms with a "lively voyce" is a "holy duty of God's worship now in the days of the New Testament;" that the Psalms of David having been "penned for Temple worship during the Pedagogy of the Old Testament" now in the days of the "New Testament, when God had promised to powre out his spirit upon all flesh, be carried on by personall spirituall gifts, whereby some one or other of the members of the church having received a Psalm by the enditement of the spirit," should sing the same "openly in the publique assembly of the church, and the rest of the bretheren say Amen to it at the close." Mr. Cotton also argued that "all should sing; with liberty for one to sing a psalm written by himself, while the church should respond Amen." In the latter part of the foregoing argument is found the first suggestion of a church solo in American religious assemblies.

The average Puritan felt that all melodies made by man were uninspired, in fact that they were a vain show of skill, therefore God could not take pleasure in praises offered in the melody made by sinful man. Mr. Cotton argued that, "Since God commandeth all men in distress to call upon him, and all men in their mirth to sing his praise, what is mortal, sinful man (Dust and Ashes) that he should forbid what God had commanded?" Mr. Cotton qualified his remarks by saying: "I can but marveile why you should put in the man of sinne, as having any hand at all in making the Melody." The arguments set forth carried such weight that the more progressive spirits sided with Mr. Cotton and those already supporting him, and efforts at improvement of congregational singing at once took shape.

The Bay Psalm Book passed into its third edition under the revision of Henry Dunster, President of Harvard College, and Richard Lyon of Cambridge University, England. Lyon added some additional hymns, which at the time was considered a most daring innovation. The third edition of this psalter, which was published in 1651, also was known as the first edition of the New England Psalm Book. This volume again and again was revised, until in 1744 it had reached its thirtieth edition, and not only was the favorite psalter in America but the churches of England and Scotland also gave it preference.

In 1698 the "Bay" or New England Psalm Book again underwent revision, this being the ninth time it had been subjected to such process, and was issued with the tunes of the psalms appended. This important edition was published for Michael Perry by A. Green and J. Allen of Boston, and without doubt was the first music published in America.

A reprint of a work bearing the title Psalms of David, fitted to the tunes used in Churches, which had been published in London in 1704, under the joint editorship of N. Brady, D.D., Chaplain in Ordinary, and N. Tate, Esq., poet-laureate to Her Majesty, appeared from the press of J. Allen of Boston in 1713, being the first American edition of this work. Its production no doubt proved an incentive to the New England clergy, who had ability in music, to compile similar works, for in 1715 the Rev. John Tufts published a work containing an introduction to the psalm-tunes, together with a collection of tunes in three parts. This is notable as the first collection of harmonized tunes issued in America.

Some five years later, Mr. Tufts put forward a more pretentious work which he designated in a preface "a very plain and easy introduction to the art of singing psalm-tunes, contrived in such a manner that the learner may attain the skill of singing them with the greatest ease and speed imaginable." In 1723 he brought out a collection of thirty-eight psalm-tunes in three parts — "treble, medias, and bass "— in which letters were used to indicate notes, this giving to the staff a clumsy and complicated appearance.

Five years before there had appeared a work which, with a little more forethought in its method of compilation, might have won for it a general and lasting popularity, for it was the most pretentious rendition of the psalms that yet had been made in America. Cotton Mather's "Psalterium Americana" is the work in question. While in this work each psalm was printed like prose and could be read or sung as such, a certain division of the words had the effect of changing them into something akin to lyrical verse. Sixteen pages of hymns or Scriptural subjects were added to the psalms, but there was not a note of music in the whole work. One scarcely can understand the reason for this omission as Dr. Mather, its compiler, was one of the strong advocates of singing, and he, as well as his contemporaries, felt the need of a variety of tunes and persistently endeavored to arouse in the people a spirit of enterprise in music. It was an excellent work so far as the arrangement of the text was concerned but it lacked the vital breath — tunes.

Contemporary with Tufts and Mather was Thomas Walter, a clergyman of Roxbury, Mass., who issued, in 1721, a work with the following title: The Grounds of Music Explained. Or an Introduction to the Art of Singing by Note; Fitted to the meanest Capacities. This was our first American musical work in which the notes were grouped by bars. Previous to this time the tunes had been rendered by each individual according to his own idea, and one can readily imagine the confusion of sounds heard in the rendering of the psalm-tunes when scarcely two of the congregation sang the same tune to the same stanza, and when no one made any effort to keep either in time or in tune with his neighbor. Mr. Walter likened this singing to "five hundred tunes roared out at the same time with often one or two words apart," and he admitted that he himself often was guilty of "pausing twice in one note to take breath."

If a new tune were introduced in fifty years it became a great event, for the whole church had to pass upon it to render a decision, and frequently it was necessary to put it to a parish vote. It was no easy matter to reconcile the congregation to such an innovation as learning to sing the psalms and hymns in time and in tune, and above all by note. All kinds of excuses were framed to oppose the introduction of new tunes in the churches and many of them prove how bitter was the sentiment against any innovation. But the ministers were firm, yet tolerant, and they met all objections either by persuasion from the pulpit or by issuing tracts on the subject.

The Rev. Thomas Symmes, a graduate of Harvard, was one of the active participators in the struggle to improve the music in the churches. He diplomatically met the advocates of the "old method" by urging that "what is now called the usual way, in opposition to singing by note, is but a defective imitation of the regular way," adding: "Your usual way of singing is but of yesterday, an upstart novelty, a deviation from the regular, which is the only Scriptural good old way of singing; much older than our fathers' grandfathers. The beauty and harmony of singing consists very much in a just timing and tuning of the notes; every singer keeping the exact pitch the tune is set in, according to the part he sings. Now you may remember that in our congregation we used frequently to have some people singing a note or two after the rest had done, and you commonly strike the notes, not together, but one after another, one being half way through the second note before his neighbor is done with the first."

An idea of the general prejudice prevailing at the time against learning to sing by note may be gained from a perusal of the files of the New England Courant. In its issue of Sept. 16, 1725, the following notice appears: "Last week a Council of Churches was held at the south part of Braintree, to regulate the disorders occasioned by regular singing in that place, Mr. Niles, the minister, having suspended seven or eight members of the church for persisting in their singing by rule." The following statement also appears: "If we once begin to sing by note, the next thing will be to pray by rule, and preach by rule."

As a general thing, however, the clergy took a decided stand for better music in their respective churches. They did their utmost to further singing by note by exhorting and pleading from the pulpit and by means of tracts which they circulated among the people. In order to conciliate both parties many congregations adopted the plan of singing by note, that is with an attempt at keeping together, and in the usual way, on alternate Sabbaths.

From the diary of Samuel Sewall may be gained a good idea as to the manner in which the singing in the churches was conducted about the time that the Tufts, the Tate and Brady, the Mather, the Walter, and other psalters came into existence. It was customary at this time for the deacon or minister to read each line of the psalm or hymn before it was sung by the congregation. The first settlers had not practised this manner of singing, but it had become generally adopted owing either to the scarcity of books or to the inability of some to read. One readily can understand the difficulty of retaining the pitch under such circumstances. It also must be remembered that there were no instruments in use in the churches at that time. Mr. Sewall was precentor of his church for over twenty years, and under date of Feb. 2, 1718, he writes: "In the morning I set York tune, and in the 2d going over the gallery carried it irresistably to St. David's, which discouraged me very much. I spake earnestly to Mr. White to set it in the Afternoon, but he declines it. p. m. The tune went well." Again, on "Lord's Day" Feb. 23, 1718, he writes: "Mr. Foxcroft preaches. I set York tune and the congregation went out of it into St. David's in the very 2d going over. They did the same three weeks before. This is the second sign. This seems to me an intimation and call for me to resign the Praecentor's place to a better Voice. I have through the divine Longsuffering and favour done it for twenty-four years, and now God by his Providence seems to call me off; my voice being enfeebled. I spake to Mr. White earnestly to set it in the Afternoon, but he declined it. After the Exercises . . . I laid this matter before them, told them how long I had set the Tune; Mr. Prince said, Do it six years longer. I persisted and said that Mr. White or Mr. Franklin might do it very well. The return of the gallery where Mr. Franklin sat was a place very Convenient for it."

On February 27 of the same year Mr. Sewall again notes: "I told Mr. White, Next Sabbath was in a Spring Month, he must then set the Tune. I set now Litchfield to a good key." On March 2 he again tells in the following quaint language of his anxiety in regard to the leadership of the singing: "I told Mr. White the elders desired him, he must set the Tune, he disabled himself, as if he had a cold. But when the Psalm was appointed, I forebore to do it, and rose up and turn'd to him, and he set York Tune to a very good key. I thank'd him for restoring York Tune to its Station with so much Authority and Honor: I saw 'twas Convenient that I had resigned, being for the benefit of the Congregation."

By the middle of the Eighteenth Century interest in church music was thoroughly aroused, as evidenced by the ever increasing number of musical publications. In 1737 Benjamin Franklin issued an edition of Dr. Watts' Psalms and Hymns, which passed into its second edition twenty years later. Dr. Watts' Songs and Hymns for Children also was published in America and became very popular with the youth of the country. In 1725 Rev. John Bernard of Marblehead edited a book of psalms and hymns which contained some fifty tunes in three-part harmony.

There was published in England, by William Tansur in 1754, a collection of music entitled the Royal Harmony. It contained hymns, anthems, and canons, arranged in from two to seven parts, and it became exceedingly popular. A copy of Tansur's book was brought to America and republished at Newburyport, Mass., two years after its publication in England. Following this collection by Tansur came a similar work by T. Williams, entitled New Harmony of Zion, also published in London and republished at Newburyport in 1769. These two works ultimately were combined in one and was generally liked by the New England singers, who now began to meet together to try this new and fascinating music. The publication of the combined work created an interest in music never before felt in this country. On account of its containing music written in a fugal style Tansur & Williams' volume is of special interest, for this style of music played an important part in our early musical development. The fugal setting of the Thirty-fourth Psalm was the forerunner of all subsequent music of that character.

From Philadelphia, in 1761, came the most pretentious of musical publications of its time, when James Lyon issued his Urania. This book contained not only a collection of psalms, hymns and anthems but had twelve pages devoted to instructions. The success of Urania undoubtedly was instrumental in encouraging others to produce works of a similar nature. One may form a fair judgment of the status of music at different periods of our musical life by scanning the pages of the various publications appearing from year to year. The fact that twelve pages of instructions was included in Lyon's work points to a desire on the part of the public for something of this character.

Josiah Flagg published in 1764, at Boston, a collection of one hundred and sixteen tunes and two anthems. This was a decided innovation upon all preceding works as it contained a variety of music from "Old Hundred," to a popular march entitled "March of Richard the Third." Most of the vocal selections were written in four parts, the melody being given to the tenor voice. Flagg had borrowed largely from Tansur and Williams and others, giving credit in his preface as follows: "We are obliged to the other side of the Atlantic chiefly for our tunes." Then the author feels impelled to apologize to the public for setting before them a "new collection at a time when there were already so many among us, there having been two or three within the past fifty years."

Flagg's work is of import apart from its musical significance, and the author is found congratulating himself upon the fact that he is under no obligation to "the other side of the Atlantic" for his paper even if he is for the music, since the former was the first manufactured in America for this purpose. The plates were engraved by Paul Revere — later the hero of the midnight ride — who also published and issued the work.

In 1764, Daniel Bayley of Newburyport, Mass., edited two volumes which were designated "A new and complete Introduction to the grounds and rules of music, in two books." The first volume really was little more than an elaborated edition of Walter's work, and the second volume was borrowed largely from Tansur's Royal Harmony. Three editions of this work were published within a year, which would intimate that there was more interest in music than formerly. The introductory page to this volume states that there were "tunes from the most approved masters." It is rather unfortunate that Bayley did not place on record the names of the individual composers; had he done so the chances are that something of American origin might be found among these early compositions.

It was in New England in the early days that the real struggle for the very existence of music itself was fought. Owing to the religious views of the Puritan settlers, conditions in New England were different from those in the other American colonies. On account of the absence of any great controversy over music elsewhere in the country there is little or no record of musical conditions in the early days outside of the New England settlements. In New York and Charleston the singing of psalms and hymns in the churches was generally accepted without controversy, and by the time Philadelphia, Annapolis, Baltimore and other pioneer American cities had come into being the crisis of the struggle had passed. The influx of Dutch, German, Swedish and Moravian immigrants, who brought with them their own music, did not affect appreciably the status of music in this country; for these colonists usually kept to themselves and, owing to the distance between settlements, for some years had little intercourse with each other.

Such further struggle as there was took place in New England and was occasioned by the opposition to the more progressive element who wished again to advance the cause of church music by abolishing the custom of "lining out" the psalms. Still later another controversy arose relative to the introduction of organs in the churches. The prejudice against instrumental music of any kind continued for many years, in the most remote districts lasting beyond the middle of the Nineteenth Century. The opposite stands taken by those in favor of doing away with the reading of the lines and their opponents long were detrimental to the cause of church music and caused Boston and its vicinity to lag somewhat behind Charleston, Philadelphia and New York. As the incoming English settlers belonging to the Episcopal Church became more numerous throughout the country the churches which they established were among the first to accept the more liberal views regarding church music. It was in the churches of this denomination that the first organs also were installed.

The leading factor in the betterment of psalmody was the advent of the singing master and the singing school. Through the influence of the singing school choirs came into existence, and with the choirs the abolition of the "lining out" process naturally followed. An instance of the tenacity with which the older members of the congregations held their views in the matter of reading the lines of the psalms is culled from the History of Worcester. On Aug. 5, 1779, it was voted: "That the singers sit in the front of the gallery, and that those gentlemen who have hitherto sat in the front seats in said gallery, have a right to sit in the front and second seats below, and that said singers have said seats appropriated to said use." "Voted, that said singers be requested to take said seats and carry on the singing in public worship."

"Voted, that the mode of singing in the congregation here be without reading the psalms line by line to be sung."

"The Sabbath after the adoption of these votes, after the hymn had been read by the minister, the aged and venerable Deacon Chamberlain, unwilling to desert the custom of his fathers, rose and read the first line according to the usual practise. The singers, prepared to carry the alteration into effect, proceeded without pausing at the conclusion. The white haired officer of the church with full power of his voice read on till the louder notes of the collected body overpowered the attempts to resist the progress of the improvement and the deacon, deeply mortified at the triumph of the musical reformation, seized his hat and retired from the meeting house in tears. His conduct was censured by the church and he was for a time deprived of its communion for absenting himself from the public services of the Sabbath."

Singing schools, or something akin to them, were organized early in the Eighteenth Century at the time when the New England churches were in such turmoil over the matter of congregational singing. In a tract written by Rev. Thomas Symmes in 1723 in favor of better singing in the churches he makes reply to his opponents who denounced those who were "spending too much time in singing" and "staying out at nights disorderly." From this it is seen that concerted efforts then were being made to learn to sing. In the announcement of one of the early singing masters he states that he is prepared to teach "the new version of the psalms with all the tunes, both of particular and common measure."

The efforts of the first singing masters in America undoubtedly were directed toward instruction in psalmody.

As the size and number of their classes gradually increased, improved congregational singing was the result. The formation of choirs naturally followed, with special seats being set apart for them. At first these bodies of singers merely took the place of the "tune setters" and served to lead the singing of the congregations. At a later date the choirs assumed very much the same position as those of today, acting not only as aids in carrying the psalm-tunes and hymns but also performing anthems and other choral pieces without the assistance, or rather the hindrance, of the congregations.

Each choir had its leader, who set the pitch and time of the tune or composition to be sung. In the early psalm-books containing the tunes directions were printed as to the pitch to be fixed on for each tune. When the compass of the notes was but five or six above the first it was stated that a high pitch should be taken; when the compass extended to eight or nine notes above the first, the tune should be pitched low. It must be remembered that in the early days no instruments were in use in the churches. The pitch pipe came as the first aid to the choir leader. Its introduction counted for much and served to insure a convenient pitch for each tune. At the time when there was absolutely nothing except the not always infallible judgment of the precentor in fixing the key it may be imagined how haphazard was the task. Following the introduction of the pitch pipe came the tuning fork; then the cello, followed by the flute, oboe, bassoon, clarinet and violin; and finally the organ.

The first heard relative to the introduction of an organ in an American church was in 1704, when the matter was brought before the vestry of Trinity Church, New York. While the first proposition did not materialize, its influence was felt some five years later, when it was thought desirable to have a "set of organs." In discussing ways and means by which to meet the expenses of the same we find this placid resolution: "What we cannot afford ourselves, we shall leave to God Almighty's good providence." It is probable that the committee was forced to take refuge in the latter alternative, for no real contributions were made toward procuring this much talked of instrument until 1739. The organ finally was constructed and installed by Johann Gottlob Klemm of Philadelphia in 1741.

In the meantime, Thomas Brattle of Boston, a man of artistic instincts, had made provision in his will for an imported organ to be set up in the Battle Square Church of that city. The liberal and broad-minded donor evidently had realized that there might be some opposition regarding the acceptance of the gift, so in a businesslike manner he had attached a proviso that the offer be accepted within a year after his death. In the event of its non-acceptance by the trustees of this particular church, which was of the Congregational denomination, the gift was to be offered to King's Chapel, which was the Boston representative of the Church of England. Mr. Brattle also stipulated that an organist should be procured, a "sober person to play skilfully thereon with a loud noise." The Puritans were scandalized to think that one of their own church should propose such an outrageous innovation to their sedate form of worship, and the vote, "We do not think it proper to use the same in the public worship of God," fully expresses the sentiment of the opposing element, whose obduracy also decided the fate of the instrument.

While the trustees of Trinity Church, New York, still were deliberating on building an organ, Trinity Church, Newport, Rhode Island, had received the gift of an instrument from Dean — afterward Bishop — Berkley. This church was considered one of the finest timbered structures in America, and from its belfry, crested by a gracefully proportioned spire, a mellow toned bell, the gift of Queen Anne, summoned the colonists to worship. It was in this church that the second organ in New England was set up, an organ which for many years held rank as the best in

America. Its workmanship in every detail was of the highest quality. The case was of English oak and was of very handsome design. It was nearly fifteen feet in height, eight feet in width, and eight feet in depth. Its front presented twenty-three gilded pipes, and a crown supported by two miters adorned its top.

The clerk was an important official of the Episcopal Church at this period. He read out the hymns and psalms, led the singing, and performed many other duties in his official capacity. Frequently he and the organist disagreed over the manner in which the tune should be sung, or in the choice of the particular tune itself. Trinity Church, Newport, with its fine organ, did not escape the trials of its sister churches, for organ, organist and clerk formed a trio to be reckoned with. Thus it came that in 1753 John Grelca, clerk, was dismissed from Trinity Church because he refused to sing the tunes played by the organist at the morning service.

An interesting anecdote is related of John L. Berkenhead, known as "the blind organist," who was appointed to Trinity Church, Newport, in 1796. Dr. Berkenhead was playing the hymn tune when he was interrupted by Joseph Dyer, the clerk, calling loudly "Berkenhead, you are playing the wrong tune!" The organist immediately stopped his playing and most emphatically told the clerk that he was a liar. The congregation naturally was greatly shocked at this unseemly conduct, and the vestry in considering the continued engagement of Berkenhead added the proviso, "during good behavior and punctual attendance."

As already has been noted, it was in the Episcopal churches of America that the first organs were installed, and it was in these same churches that music first assumed any recognized place apart from the singing of the psalms and hymns. The installation of organ after organ called for persons qualified to perform on the same, and as there were few or none of the colonists with the necessary endowments and preparation, organists were imported from England to fill the positions thus created. It is to these men that we owe our first introduction to church music such as was produced in the English cathedrals. Among the most prominent of these early organists were Edward Enstone, William Tuckey, Theodore Pachelbel, Benjamin Yarnold, James Bremner, Raynor Taylor and Benjamin Carr. In addition to their organ playing these men conducted schools "for the improvement of psalmody;" they gave lessons on various instruments and in dancing, and some of them sold musical merchandise as well.

Through the influence of the singing schools choirs came to be formed about the middle of the Eighteenth Century. As always the case, much opposition was shown to the innovation, but through the efforts of those who had the desire for better church music at heart and on account of the general interest taken in singing, choirs came to be generally adopted. But even in the churches where choirs had been formed the "lining out" process was for some years not altogether given up. William Billings, one of our first composers and apostles of reform in church singing, put forward an argument against the custom which must have had its effect. He stated: "As all now have books and all can read, 'tis insulting to have the lines read in this way, for it is practically saying, 'We are men of letters, and you, ignorant creatures.'" Billings also is said to have been the first to introduce the "viol," or cello, as an aid to the singing of the choir.

The adoption of the choir system became general about the latter part of the Eighteenth Century. It was in New England, of course, that the conflict in regard to the matter was most pronounced, the New Englanders thus keeping up their record for conservatism concerning changes in anything relating to the church. The History of Rowley states that in 1765 the parish voted that "those who had learned the art of singing may have the liberty to sit in the front gallery." The singers did not take the "liberty" however, as they objected to singing after the clerk's reading. In 1780 it is recorded that the parish requested Jonathan Chaplin, Jr., and Lieutenant Spafford "to assist Deacon Spafford in Raising the tune in the Meeting house." Five years later the parish desired "the singers, both male and female to sit in the gallery, and will allow them to sing once upon each Lord's Day without reading by the Deacon."

The leaders of these parish choirs either were chosen by the town or church or occupied the position by common consent. When choirs first were introduced the leader was expected to sound the key-note and then to give the pitch successively to the other parts, all this without the aid of any instrument. He also was expected to beat time in some conspicuous way. The part sung by the choir leaders was what now is known as the soprano or air but which then was designated the tenor. Usually the choir sounded the chord before singing. They sang without the aid of notes, the music having been memorized previously, either at the singing school or in the home.

During the early period of the choir system the music of necessity was of the simplest possible kind, such as psalm-tunes and hymns. The use thus made of this class of music called out many collections, and by the last of the Eighteenth Century at least sixty books, largely composed of sacred selections with a few secular pieces added, had appeared in New England alone. After the singing schools and choirs had become firmly established a new era of church music began. This was the age of the fuguing pieces of Billings and other American composers of his time.

There seems to have been considerable confusion in the minds of our early composers as to what constituted a fugue, for they were in the habit of designating any composition written in contrapuntal style a "fuge." A quantity of music of this type was introduced from England and became exceedingly popular with the singing schools.

From the singing schools it was adopted by the choirs and thus came to take the place previously occupied by the more simple hymn-tunes. The fuguing music seems to have made a profound impression when it first came into use, and William Billings is found voicing its praises in the following extravagant terms: "It has more than twenty times the power of the old slow tunes; each part straining for mastery and victory, the audience entertained and delighted, their minds surpassingly agitated and extremely fluctuated, sometimes declaring for one part, and sometimes for another. Now the solemn bass demands their attention — next the manly tenor — now, the lofty counter — now, the volatile treble. Now here — now there, now here again. O, ecstatic! Rush on, you sons of harmony!"

It is seen that such music was not calculated to inspire any deeply religious feeling — in fact quite the reverse — for many of these fuguing choruses were decidedly secular in character and were very much out of place in the services of the church. Their long continued popularity no doubt was due to their value as show pieces. They were sung from beginning to end without any attempt at expression, each part trying to outdo the other in vigor and in volume. According to the custom of the time the air, then termed the tenor, and the bass were sung by the men; the true tenor part, which then was known as the treble was sung by the women; while the alto or counter was taken either by the men falsetto or by women and boys.

Church music in America received a decided setback on account of the prevalence for so many years of this fuguing. Those of the congregation who were unlearned in music were unable to participate in the singing, and the choirs thus appropriated the entire tonal service unto themselves. Not that it always was smooth sailing for the choristers however, for it is related that the Rev. Dr. Bellamy on one occasion turned to the choir and remarked: "You must try again, for it is impossible to preach after such singing." Because the singing in the church devolved entirely upon them some of the choirs became arrogant, and at times refused to sing. At one of the New England churches just such an occurrence is recorded. The officiating clergyman in some way had offended the singers and they consequently declined to take part in the service. Finally they were brought to see the error of their ways by the pastor reading the hymn:

Let those refuse to sing
  Who never knew our God!
But children of the heavenly King
  May speak their joys abroad.

Relative to the behavior of the choirs during the service there early is record of an undesirable feature which unfortunately has not yet been entirely eliminated. "The result of my observations," writes a pastor early in the Nineteenth Century, "is that there is a great lack of devotion (not to say of common good breeding) in choirs of all denominations. Especially is this manifested by smiling and whispering, and looking over the tune-book in the time of the sermon." Again another writer states: "I boarded when very young with a family in the South, the head of which was the organist in the church. Not being attached to any church or form, I sometimes attended divine service with him and for convenience sat in the organ loft . . . The loft was railed in and furnished with substantial thick, crimson curtains which, when drawn, were sufficient to exclude vulgar eyes from the hallowed interior. It was customary when the excellent ritual of devotion was gone through and the rector had named the text, for the singers to draw the curtain around them, and read or sleep, as it suited them best. In very warm weather they also took care to be supplied with refreshments, and thus the tedious half hour allotted to the sermon was pretty easily consumed without much weariness. I recollect that on a very warm Sabbath afternoon the singers had watermelon and lemonade wherewith to console themselves, and it happened that one of the gentlemen in handing a slice of the melon to a lady singer, overset the pitcher of lemonade. This might not have been of much consequence had the floor of the organ loft been liquor tight. But there were many chinks in it and the lemonade trickled through quite freely down into the broad aisle, to the discomfiture of the rector and such of his congregation as were wakeful enough to notice passing events."

The music sung by our early choirs usually was of a low order, being without much intrinsic merit and badly arranged. Owing to the then prevailing prejudice against everything English the better class of church music generally was thrust aside and was to be heard only in the churches of the Episcopal denomination. As the first American composers almost entirely lacked the necessary preparation it may be judged that their compositions were not of high order. Many unwarranted and grotesque liberties also were taken by the singers, such as "singing flat with a nasal twang, straining the voice to an unnatural pitch, introducing continued drawls and tasteless ornaments, trilling on each syllable, running a third above the written note." Thus it is seen that at the beginning of the Nineteenth Century there was much chance for improvement in the matter of church music.

It will be remembered that the first controversy regarding music in the churches was as to whether any singing whatsoever should be countenanced. When finally this was decided in the affirmative the next question that arose was as to the manner of singing — whether singing should be by rule and note or otherwise. After much discussion this also was carried and there was a lull for a time until the advisability of the adoption of the choir system and the doing away with the "lining out" of the psalms and hymns again caused discord. Once more the reformers came out victorious, but their very success eventually became a stumbling block through the class of music which they elected to sing. So finally, on account of the choir abuses, about the year 1790 the question of doing away altogether with the music in the services of the church again arose. Thus at the close of the Eighteenth Century church music in America was in sorry straits; but again it was destined to arise purified and strengthened.

When the reaction against the fuguing pieces of Billings and his school became evident the reformers could do naught else but turn back to the hymn and psalm-tunes of their forefathers. Because of the renewed interest shown in the old hymnody many new collections made up of music of this class began to appear. Among the first of these was a collection of Sacred Dirges, Hymns and Anthems published by Isaiah Thomas and E. T. Andrews in 1800. The following year Timothy Swan brought out his New England Harmony. This was a book of one hundred and four pages and it contained among other original compositions the well-known tunes "China," "Pownal" and "Poland," which are still in vogue. Following this, William Cooper and Jonathan Huntington published in 1804 The Beauties of Church Music and Sure Guide to the Art of Singing.

In 1805 three publications appeared: The Christian Harmony by Jeremiah Ingalls; The Salem Collection by Cushing and Appleton of Salem, and The Delights of Harmony or Norfolk Compiler by Stephen Jenks. The latter collection is described on the title-page as "A new collection of psalm-tunes, hymns and anthems, with a variety of set pieces from the most approved American and European authors, likewise the necessary rules of psalmody made easy." In 1806 Abijah Forbush produced The Psalmodists Assistant which included one hundred and eight original melodies.

In 1807 Prof. John Hubbard of Dartmouth College delivered an essay on music before the Middlesex Musical Society. This lecture evinces a high degree of acquaintance with the æsthetics of music, and in it Professor Hubbard bewails the fruitfulness of ambitious dulness. He says: "Almost every pedant after learning the eight notes, has commenced author. With a genius sterile as the deserts of Arabia, he has attempted to rival the great masters of music. On the leaden wings of dulness he has attempted to soar into those regions of science never penetrated by real genius. From such distempered imaginations no regular productions can be expected. The unhappy writers, after torturing every note in the octave have fallen into oblivion and have generally outlived their insignificant works."

In an address delivered before the Handel Society at Dartmouth College in 1809 Francis Brown assails the prevailing style of church music and explains its shortcomings by saying that "The greater part of those in our country who have undertaken to write music have been ignorant of its nature. Their pieces have little variety and little meaning. . . . As they are written without meaning, they are performed without expression. . . . Another very serious fault in the greater part of American music denominated sacred, is that its movements and air are calculated rather to provoke levity than to kindle devotion."

Brown claims for American musical talent as much merit as he attaches to that of the European authors, but he says: "Our best musicians, instead of being awakened to exertion by a call for splendid talents, have been discouraged by the increasing prevalence of a corrupt taste." He traces this evil to the following causes: First, the passion for novelty; second, the antipathy of the higher classes, more particularly of the ladies, to taking part in the music of the sanctuary; third, the lack of attention to the character and qualifications of the instructors.

In 1809 Joel Harmon, Jr., of Northampton, Mass., published the Columbia Sacred Minstrel, a book of some eighty pages, containing original compositions in three, four, five and six parts. Harmon had endeavored to eliminate from his collection all compositions in which levity had supplanted dignity, and in his preface he states: "It is with pleasure that the author discovers that fuguing music is generally disapproved of by almost every person of correct taste." Three years later than Harmon's production Brown, Mitchell and Holt of Boston brought out Templi Carmina or Songs of the Temple, which afterward was called the Bridgewater Collection. This was a book of three hundred and fifty pages of music taken from English sources, and it became extremely popular. It was the most important publication of its time and was recommended by the Handel and Haydn Society of Boston. Another work of note which made its appearance about this time was the Village Harmony or Youth's Assistant to Sacred Music. This book was of about the same size as the Bridgewater Collection, and its popularity is attested to by its having passed through seventeen editions.

A book of Chants Adapted to the Hymns in the Morning and Evening Service in the Protestant Episcopal Church was issued in 1819 by Jonathan M. Wainwright of Hartford, Conn. The preface to the work states: "Metrical music is but a modern invention and adds nothing to true devotion and the worship of God; the conceit of versifying the psalms, though it seems in some degree to unite the peculiar advantages of the anthem and chant, in no less degree excludes the excellence and effects of both." The first heard of chanting in New England was in St. Michael's Church at Marblehead, Mass. In a letter dated Dec. 24. 1787, the rector, Rev. Thos. F. Oliver, writes: "As tomorrow is Xmas we intend to introduce chanting into our church." It is quite probable, however, that chanting had been used to some extent in the Episcopal churches in other parts of the country previous to this time.

During the early years of the Nineteenth Century, in addition to the attempted reform touching on the singing and music in the churches, a controversy also was waging over the use of instruments. The old Puritan admonition, taken from the Scripture, "I will not hear the melody of the viols"

(Amos 5-23) again was cited; but in spite of all opposition the use of instruments became general. Another point of contention among the musicians themselves was the proper disposition of parts among the singers. It was suggested by the singing masters of better taste that the air, which previously had been sung by the men, be given to the women. This was held by some to be an interference with the rights of man and contrary to Scripture. It was agitated for some years and finally was put into practise by Andrew Law about the year 1825.

The singing of solos and duets also came to be practised about this time. Formerly it had been the custom for all the voices attached to each part to keep on wherever they found notes. If a solo passage occurred it was marked "pia," or soft, no matter what might be the character of the words. It took some time before either male or female singers could decide to make the attempt at solo singing, and when finally they did they often were sneered at as being immodest.

One of the best known among the early choirs was that connected with the Park Street Church in Boston. In spite of the conservative tenets held by this body, which indeed were so severe that it refused to use an organ until well on in the Nineteenth Century, the singing of the Park Street choir was of a high order. Gen. H. K. Oliver, the composer of the well-known tune "Federal St.," gives some interesting reminiscences relative to this choir. He states: "From 1810 to 1814, the writer, a Boston lad, having a high soprano voice, was a singing boy, with two or three others, in the choir of Park Street Church, a choir consisting of some fifty singers and deservedly renowned for its admirable rendering of church music, ignoring the prevalent fugue-tunes of the day, and giving the more appropriate and correct hymn-tunes and anthems of the best English composers. Out of this choir came many of the original members of the Handel and Haydn Society. There was no organ at Park Street, the accompaniment of their singing being given by a flute, a bassoon and a violoncello. At that remote date very few musical instruments of any sort were to be found in private houses. In the entire population of Boston, of some six thousand families, not fifty pianos could be found."

The first genuine reform in church music in America was due to the efforts of three men: Thomas Hastings (1787-1872), Nathaniel Gould (1789-1854) and Lowell Mason (1792-1872). To these three do we owe the chief credit for first placing church music on a proper basis. At the period of their early manhood psalmody and hymnody were just emerging from the deleterious influence of the Billings school, and the churches were reverting to the hymn-tunes sung in earlier times. These pioneer reformers to some extent encouraged this process, but they also brought forward original compositions and arrangements of airs taken from the works of Haydn, Mozart, Beethoven and other of the masters, thus augmenting the rather small repertory possible at the time. Their efforts were in the line of music suitable for congregational singing rather than of that for the choir. With them music was looked upon not so much as an art but as a factor subservient to religious purposes. It is certain that Hastings and Gould, and to some extent Mason, hardly were able to realize that music might serve the double end of art and religion. While Mason was somewhat shackled by his religious views, his attitude toward music was much more liberal than either of his contemporaries. So far-reaching have been the results of his labors that he justly has been termed "the father of church music in America."

Thomas Hastings began his career as a singing master. He taught for some years in the vicinity of his home in Connecticut, later changing the field of his labors to New York State. The scope of his usefulness was limited by his extreme views relative to the place of music in religious devotion. His one idea was that its mission lay in the furtherance of gospel teachings to the total exclusion of any inherent artistic merit. In spite of his narrow views, however, he did much to promote correct singing of the music then in use in the churches and supplied as well new and original work of real merit. Hastings published many collections of psalm tunes and books of elementary instruction, and he also was the author of versification which indicates more than ordinary talent in that branch of literary musical endeavor. In 1832 he settled in New York and the balance of his life was devoted to the improvement of church choirs according to his light.

The career of Nathaniel D. Gould was similar to that of Hastings, both of these men leading the lives of the singing masters of their age. In addition to his work in connection with the various singing schools, Gould composed and adapted many psalm and hymn-tunes; he also compiled several collections of church music and instruction books as well as a History of Church Music in America which was published in 1853. Probably his most noteworthy achievement was in connection with the juvenile singing classes which he established. Of his work in this field he states: "The writer is constrained to say that, if he had any one thing more than another that he can look back upon with satisfaction during a long life, it is the fact that he was the first to introduce the teaching of children to sing." His first juvenile schools were in Boston, Cambridge, and Charlestown in the year 1824.

The effect of what Lowell Mason accomplished in his labors for church music in America hardly can be overestimated. Judged in the light of today the work itself was not on a high artistic plane, but when referred to the period in which it was performed it is found that Mason was far in advance of his time. Taking his place as a laborer in the field of musical endeavor, he found matters in a bad shape. The music itself was of a low order and illy arranged; and in addition, it commonly was rendered with no attempt at giving expression to the context of the words. In both of these spheres Lowell Mason worked a marked change. First of all he brought forward good singable music correctly and fittingly harmonized and he further saw to it that it was properly sung. His first compilation, The Boston Handel

& Haydn Collection of Music, was published in 1822 under the auspices of the Society. This work included adaptations of music taken from various sources as well as many original compositions. It won an immense success and received creditable comment from the German theorist, Moritz Hauptmann. So popular did it become that it passed through seventeen editions and was generally adopted by church choirs and singing societies throughout the country.

Mason's works were the first of their kind in America which were respectable from a musical standpoint. Many of his tunes are still sung in our churches and the compositions of later writers in the same field largely are patterned on the same lines. The marks of expression always are natural and appropriate to the sentiment of the words and they thus call attention to the spirit of the text. In all phases of church music Lowell Mason was indefatigable in his efforts toward improvement. As author, teacher, lecturer, organist, director and composer he was equally prominent, and his name acts as the connecting link between the time of Billings and the present. Following Mason came his pupils and associates among the most prominent of which were Henry K. Oliver, Geo. J. Webb, Wm. B. Bradbury, Geo. F. Root, Isaac B. Woodbury, W. F. Sherwin and Horatio R. Palmer. None of these men, however, has exerted the same power for reform as did Lowell Mason.

Before Mason's death, in 1872, music had assumed practically the place it occupies in the church today. But there is one name, that of Dudley Buck, which must be mentioned on account of the excellent work he performed in the production of suitable choir music. Mason's efforts largely were directed in the line of music for the congregation, while on the other hand Buck confined himself principally to choir music. He has written many anthems, motets and services which are found in the repertory of almost every church choir. Mr. Buck was one of our first properly qualified church musicians, and the efforts he exerted as organist, conductor and composer have been of lasting benefit. There are many other workers in the same field who well deserve mention in this connection but who, on account of their special performances in other directions, are noted elsewhere in this volume.

A special feature of church music in America is the establishment of boy choirs. This idea has been carried out principally in the Episcopal and Roman Catholic churches and never has obtained a firm hold in those of other denominations. In the great majority of Episcopal churches and in an ever-increasing number of those of the Roman Catholic denomination, especially since the recent Encyclical Letter of Pope Pius X. the surpliced choir of men and boys has been generally adopted. The first person to take a step in this direction was Rev. Francis Hawks, D.D., of St. Paul's College, Flushing, L. I., about the year 1839. The opposition was so marked, however, that the custom of putting the college choir into surplices was dropped for the time, but the use of the boys' voices in the service was continued under the guidance of Rev. Dr. Muhlenberg. In 1845 Dr. Muhlenberg removed to the Church of the Holy Communion in New York where he installed a boy choir (without surplices) which rendered the entire musical service.

The feasibility of boys' voices for choir use thus having been demonstrated, it was not long before other churches, in which special attention was paid to liturgical matters, adopted the vested choir. Among the first to do so was the Church of the Advent in Boston. In 1856 a full choir of men and boys was installed under the direction of Dr. Henry Stephen Cutler, who had made a special study of the subject in the English cathedrals. Here services and anthems of the best type were produced, and the Advent choir reached the high level it has maintained for so many years. In course of time Dr. Cutler was offered the post of organist and choirmaster at Trinity Church, New York, which position he accepted with the understanding that a vested choir should shortly be established. Nevertheless, the matter was delayed for some time, and it was not until the Prince of Wales visited

New York and attended Trinity Church that the choir appeared in surplices. Since that time the vested choir has been a feature of the services there.

It was long, however, before the movement gained much headway, for there was a strong prejudice to be overcome. For some years there were but two places in New York where vested choirs were to be seen, at Trinity and in the Madison Street Mission Chapel. From these two sources emanated the movement which since has resulted in the formation of choirs of men and boys throughout the country. It was not until the idea obtained a firm hold in the West that its possibilities were recognized. The first vested choir in that part of the country was formed at Racine College in Wisconsin. Shortly after, in 1867, a similar choir, under the direction of Rev. J. H. Knowles, was installed in the Cathedral of SS. Peter and Paul in Chicago. Since then the growth of the movement has been remarkable. In the Episcopal churches it corresponds with a similar movement in the Roman Catholic communions — the result of the Cecilian Society — whose object is to secure for the liturgy of the church a dignified and reverent rendering and the use of strictly appropriate music.

There are no data available as to the number of surpliced choirs in the United States today, but wherever adopted they have proved to be generally satisfactory and it is indeed rare that a church reverts to a quartet or mixed choir. The most pronounced drawback has been the absence of suitable altos and the scarcity of competent choirmasters, In the English choirs the alto part usually is strengthened by men's voices trained to sing falsetto, and the result is most gratifying; but in this country we seem to have no such voices. The inadequate remuneration offered by the majority of churches has steadily militated against the taking up of this special line of musical endeavor by men who otherwise would be glad to qualify themselves for such work Many special benefits accrue to the boy singers through their choir connections, for they early become proficient sight readers and gain a familiarity with the best class of church music. The average size of the boy choir in America is about thirty-five voices. Twenty-four is about the smallest number of singers desirable, while there now are several vested choirs in this country numbering from fifty to seventy-five active members. Among the most noted of such choirs are those connected with the Cathedral of the Incarnation at Garden City, L. I., Emmanuel Church in Boston and Grace Church in Chicago. These and similar choirs sing only music of the highest grade, such as anthems by Barnby, Tours, Dyke, Smart, and Sullivan, as well as oratorio choruses, services, and masses.

Undoubtedly the best music heard in American churches today is to be found in those of the Episcopal and Roman Catholic communions. In the churches of these two denominations where it has been found inexpedient to adopt the vested choir of men and boys similar efforts nevertheless have been put forth for the best church music. It has been much easier, however, for these churches than for those of other persuasions owing to the authoritative traditions inherited from the mother country. But in the non-liturgic churches of America conditions have not been favorable for the development of any standard of taste. The make-up of the choir largely rests with the ministers and individual congregations, while the style of music sung usually is left in the hands of the choir leader or music committee. The result is that there is too much diversity of effort. This is unfortunate inasmuch as it has not been conducive to the elevation of church music at the same rate at which other lines of musical endeavor have progressed. There is no doubt that the American churches have fallen far behind in the general trend of music culture. Such a state of affairs can be remedied only when the religious bodies come to realize that if the worshipers hear the music of the masters without, they will not be content with that of lesser merit within the church doors.

There is urgent necessity for improvement both in the music of the congregation and in that of the choir. If the chuıch powers could but realize the need for betterment they would see that much good could be done by the adoption of hymn-books in which the style and arrangement of the tunes is in keeping with the dignity of worship. Another pressing need is the general distribution throughout the edifice of books containing the musical settings of each hymn. The majority of worshipers now are able to read music to some extent, and it seems strange that this simple change is so long in being brought about when undoubtedly it would prove efficacious in improving congregational singing.

As regards choir music the necessity for correction and progress equally is eminent. The question of what is the most satisfactory form of choir — whether solo, quartet, or chorus — largely is dependent on the individual communion. It has been found that churches having a chorus choir usually have the best congregational singing. Wherever expedient, the adoption of a combination choir of solo, quartet and chorus seems to be most suitable in every way, for it allows of adequate presentation of almost every species of church music. Without the aid of a chorus, quartet singing in the church never is wholly satisfactory, for of necessity it lacks the dignity and grandeur naturally associated with the worship of God. Apart from the choir itself, it is to be hoped that more noteworthy advancement in the class of music sung will be made in the future than has been the case in the past, and that all music of a trivial nature will be banished to the place it rightfully belongs. It is pleasing to know that in many individual cases a high standard of music is maintained, but the improvement could be and should be effected through the governing bodies of the various denominations. Until some such step is taken, progress in this direction will be haphazard and uncertain. The liturgic churches of America are far in advance of those of a non-liturgic character, and they will maintain their musical supremacy until a wider and deeper interest be taken in the subject by the latter bodies.

MUSICAL EDUCATION

The era of musical education in America dates back about two hundred years. From the most obscure and crude beginnings and in the face of many difficulties the country has undergone such a remarkable evolution that at the present time the United States of America stands on a truly high plane in artistic appreciation and in general educational advantages. From a condition of almost entire ignorance of what is best in music the American public has progressed to the state where it is enabled to form a palpable judgment of what is presented for hearing. Again, it is but a short time since it was considered necessary for the prospective professional musician to go to Europe for purposes of study, but this state of affairs fortunately has been changed until now musical training can be secured in this country which is equal if not superior to that to be obtained elsewhere.

The progress of musical education in America has been brought about in two ways: first, by reason of the study of the art by many individuals; and, second, through the public presentation of good music of every description by properly qualified performers. When the educational movement began in this country the efforts were confined to vocal music almost exclusively, but here again the trend has changed entirely until now instrumental music occupies a much more prominent place than does its sister art. The means of our educational growth also have changed. First there was the singing school for instruction in psalmody; then came the musical convention, followed by the institutes, normals, and festivals. Latterly the work has devolved almost wholly upon the musical institutions and private teachers scattered throughout the country. These factors have cared for the training of the individual; for the general public, from early times there have been concerts and recitals of all descriptions.

Our earliest educational advantages in music were offered by the singing schools. These schools were the outcome of the endeavor to improve the music in the churches. They were conducted by men drawn from all the walks of life, men who in addition to their business occupation contrived to derive both pleasure and profit by means of their inherent musical gifts. In the early days there was a strong prejudice against any one devoting himself exclusively to music, and in 1673 the Commissioner for Plantations reported that there were no "musicians by trade" in the whole country. This condition continued, so far as may be learned, for about half a century, and even when a few had adopted music as a "trade" they were forced to follow other pursuits as well in order to obtain a living.

Our first music instructors and singing masters, apart from their natural aptitude, were not well qualified for their work, for they had had little or no training. But when the time came that a desire was shown for instruction in the art, those men who had, or thought they had, any musical ability at once came forward. Some one had to do the work, and crude as were these early efforts they were instrumental of much good. At the time our first singing schools came into existence the singing of the psalms was the only music practised to any extent in the colonies, and it was on account of this that our earliest educational endeavors were made in the line of improved psalm singing. When the interest in music became more general some few musicians who had drifted across the Atlantic, chiefly from England, offered instruction on the spinet, clavichord and other instruments, and most of them taught dancing as well. From these simple beginnings America has progressed until today the country supports scores of schools devoted to music instruction, to say nothing of thousands of individuals earning their livelihood by this means.

Singing schools were first established in New England about 1717, with the object of teaching sight reading and thus improving the psalmody of the church. As the would-be singers had but a scant knowledge of the rudiments of music, psalm-books containing explanations of the various signs, clefs, method of counting, etc., were used. In a book entitled The Grounds and Rules of Musick explained, Or an Introduction to the Art of Singing by Note: Fitted to the meanest Capacity, which the Rev. Thomas Walter published in 1721, he makes the following remarks: "Musick is the art of modulating Sounds, either with the voice, or with an Instrument. And as there are Rules for the right Management of an Instrument, so there are no less for the well ordering of the Voice. . . . Singing is reducible to the Rules of Art; and he who has made himself Master of a few of these Rules, is able at first Sight, to sing Hundreds of New Tunes, which he never saw or heard before; and this by the bare Inspection of the Notes, without hearing them from the Mouth of the Singer: Just as a Person who has learned all the Rules of Reading, is able to read any new Book, without any further help or Instruction. This is a Truth, although known to, and proved by many of us, yet very hardly to be received and credited in the Country."

From the above it is clearly seen that the art of singing by note at this time was looked upon by some as almost incredible, and it is small wonder that the idea was not readily grasped as the rules and directions given were exceedingly hazy and indefinite. The same uncertainty is shown in a later publication, Lyon's Urania, which appeared in 1761. In it the author formulates "some directions for singing." such as the following:

"1. In learning the eight Notes, get the assistance of some Person well acquainted with the Tones and Semitones.

"2. Chuse that Part which you can sing with the greatest ease and make yourself Master of that 'first.'

"3. Sound all the high notes as soft as possible, but the low one hard and full.

"4. Pitch your Tune that the highest and lowest Note may be sounded distinctly."

But in spite of the lack of any adequate directions and explanations good results were achieved by means of the supplementary work of the singing masters in their classes and through the persistent efforts of their pupils. The members of the singing schools thus learned sight reading and singing in parts. An excellent description of the methods adopted for the conduct and maintenance of the early singing classes appeared in the Boston Musical Visitor in 1842. It was written by Moses Cheney, who was born in 1776, and who himself as a boy attended such institutions. Mr. Cheney states that when he was twelve years of age news came that a singing class was in process of formation within a few miles of his home in New Hampshire, and quite a number came from considerable distances in order to join it, he being the youngest among them.

The sessions were held either in the homes of the members or in the schoolhouse. At the first meeting boards were placed on kitchen chairs to answer for seats and all the candidates for membership "paraded around the room in a circle, the singing-master in the center." The master then read the rules, instructing all to pay attention to the "rising and falling of the notes." Books containing individual parts, treble, counter, tenor and bass, were distributed, and directions for pitch were given. Then the master commenced. "Now follow me right up and down — sound!" So the master "sounded" and the pupil "sounded"

STEPHEN COLLINS FOSTER. 1826-1864

Born at Lawrenceville, now a part of Pittsburg, Pa. Foster was one of America's most noted song-writers, whose chief title to fame is "The Old Folks at Home," better known as "The Suwanee River," and "My Old Kentucky Home."

Foster received only the merest pittance for any of his songs and died in the direst poverty at Bellevue Hospital, New York. His life was singularly like that of Burns in that he was of an irresponsible, pleasure-loving nature, too fond of drink, but very gifted and of a lovable disposition.

STEPHEN COLLINS FOSTER. 1826-1864

Born at Lawrenceville, now a part of Pittsburg, Pa. Foster was one of America's most noted song-writers, whose chief title to fame is "The Old Folks at Home," better known as "The Suwanee River," and "My Old Kentucky Home."

Foster received only the merest pittance for any of his songs and died in the direst poverty at Bellevue Hospital, New York. His life was singularly like that of Burns in that he was of an irresponsible, pleasure-loving nature, too fond of drink, but very gifted and of a lovable disposition.

and in this way some learned to sing by note and others by imitation. At the close of the session the singing master agreed to give instruction for one shilling and sixpence per night, and to take his pay in Indian corn. It seems that the men paid for instruction for all, while the girls supplied the candles used for lighting purposes. This class which Mr. Cheney attended was typical of our earlier singing schools — simple organizations which served to diffuse a knowledge of and love for music until gradually they died out in the latter half of the Nineteenth Century.

The first record of music instruction offered in the South dates from about 1730, when John Salter is found teaching music at Charleston, South Carolina, in a boarding school for young ladies conducted by his wife. Singing schools were established in Philadelphia about the middle of the Eighteenth Century. On March 25, 1757, an announcement appeared in the Pennsylvania Journal to the effect that Josiah Davenport would hold a Summer Season Evening Singing School for the purpose of instruction in psalmody. Two years later, from the same source we learn that part singing was taught on three evenings each week "in the best manner in the School House behind the Rev. Dr. Jenny's, near the Church," and that the second and fourth Wednesday of each month was set apart for public performances. James Lyon either founded or conducted a singing school in Philadelphia in 1760, for advance sheets of his collection of tunes were prepared for this particular school, the same afterward being published under the title of Urania. In 1764 the children of Philadelphia were receiving instruction in the art of psalmody, for the vestry board of St. Peter's and Christ Church extended a vote of thanks to Francis Hopkinson and to William Young for their "kind services in teaching and instructing the children in psalmody."

The name of Andrew Adgate becomes prominent in Philadelphia in 1784 as a moving spirit in the establishment of a singing school designated "Institution for the Encouragement of Church Music." It held monthly concerts at the University, and from its inception was dependent upon public subscription for support. Shortly after its formation the trustees made objection to the "indiscriminate assemblage of persons at the public singings," and on the first day of April, 1785, directed that admission tickets be prepared for the use of subscribers. Two months later the organization ceased to exist, but Adgate was equal to the emergency and he immediately established a free school — "Adgate's Institution for diffusing more generally the knowledge of vocal music." Many influential people of the Quaker City rallied to his support, and his plans regarding the conduct of the singing school were given publication, one of which was his pledge to give twelve concerts of vocal music before June, 1786. The subscribers to the new organization elected their trustees, and under this patronage Mr. Adgate opened classes at the University and invited interested parties to join at once without compensation, adding, "the more there are who make this application, and the sooner they make it, the more acceptable will it be to the trustees and the teacher." Mr. Adgate continued in his choral work — a work that had a marked influence upon the musical life of Philadelphia — until his death from yellow fever in 1793. But before this time through his earnest efforts Philadelphia had become seriously and earnestly interested in music. The enthusiasm of Andrew Adgate, Francis Hopkinson and James Lyon, left an influence that was felt for more than fifty years.

Something may be said here of the singing societies conducted by the Moravian Brethren who had established a settlement at Bethlehem, Pennsylvania, in 1741. Although this and similar organizations of foreigners have played little or no part, per se, in our educational uplift (for they have continued as exotics), they have exerted an undeniable influence for good among themselves, which in turn has reacted upon the American people in general. Coming from a country where various singing societies existed for the people, a deep love for song naturally was implanted in each breast, and change of environment could not altogether eradicate these earlier impressions. So the Moravian colony soon became famous for its general musical atmosphere, which was a part of the daily life of the people. It was found not only in the church but in the home, and the laborer carried the song to the fields and on the streets, where it lightened toil and encouraged contentment even under the most trying conditions. It was a cultivated art, and in order that the people still might cherish a love for good music, about 1750 a school was founded where the members met for the purpose of singing. Weekly serenades were instituted and both sacred and secular song were cultivated, while orchestral music also had its place. So while English influence was felt in Charleston, Philadelphia, New York and Boston, German music was the essential feature in all the Moravian settlements. From the diaries of Franklin, Washington, Samuel Adams and other prominent men of the colonial period, much may be learned of the powerful impression which the music of the Bethlehemites made upon those who came into contact with it.

Singing schools were early established in Maryland. In the month of July, 1765, Hugh Maguire announces that he has opened a singing school at St. Anne's Church. He probably was the organist there, supplementing his salary by teaching "the new version of the psalms with all the tunes, both of particular and common measure." Mr. Maguire also announces that he will "if agreeable to young ladies, attend them at their own homes, where such as play on the spinet may in a short time and with the greatest ease, learn the different psalm-tunes." He made the following concession for the benefit of the musically inclined young men: "In order that those youths who are engaged on other studies may not lose time from them, I have appointed the hours of attendance at church on Thursday and Friday, from five o'clock in the morning till eight, and from five to seven in the afternoon; and on Saturday the above-mentioned time in the morning, and in the afternoon from two to six. Price fifteen shillings per quarter, and one dollar entrance."

At Newport, Rhode Island, a public announcement was made in 1770 of a singing school being opened by a schoolmaster named Bradford, who had "taught the various branches of psalmody in the provinces of New York, Massachusetts Bay and Connecticut." An advertisement of a singing school appears in a Salem newspaper in 1772. Apart from the display type and quaint spelling of the period it reads as follows: "Samuel Wadsworth begs leave to inform the public, but the female sex in particular, that he has opened a singing-school for their use, at his Dwelling House near the Town House, to be kept on Tuesday and Friday evenings, from six to nine o'clock. If any of the sex are desirous of being instructed in this beautiful science, they shall be instructed in the newest method."

One of the most important of the early New England singing schools was formed in 1774 by William Billings. This class, a record of whose membership still is preserved, was formed of forty-eight singers, eighteen of whom were women. It met at regular intervals at the home of Robert Capen at Stoughton, Massachusetts. From this class there developed, in 1786, an organization which has become familiar as the "Stoughton Musical Society," and which still is in existence. Singing schools also existed in the neighboring parishes, and naturally a spirit of rivalry regarding the respective merits of individual organizations sprang up. Singing contests were in order, as a matter of course, the earliest of these probably arising from the fact that the clergy were in the habit of exchanging pulpits, and whenever opportunity offered made laudatory comments upon the excellence of the singing in the various churches at which they officiated.

One parish no longer could withstand the temptation of being heard in competition with the much-lauded choristers of the adjacent parish, and so it happened that in 1790

Dorchester challenged Stoughton to a contest, the choristers of the latter parish accepting the same. Boston turned out in full force to hear the singing of the rival societies, an event which took place in a large hall in Dorchester. The musical contingent of the latter parish consisted of men and women vocalists assisted by a bass viol; the choristers from Stoughton were made up of selected voices — all male — and no instruments. It is a matter worthy of record that the Stoughton singers selected as their initial piece a composition, "Heavenly Vision," by a fellow townsman Jacob French, who was one of the charter members of the Billings singing class. The concert proceeded with the Dorchester choristers feeling the superiority of the men from Stoughton, and when the latter ended by singing Handel's "Hallelujah Chorus" without the aid of notes, the Dorchester singers with the best grace possible acknowledged defeat. Considering the musical conditions at the time, the rendition of this now universally known chorus was a noteworthy achievement and speaks well for the educational work accomplished by the early singing schools.

In 1754 William Tuckey is found advertised in New York as a singing master. Coming to America in the preceding year, with ambitious expectations in his profession, Mr. Tuckey seems to have become discouraged, for in March, 1754, when his "singing-master" advertisement appears, he distinctly states that he will teach "no longer than one year more." But fortunately he remained and continued to urge the necessity for improvement and amendment of the singing in "public congregations." He became a moving spirit in the musical life of New York until the beginning of the Revolutionary War, dying in Philadelphia in 1781 in his seventy-third year. Tuckey was affiliated with Trinity Church in New York City, and in the charity school of that church commenced the musical training of the youthful inmates. He also occupied the vestry of the church for two evenings each week, conducting a singing school there, from which originated the trained choir. He was a composer of merit as well, and his anthems appeared on concert programs in New York, Philadelphia, and Boston during the period of his activity and indeed for long after. The singing schools conducted by him were greatly in advance of the majority of similar institutions existing at the time as his early training had been of the proper kind, and the results he obtained were proportionately higher.

Early in the Nineteenth Century, the following advertisement appeared in the Cincinnati Western Spy: "Those gentlemen and ladies who feel themselves disposed to organize a singing school will please to convene at the court house tomorrow evening at candle light, as it is proposed to have a singing. Those who have books will please bring them." Shortly after, the name of a Mr. McLean is found in the same connection. His advertisement has a few unique features worthy of record since they afford a glimpse into the methods of remuneration adopted for the singing teacher's benefit. After declaring his intention of opening a singing school, Mr. McLean stipulates that all persons desiring to join the class "may become members at the honorarium of one dollar each for thirteen nights, or two dollars per quarter," and that "subscribers are to find their own wood and coal." This class evidently met in the winter evenings, and its members were expected to furnish light and heat. Small beginnings in our musical development in the West, but every plan for diffusing a knowledge of music among the people left its influence, and today we are reaping the harvest.

Singing schools did not altogether lose their identity in the more pretentious and later organizations designated "Societies," "Institutes," and "Normals," until the latter part of the Nineteenth Century. The promoters of musical education worked steadfastly and unceasingly in the "good old way," and not without good results. They were the pioneers of our musical evolution, and by perseverance and energy eventually they brought order our of chaos. It was through the effort of our early singing masters that the subject of musical education was brought more prominently before the public, and to the general interest thus first promoted in the matter do we owe our present high status in this field.

Out of the desire, fostered by the singing school contests, for a truer understanding of the art, grew the musical convention. The latter term implies that more than one society takes part, that lectures be given, and that classes be held; in this way disseminating a knowledge of music throughout the more remote communities. Such conventions had their origin at Montpelier, Vermont, and directly through the influence of the singing school masters. The first convention of this character was instituted by two men, Elijah K. Prouty, who combined the occupations of peddler with that of singing school instructor, and Moses Elia Cheney, who devoted his time almost exclusively to the latter pursuit. Cheney was the choir leader in the "brick church" at Montpelier and was in great demand as a teacher of singing.

Soon after the meeting of the two musical enthusiasts they decided that they must have a convention and at once proceeded to consider ways and means of bringing the matter about. They were successful in getting some of the most influential people of the town interested in the plan, and upon the suggestion of one of these, Judge Howes, an announcement was inserted in the Vermont Watchman. Mr. Cheney, realizing that considerable preparation was necessary, immediately went to work to train classes desirous of taking part in the prospective convention. They practised "unusual tunes, anthems, male quartets, and duets and solos for both sexes," for the secular music using the Boston Glee Book and two volumes of the Social Choir, by George Kingsley — the latter work being one of the best and most extensive collections in use in America at the time.

When the date set for the convention came, about two hundred singers had responded. The sessions were held in the church at Montpelier on May 22 and 23, 1839; Moses

E. Cheney, the originator and promoter as well as director, then being twenty-six years of age. Thirteen clergymen were present, and thirteen questions, interspersed with the singing of anthems, tunes and glees, were discussed, in which ministers, doctors and lawyers as well as musicians took part. The singers were arranged on three sides of the gallery, with the organ in the center. So successful was the outcome of the convention and so enthusiastic were singers and audience, that those interested resolved themselves into a permanent institution in order to hold such meetings at regular and stated intervals throughout the State of Vermont. Thus the Green Mountain State became the birthplace of the American musical convention in the fullest significance of the term.

The second convention was held in 1840 at Newberry. Elijah K. Prouty, whose name now had become well established not only as a singing school teacher, but also as a private vocal teacher, composer and instructor of harmony, was the director. The third convention was held in 1841 at Windsor; the fourth in 1842 at Woodstock; and the fifth in 1843 at Middlebury, where a committee was appointed to arrange for the convention in 1844, but as it failed to report the organization drifted apart. In later years Prouty became a piano tuner. The influence which he exerted upon the early musical life of Vermont through the singing schools which he established in the towns of Burleigh, Plattsburg and St. Albans hardly can be overestimated. He was the first Vermont singing master to adopt the Pestalozzian system of instruction, to use the blackboard by way of illustration, and to introduce the modern method of beating time. Many singers would not submit to the innovations of singing the syllables, do, re, mi, etc., and quit the choir, showing that the singing teacher and choir leader had no easy task even in the early beginnings of our musical culture.

Immediately after the convention at Middlebury in 1843, Moses E. Cheney left for Buffalo, New York, but returned to re-establish himself in Vermont, in 1850, finding that in the meantime the Green Mountain State had become the meeting place of several musical conventions now directed by "Boston Professors." The Cheney family became a well-known concert troupe and when they commenced this career in 1845 there were four brothers: Moses, Nathaniel, Simeon, and Joseph, with a sister, Elizabeth. This family became pioneers of vocal culture and choral singing in the West. Moses E. Cheney lived for many years in South Dakota. He was an original and practical teacher as well as a lecturer on musical subjects. Nathaniel went to Illinois. Joseph Cheney spent his later years in New Hampshire, and was a life-long teacher of singing. Elizabeth, besides being a gifted singer, was a fairly good pianist and gave instruction on this instrument. Simeon Pease Cheney taught singing classes all his life, teaching with good success in California. He also was a composer of simple sacred music and published The American Singing Book in which, in addition to a variety of sacred and secular music, appear short biographies of some of the early American composers.

The influence of the singing master drifted across the country in the wake of explorer, hunter, trapper and settler. The singing school, with its accompanying periodical convention, was established in towns just as soon as the people had built their churches and schoolhouses, and installed ministers and teachers. Singing was needed in the church, in the schoolhouse and in the home; and as connecting links for commerce were established towns grew and multiplied and church and school became frontier posts, so to speak, of educational and musical ambitions.

In the early thirties of the last century, Chicago was but a frontier town. It was incorporated as a town in 1833, and as a city in 1835, its population at that time numbering about four thousand. Among its people were some of a decidedly musical taste and a singing society was established in 1835, with the ambitious title of "Chicago Harmonic Society." Dec. 11, 1835, was the date of its first concert, which was held in the Presbyterian Church, and a lively interest must have been awakened at this particular time, for a second concert was given by the same organization about a year later. Mention is made, in 1844, of the first professional singing master in the person of T. B. Carter. Two years previous to his coming an organization known as the "Chicago Sacred Music Society" was established, and in 1846 a "Choral Union" was organized.

In May, 1848, in the First Baptist Church, a Musical Convention was held in which singers and those interested in music gathered together to discuss the best means for securing the advantage of general musical education for the young of the city; the adoption of the study of music in the public schools; and the improvement of singing in the church services. Four years later a second and more important convention was held under the direction of William Bradbury. The following extracts from a newspaper advertisement of the event will serve to show the aims and scope of these periodic meetings. It is announced as a "Convention of Teachers of music, choristers, singers and the lovers of music generally." The announcement states that "it will continue for three days, closing with a concert of miscellaneous music on Thursday evening, October 26, at Warner's Hall." The work of the convention embraced: (1) Instructions in the best method of teaching music both in adult and juvenile classes; (2) The practice of glees and social music; (3) Instruction and exercises in vocalization, with reference to the improvement of the voice, style, delivery, etc.; (4) Church music, including the departments of choir singing, congregational singing and chanting, with instructions in articulation and expression, adapted to singing schools; (5) Classification of church tunes, being a methodical arrangement of the different styles of tunes required in public worship — a great assistance to choristers; (6) Practical anthems, choruses, solos, etc. Tickets for the course (Gentlemen) two dollars. (Ladies — singers) free. The Psalmista and Alpine Glee Singer will be the standard works used at the convention. Some new glees may be introduced from the Metropolitan Glee Book (a new collection) if ready.

By the early fifties musical conventions had become established features in all parts of the country. Many of these were under the direction of George F. Root, who became extremely well known in this connection. At Rochester, New York, Mr. Root conducted several such enterprises. Later in New York City he held a number of conventions which were designated "Normal Musical Institutes." One of the first musical conventions which Mr. Root conducted in the South was held at Richmond, Virginia, and shortly after a second was convened at the Smithsonian Institution at Washington. At Quincy, Illinois, two conventions were held, with a "Normal" (note the change in title) at Jacksonville in the same state. In 1856 the musical convention at North Reading, Massachusetts, under Mr. Root developed into a more permanent organization known as the "Normal Musical Institute." Here came Dr. Mason, J. G. Webb, George F. Root, and others, and under the guidance of these leaders the North Reading Institute became known far and wide.

The conventions held throughout the country were the means of accomplishing much good, for they served to bring the music lovers and country singing schools into touch with each other. The meetings, usually held in spring and autumn, were looked forward to as important events, and they acted as a source of inspiration to all who were musically inclined. Some distinguished leader always was in charge, and at the sessions, occupying some three or four days, the local teachers alternately were given a chance to take part. True, the work taken up was not of the highest significance, but this pioneer movement of musical instruction was useful in developing a knowledge of the fundamental principles of the art and of instilling a love for music in general. The country singing school was the means of developing singing by note. The members prided themselves on being able to sing at sight, and the conventions fostered this spirit of ambition by bringing the singers together at stated intervals and circulating among them music of a recognized higher grade and encouraging them in efforts to accomplish.

Something may be said here as to the nature of the Normals which originated with Mr. Root. They were organized for a term of a few weeks, usually in the summer so as to afford teachers the opportunity of attending, and were the means of bringing together earnest musicians who lived in remote districts where they could not possibly attend any musical institution of benefit to them. The stimulus which these Normals exerted was seen in the widespread musical culture wherever a member of the Normal happened to be located. These Normals were popular and beneficial and supplied a real need in our musical evolution.

Owing to their nature, the conventions, institutes, and normals had but an ephemeral existence; but from these beginnings sprang the musical festival, which still exists in all its glory. The musical festival is the direct descendant of the singing school convention. From its earliest inception as a convention of singing societies gradually it has evolved until it includes, in addition to the choral work of the local bodies, orchestral performances by well-known organizations and the appearances of both instrumental and vocal soloists of the highest rank.

Probably the oldest and best known of the music festivals now regularly held is that annually convened in the fall of the year at Worcester, Massachusetts. For forty-three successive years it has been maintained with excellent artistic if not always the best of financial success. What now is considered the first Worcester Festival was held on September 28, 29, 30, October 1, 1858, through the efforts of Edward Hamilton, a local musician, and Benjamin F. Baker of Boston. The announcement of the project states: "Lectures will be given upon the voice; the different styles of church music, ancient and modern; the philosophy of scales, harmony, etc., with singing by the whole class and by select voices; solos by members of the convention and ladies and gentlemen from abroad." It further stated that congregational singing would be a prominent subject for discussion and that "the platform would be perfectly free." The circular continues: "It is the purpose of the mover in this enterprise to make it a permanent annual meeting of those interested in music throughout the county of Worcester — It is even hoped that at no very distant day it may be possible to achieve the performance of the oratorios and other grand works of Handel, Haydn, Mozart, Beethoven and Mendelssohn."

In 1863 the institution assumed for the first time the title of "The Worcester County Musical Convention" and elected Samuel E. Staples of Worcester as President, a long list of officers representing more than twenty towns. In 1866 a constitution was adopted whereby all persons who bought tickets, fifty cents for singers and seventy-five for visitors, were declared members of the convention, and financial deficits (which never occurred) were to be covered by assessing the men. At the annual meeting on Oct. 26, 1871, the name of the organization was changed to "The Worcester County Musical Association," and it was decided that thereafter the annual gatherings should be termed "festivals." In 1879 the association was incorporated under the general laws of the state and a new policy assumed.

The growth and development of the Worcester Festival may be noted from a comparison of the constitution of 1866 with that of 1879. In the former it is stated that the object of the institution is "the improvement of choirs in the performance of church music, the formation of an elevated taste through the study of music in its highest departments, and a social, genial harmonious reunion of all lovers of music." In the charter of 1879 the social element is entirely omitted and the stated object is narrowed to "the cultivation of the science of music and the development of musical taste."

During the first fifteen years of its existence the Worcester Festival to all intents and purposes was a musical convention. In 1858 but one formal concert was given; in 1860 there were two, and in 1866 four, three of a miscellaneous character and the fourth an oratorio. Carl Zerrahn was appointed conductor in 1866 and served for thirty-two years, resigning after the festival of 1879. For eleven years he had sole charge, but previous to 1879 he conducted only oratorios and similar works, the church music and smaller choruses being intrusted to W. O. Perkins, Geo. F. Root, Dudley Buck, and others of lesser fame. From 1889 to 1891 Victor Herbert acted as associate conductor, directing the purely orchestral works and accompaniments. Mr. Herbert was followed by Franz Kneisel and later by others.

When Mr. Zerrahn first assumed charge the Mendelssohn Quintet, reinforced by a doublebass, performed the accompaniments to the choral works. Gradually the orchestra was increased to sixty-five players. From 1868 to 1873 the Boston Orchestral Union served; then came the Germania Orchestra until 1887, when they were succeeded by the Boston Symphony Orchestra, which has been employed up to the present. In 1878 the scheme of performing two choral works requiring an entire evening for each was inaugurated. Since 1884 three such works have been given annually.

One of the features of the early festivals which has been abolished was the frequent appearance of singing and instrumental clubs. Many of the most important clubs of New York and Boston as well as local German and Swedish singing societies and even surpliced choirs have appeared in the festival concerts. As conducted today the Worcester Festival includes the performance of choral and orchestral works, and the appearance of leading artists in all the branches of music such as singers, pianists, violinists, cellists, etc. There are few prominent soloists now before the public who have not been heard at Worcester, and many works by American composers also have been heard at this, the best known of all America's music festivals. Upon the resignation of Carl Zerrahn in 1897 Geo. W. Chadwick took up the baton which he held for some years. He was succeeded by Wallace Goodrich in 1902. Arthur Mees has been the conductor since 1907.

Another permanent Festival Association conducted along similar lines is that of Cincinnati. The first performances instituted by this body were given on May 6-9, 1873, under the guidance of Theodore Thomas. Thirty-six societies, aggregating about a thousand singers, of whom six hundred and forty were residents of Cincinnati, made up the chorus. The orchestra numbered something over a hundred and included members of Mr. Thomas' own orchestra, resident orchestra players, and members of the New York Philharmonic. A second festival was held in 1875 and was so successful that it started the movement which gave to Cincinnati the finest music hall and organ which America up to that time had possessed. The third festival took place in 1878, and succeeding ones have been held every two years since. Subsequent to 1880 the assistance of outside choral contingents has been dispensed with. Among the more prominent men who have been associated with the Cincinnati festivals, in addition to Theodore Thomas may be mentioned Dr. Otto Singer, Arthur Mees and Frank Van der Stucken. An offshoot of the regular music festivals, resultant of a difference of opinion between Col. Geo. Ward Nichols, one of the directors, and Mr. Thomas, was the opera festivals instituted by the former. The first of these took place in 1881 and subsequent ones occurred annually for some years, that of 1884 lasting over two weeks.

The festival idea seems to have become a fixture in the musical life of America, for every year sees a large number being held in all parts of the country. From Maine to California each succeeding May brings to many of the smaller towns and cities the one opportunity of the year for the gathering of the musical forces of the community and the hearing of choral and orchestral works of the highest type.

It is the custom for several adjoining towns to combine their forces and to import soloists, a director, and orchestra, and hold a three days' festival in which the local bodies present the choral offerings. These scattered festivals have proved of great benefit in educating both the public, and more particularly those who take part, in the appreciation of concerted music and the larger musical forms. It is impossible to individually note here either the places where festivals are held regularly or those who have been instrumental in bringing them about. Suffice it to mention the more prominent, among which are the Maine festivals, so successfully conducted by William R. Chapman since 1897; those held at Birmingham and Spartanburg in the South and at Bellingham, Seattle and Los Angeles on the Pacific coast.

All the leading American cities at one time or other have had their music festivals, but owing to the scale assumed by the regular offerings of the musical season, there is no longer a call for events of this nature, and consequently the field has been left to the smaller and more remote communities. Among the notable festivals of bygone days were those conducted in Boston by the Handel and Haydn Society, the Peace Jubilees held in 1869 and 1872, and the festivals inaugurated by Dr. Leopold Damrosch and Theodore Thomas in New York and by Thomas in Chicago in the early eighties. The first Handel and Haydn Society festival was held in 1857. Eight years later a second one lasting a week took place, commemorative of the fiftieth anniversary of the founding of the society. At the festival of 1871 the Bach "Passion Music" was given for the first time in this country.

The Peace Jubilees, promoted by P. S. Gilmore, were the most stupendous attempts America ever has seen in the way of a music festival. But the huge unwieldy forces enlisted were not at all satisfactory from an artistic point of view, for good ensemble cannot be obtained where the chorus numbers twenty thousand and the orchestra two thousand, as at the second Jubilee. The Peace Jubilees, however, were the means of bringing together many enthusiastic music lovers and of raising the standard of taste in the music sung by the societies who came from all parts of the country to join in the undertaking. Several famous composers were present and conducted their own works. The solos were sung by celebrated artists, who vainly endeavored to be heard in the vast hall. Some of the solo parts were given by forty voices singing in unison. Another feature was the appearance of famous English, French and German military bands.

Since the first introduction in America the various conventions and festivals have served the purpose of diffusing a knowledge of and an interest in music among the general public. But more specific efforts have been made in educational lines by individual musicians and by conservatories of music and similar institutions. The early singing masters were our first music instructors, and it was one of these men who first promoted an interest in the serious study of the art. Although schools of music had been instituted by the Moravians in Pennsylvania about 1750 and by the Musical Fund Society in Philadelphia in 1825, it was due to the persistent efforts of Lowell Mason that the subject of music education was brought prominently before the public. There were others, among them Thomas Hastings and Nathaniel Gould, who entered the field even before Mason, but they lacked the benefit of the preparation which Mason had received and consequently their efforts neither were so well founded nor so successful as those of the latter. Mason performed a great and lasting work in his desire to implant music instruction as a regular part of the education of the young. In 1833, in conjunction with Geo. J. Webb, William C. Woodbury and Hon. Samuel A. Eliot, he established the Boston Academy of Music, an institution which accomplished untold good during its fourteen years of existence. It established many normal classes, and sent its graduates through every section of the Union; it trained children in vocal work, and established a system of popular lectures in which music was discussed as a fine art; it gave choral concerts in its earlier incipiency, but ultimately left these to the musical organizations making a specialty of this feature; it also gave to Boston its first properly equipped and conducted orchestra. For fourteen years the Boston Academy of Music carried on its philanthropic work, financial loss attending it for many years, and the school, which had been instrumental in disseminating an advanced musical knowledge throughout the country, wound up its affairs in 1847.

There was associated with Lowell Mason in this enterprise William C. Woodbridge, who had journeyed to Europe in order to study the Pestalozzian method of training the young. Mr. Woodbridge converted Lowell Mason to the new system, and he himself went to work to put its principles into practise. Lectures were given on the subject, and singing was taught according to the Pestalozzian method, which finally was carried from the Boston Academy into the public schools of the city in 1836 by Woodbridge and Mason, who gave their services, books, and instruments gratis. For two years they carried on the experiment in the public schools; the school board then decided that it was a success, and music as a part of the public school curriculum first was established in America.

Since the time of the Boston Academy America has witnessed a remarkable evolution in music education. From its first introduction in the public schools of Boston the subject of music instruction has advanced until it has been accepted as a regular part of the course in the public schools everywhere. The number of private teachers and conservatories ever is on the increase, and by means of the numberless recitals and concerts the general public has received a most pronounced educational uplift.

The oldest and perhaps the most important school of music in America today is the New England Conservatory of Music. This well-known institution was founded by Dr. Eben Tourjée in 1867. It was incorporated in 1870, and for some years occupied quarters in Music Hall Building. To quote from the catalog: "In the year 1882, the growing needs of the institution led to the purchase of an estate on Franklin Square, which it occupied until the close of the school year, 1901-1902, when it became necessary to seek more ample accommodation. Anticipating the removal of the Conservatory from the old site, the Trustees decided in 1901 to dispose of the building on Franklin Square, and to erect a modern Conservatory building on a location more convenient to the new art center of the city. This was accomplished in the most satisfactory manner, and with the opening of the school year, 1902-1903, the Conservatory took possession of its new building on Huntington Avenue, corner of Gainsborough Street.

"This building is constructed on the most approved modern plans, is fire-proof, and is especially adapted to the needs of a school of music. The material used in the exterior construction is steel-gray brick and Indiana limestone. As separate arrangements have been made regarding residences for young women students, the new Conservatory building is devoted entirely to educational purposes. On the first floor are the business offices, reception rooms, a few classrooms, the music store and two auditoriums, the basement being given over to the printing-room, tuning department, and electric plant.

"The larger auditorium, Jordan Hall, is the gift of Mr. Eben D. Jordan, and seats over one thousand people. In this hall the recitals of the faculty and advanced students are given. The equipment of the hall includes a large pipe organ and a spacious stage especially adapted to orchestral and choral concerts and to operatic performances. The acoustics of this auditorium have been pronounced by leading experts to be exceptionally fine.

"The smaller auditorium, seating over four hundred, is used for lectures and pupils' recitals and for the training of the opera classes. It is equipped with a stage, scenery and dressing rooms.

"The second floor of the building contains the musical library and a large number of classrooms. The third floor is devoted to classrooms and to rooms for organ practise, for which the Conservatory provides unequaled advantages.

"Ten new two-manual pipe organs have been built and installed in the practise rooms for the use of the pupils in the organ department. Two large new three-manual organs have been placed in the organ teaching rooms. With the large concert organ in Jordan Hall there are thirteen pipe organs in use in the Conservatory, which is more than double the number of organs contained under any other single roof in the world.

"No detail which will in any way add to the convenience or practical utility of the building has been omitted, a full equipment of electric bells, telephones, elevator service, etc., having been provided."

The New England Conservatory has enlisted the services of several of the leading musical educationists in America. Upon the death of Dr. Tourjée, Mr. Carl Faelten, who had been one of the most prominent piano teachers in the institution, was appointed to the directorship. Mr. Faelten resigned the position in 1897 in order to establish his own school, which, by the way, has developed into one of the largest piano schools in existence. Mr. Geo. W. Chadwick succeeded Mr. Faelten and has occupied the position ever since. Through his efforts the curriculum has been broadened and has taken on a more severe trend. In addition to its distinguished directors, many teachers of note have been connected with the New England Conservatory. Mr. Stephen A. Emery for many years was the leading instructor in harmony. Another teacher whose influence long was felt was Mr. A. D. Turner. Other prominent musicians connected with the institution were Carl Zerrahn, as instructor of conducting; Carlyle Petersilea and Otto Bendix, piano teachers; Geo. E. Whiting, organist; John O'Neill and Signor Augusto Rotoli in the vocal department. At the present time the conservatory numbers many well-known names upon its teaching staff. An excellent orchestra is conducted in connection with the institution and a musical brotherhood, the Sinfonia, founded by Ossian E. Mills, now has branches in all parts of the country.

In addition to the New England Conservatory Boston has several other musical schools of note. The Boston Conservatory, established in 1866 by Julius Eichberg, during its early years was a competitor of the New England Conservatory, especially in the field of violin music, but since the death of its founder in 1898, it has dropped somewhat into the background. The Faelten Piano School, under Carl Faelten, has shown a remarkable growth since its establishment in 1897. The possibilities of a school of this kind, in which the instruction is limited to piano playing and theoretical work, are well illustrated in this unique institution. Another successful music school of Boston is the International School for Vocalists and Pianists, established by William L. Whitney in 1903.

The second conservatory of importance in America is the Chicago Musical College, founded by Dr. F. Ziegfeld in 1867. It is the leading musical institution in the West and its curriculum embraces all branches of the art. While not having the facilities of the New England Conservatory nevertheless it has exerted a widespread influence in musical education. On its teaching staff are many men of wide reputation. It is the purpose of the college to erect its own building within a short time (1908) when, with enlarged and more suitable quarters, it will be enabled to pursue its work under more favorable conditions. Chicago has several other excellent musical institutions. The American Conservatory, John J. Hattstaedt, director, which was established in 1886; the Chicago Conservatory, established in 1884, Walter Perkins, director; the Cosmopolitan School, Clarence Dickinson, director; the Sherwood School, and the Bush Temple Conservatory all occupy a prominent place. The Chicago Piano College, under Charles E. Watt, and the Walter Spry Piano School devote themselves to piano instruction and theoretical work, while the Gottschalk Lyric School and the Groff-Bryant Institute make a specialty of the voice.

In common with Chicago, Cincinnati offers many advantages in the field of music education. In the Cincinnati Conservatory the city possesses one of the oldest established schools of music in the country. It was founded in 1867, and under the directorship of Miss Clara Baur it continues to cater to the needs of a large number of students. The Cincinnati College of Music, of which A. J. Gantvoort is the present director, long has been recognized as one of the leading institutions of its kind in the West. It was organized by Col. Geo. Ward Nichols and Reuben Springer in 1878 and has numbered among its directors such distinguished men as Theodore Thomas and Frank Van der Stucken.

Although New York has been most active in all other lines of musical endeavor the city never has developed any educational institutions conducted on the scale of either the New England Conservatory of Boston nor of the Chicago Musical College. Neither are her music schools of such historical import as the above, but nevertheless they have become eminent factors in music education in America. The National Conservatory, established by Mrs. Jeannette Thurber in 1885, has enlisted the services of the famous composer, Antonin Dvořák, as director, and of Rafael Joseffy at the head of the piano department. Carl Hein and August Fraemcke conduct two schools, the New York College of Music and the German Conservatory. The Institute of Musical Art, directed by Frank Damrosch, and the American Institute of Applied Music, Kate S. Chittenden, Dean, both are large institutions. Another conservatory of note is the Grand, founded by Ernest Eberhard in 1874. In the Guilmant Organ School, of which Wm. C. Carl is the director, New York has a school devoted to organ instruction, while in the Virgil School and the Granberry Piano School piano study is the specialty.

There hardly is a town in America but has its music school, many of them with large and distinguished faculties. The leading institutions of Philadelphia are the Academy of

Music, founded by Richard Zwecker in 1869, and the Sternberg School of Music. The Strassberger Conservatory of St. Louis dates from 1886. Indianapolis has an excellent conservatory of which Edgar M. Cawley is the director. The Peabody Conservatory of Baltimore, established in 1857, is the leading musical institution of the South. Harold Randolph is the director. Another well-known southern school is the Birmingham Conservatory which dates from 1895. Mrs. Emil J. Valentine is at the head of a conservatory which was established in Los Angeles in 1883. The Southern College of Music is the leading school in New Orleans. Toledo, Ohio, has an excellent conservatory conducted by Bradford Mills; in Detroit, Alberto Jonas has conducted the Michigan Conservatory since the year 1900. It is impossible to make special mention here of each of the many excellent schools scattered throughout the country, but it will be seen that institutions devoted exclusively to music instruction are not confined to any particular district. The last twenty years show wonderful strides in the development of educational facilities in America.

Within recent times the American colleges have shown an ever-increasing interest in music, and the art rapidly is taking its place as a regular feature of the curriculum. A singing club was in existence at Harvard as early as 1786 and the Pierian Sodality, which was formed in 1808, still is flourishing; but it was not until the year 1875 that the college established a professorship of music. John K. Paine, the Nestor of American composers, was the first to occupy the chair, and he continued to fill the position until 1905, when he retired on a pension. Previous to 1875 Harvard had offered a course in music, but it was not until the above named year that the subject obtained complete recognition and came to count toward a degree. At the present time the course is entirely theoretical and includes harmony, counterpoint, composition, musical history and æsthetics.

A chair of music was established at the University of Pennsylvania in the same year as was that of Harvard,

Professor H. A. Clarke being appointed to the position which he still occupies. The University of Michigan at Ann Arbor has made much of the study of music and in 1888 called Mr. Albert A. Stanley to fill the chair. The course offered by this college includes both technical and theoretical work, Yale fell into line in 1894 when Horatio W. Parker was called to the chair of music then created. Two years later Edward MacDowell was appointed to the professorship of music at Columbia. In 1895 Leo Rich Lewis was installed in the chair of music established at Tufts College in that year.

Several of the larger colleges conduct conservatories of music as special departments, among the most prominent pursuing this course being Northwestern University, of which P. C. Lutkin is the Dean. A conservatory has been associated with Oberlin College since 1867. At the University of Wisconsin Rossetter G. Cole has charge of the music department. All of the leading women's colleges such as Vassar, Smith, and Wellesley have offered musical instruction from the time of their beginnings. In the preparatory schools and in the convents music always has been a popular study.

Since its first trial introduction in the public schools of Boston, in 1836, the subject of music instruction has obtained a fixed place. There are several men who have been especially active in this field and whose influence has been both widespread and lasting. Among the number are Luther W. Mason, H. E. Holt, W. L. Tomlins, John W. Tufts, S. W. Cole and Frank Damrosch. The aim of music instruction in the public schools is to give to the child a working knowledge of the rudiments of the art especially as applied to singing. In the attempt to achieve this result much serious thought has been given to the matter and many diverse views have been propounded, but at the forty-fifth annual convention of the National Education Association held at Los Angeles, California, in July, 1907, it was resolved that a uniform course of music study be adopted.

An institution which has striven to assist the cause of public school music is the Music Teachers' National Association. This organization was formed in 1876 and has held annual sessions since that time. Its object is stated as follows: "First, Mutual improvement by interchange of ideas. Second, To broaden the culture of music among us. Third, To cultivate fraternal feelings." While these aims are just as desirable today as at the time they were formulated yet an association especially devoted to such an object hardly is longer necessary. Nevertheless, the Music Teachers' National Association has been the means of accomplishing much good and still is a live organization. Dr. Tourjée was its first president, which position now is held by Mr. Waldo S. Pratt. For many years Dr. H. S. Perkins has been one of its most enthusiastic supporters and was its secretary for a considerable period. In addition to the National Association almost every State in the Union has its local body which, however, has no organic connection with the larger society. Annual conventions after the plan of the National Association are held by the State organizations.

A fact which has tended toward the dissemination of a more general knowledge of music has been the special attention paid to the subject by the public libraries. In the Allen A. Brown collection the Boston Public Library possess the largest list of scores and of books on general literature dealing with the art to be found in America. The Newberry Library of Chicago and the Drexel Institute of Philadelphia also have large music libraries. Of a semi-private nature are the collections found in the music schools and in the various college libraries throughout the country. Another phase of the musical art touching on the educational side has been the production of many excellent works on musical subjects. America has produced many writers of note in this field, among the most prominent being Geo. P. Upton, W. S. B. Mathews, H. E. Krehbiel, H. T. Finck, W. J. Henderson, Louis C. Elson, Edward Dickinson, Gustave Kobbé, W. F. Apthorp and James G. Huneker. As writers of theoretical and technical works many American musicians also have found success. J. H. Cornell, Stephen A. Emery, Arthur Foote, Geo. W. Chadwick, A. J. Goodrich, Percy Goetschius and others have written text-books of a high order.

While music as an art has been treated by the above named writers and by others, since the year 1852, when J. S. Dwight established his Journal of Music, passing events and educational matters have received special attention. America now has many journals devoted to music in all its phases — happenings of the day, criticism, education, the trade, etc. As stated above, Dwight's Journal of Music was the first important American musical periodical. It had an existence of twenty-nine years (1852-1881), at first appearing weekly but later being changed to a fortnightly publication. Dwight's paper was one of the most important music journals ever published in this country and offers a record of the progress of music in America during its period of existence. In 1891 W. S. B. Mathews started the publication of a monthly magazine called Music, which continued in existence until 1902. It was devoted largely to critical studies and pedagogical subjects. The Étude, another pedagogical journal, has been published by Theo. Presser since 1883. W. J. Baltzell has been the editor since the year 1900. In 1896 the Hatch Music Company brought out The Musician, a similar publication, which in 1904 was acquired by the Oliver Ditson Company; Thomas Tapper is the editor. The Choir and Choral Magazine, Church Music, and the New Music Review are devoted chiefly to church and choral music. A journal published in the interest of music in the public schools is the School Music Monthly, which has been issued by P. C. Hayden since 1900.

The leading American musical weekly is the Musical Courier, founded in 1880. This magazine has correspondents in all the principal cities both in this country and in Europe and furnishes a record of the doings of the musical world. Marc. A. Blumenberg is the editor. Two other journals of the same nature are the Musical Leader and Concert-Goer, established by its editor, Mrs. Florence French, in 1895, and Musical America, edited by John C. Freund. The Musical Courier Extra, the Music Trades, the Presto, the Music Trade Review, and the Musical Age are journals devoted to the music trade. From the above named list of periodicals it clearly is seen that the American public has every chance to keep itself posted regarding the progress of music in all its phases. In every branch of musical education, either for the individual or for the people collectively, America has seen a remarkable development in its comparatively short musical life. Music teachers now are numbered by the thousands, schools and conservatories have been established, the art has found a place in practically all the educational institutions of the land, libraries have been formed, literature has been written, periodicals issued, innumerable concerts and recitals have been heard, opera has been performed, in fact every side of the art has received due attention until today the country truly may be said to have received the rudiments of a thorough musical education.

CONCERTS AND ORATORIOS

Early in the Eighteenth Century a general interest in music was awakened in this country primarily through the instrumentality of the church but also through the efforts of the dancing and fencing masters who gave instruction in singing and on the spinet, harpsichord, etc., as well. It was these latter who first inaugurated public concerts in America. Later, when organs were installed in the churches, it was the church organist who became the concert promoter, and it was one of these men, William Tuckey, who first introduced oratorio to the American public. At a still later date, when choral and oratorio societies had come into existence as a result of the work of the singing schools, these associations stepped into the place they now occupy in the concert field, The growth of recitals and miscellaneous concerts has continued along the lines first laid down, although of course in ever increasing numbers and with a more exalted standard both in subject matter and in manner of performance. In the larger cities, however, the mixed concert to a great extent has given way to the solo recital, elsewhere the former still holds sway.

The first announcement of a public concert in America of which there is record appears in the Boston Weekly News Letter dated Dec. 16-23, 1731. Doubtless other similar performances had been offered before that time, but unfortunately the data at hand relative to such matters are very meager and up to the present nothing of earlier date has been unearthed. The announcement of this concert reads as follows:

"On Thursday the 30th of this instant December, there will be performed a Concert of Music on sundry Instruments at Mr. Pelham's great Room, being the House of the late Dr. Noyes, near the Sun Tavern.

"Tickets to be delivered at the place of performance at Five shillings each. The Concert to begin exactly at Six o'clock, and no Tickets will be delivered after Five the day of performance.

"N.B. There will be no admittance after Six."

Nothing further is known concerning this, America's first recorded public concert. As to who took part or of what the program consisted, other than the bare announcement that it would be performed "on sundry Instruments," we have no means of knowing. Peter Pelham, at whose "great Room" the concert was given, was a dancing master who conducted a boarding school and who was a dealer in tobacco as well. It was not customary to publish the program in the advance notices of concerts until about half a century later. The first concert promoter to offer this species of advertisement in Boston was Josiah Flagg, of whom mention is made elsewhere in connection with his work in other fields of our musical development. In the Evening Post of May 13, 1771, appears the first announcement in a Boston paper in which the program is given in full. In it Josiah Flagg solicits the patronage of the public with the following selection of "vocal and instrumental musick accompanied by French horns, hautboys, etc., by the band of the Sixty-fourth Regiment:"

ACT I

Overture Ptolomy .... Handel
Song, "From the East Breaks the Morn"
Concerto 1st .... Stanley
Symphony 3rd .... Bach

ACT II

Overture 1st .... **Schwindl**
Duetto, "Turn Fair Clora"
Organ Concerto
Periodical Symphony .... **Stamitz**

ACT III

Overture 1st .... Abel
Duetto, "When Phœbus the Tops of the Hills"
Solo, Violin
A new Hunting Song set to music by Mr. Morgan
Periodical Symphony .... Pasquale Ricci

It is seen from the above that by 1771, at least, the Boston public was privileged to hear really excellent programs, considering the uncertain status of music in America at the time. During the period intervening between the first announcement of a public concert and the one quoted above, in which the program is given in full, it must not be supposed that Boston and its vicinity was without concert performances; but owing to the lack of data it is impossible to form any very definite idea as to the make-up of the programs. Another matter which is not clear is the distinction drawn at the time between "public" and "private" concerts. It is supposed, however, that a "public" concert implied that it was given, not for the benefit of any particular musician nor as one of a series of subscription concerts (a plan then prevalent), but as a venture of the proprietor of the concert hall. The use of the term "for the benefit," so often found in connection with our early concerts, did not have the meaning usually accepted today. It was used merely to draw the distinction between the performances offered by professional musicians for financial gain and those given by amateurs for their own amusement.

The concert life of the American colonies had its beginnings in the North and in the South at about the same time. As already noted, Boston had its first recorded concert on Dec. 30, 1731. It was but a few months later that the South Carolina Gazette in its issue of April 8-15, 1732, announced that "On Wednesday next will be a Consort of

Musick at the Council Chamber, for the Benefit of Mr. Salter." Charleston evidently appreciated this "consort" for the same year witnessed several others. In some of these the program was followed, after the European custom, by "Dances for the Diversion of the Ladies." Nothing is said in any of the public notices of these early concerts regarding the program. The announcements usually stated merely that there would be "Vocal and Instrumental Musick."

The first concert advertised in New York, of which there is record, took place on Jan. 21, 1736. The notice appearing in the Weekly Journal reads as follows:

"On Wednesday the 21st of January Instant there will be a Consort of Musick, Vocal and Instrumental for the Benefit of Mr. Pachelbell, the Harpsichord Part performed by himself. The Songs, Violins and German Flutes by private Hands.

"The Consort will begin precisely at six o'clock in the House of Robert Todd, Vintner. Tickets to be had at the Coffee House and at Mr. Todd's at 4 shillings."

There is no record of public concerts being given in Philadelphia until 1757, but it is probable that the Quaker City had witnessed "benefit" performances some years previously. Philadelphia, however lagged somewhat behind the other leading American cities in her concert life, although church music and opera early obtained a hold. It was not until the time of Francis Hopkinson and James Bremner (an English organist who came to the city in 1763) that Philadelphia was offered any concerts of note.

It is to the South that we owe our first introduction to the song recital. On Feb. 26, 1733, a benefit concert was given in Charleston in which it was announced that "none but English and Scotch songs" would be sung. But the programs of the larger number of our early concerts were made up principally of instrumental music. However, with the increasing interest in church music and the coming of the church organist this state of affairs changed to some extent. The advent of the singing school served to instill an interest in concerted vocal music and this side of the musical art also was brought forward. It was the concerts at which such performances were given that led to the production of oratorio.

One of the first important concerts given in America in which the chorus had a prominent part took place in Philadelphia on April 10, 1765. This performance marks an epoch in the evolution of music in this country. A part of the announcement reads as follows:

"College of Philadelphia, April 4, 1765.

"For the benefit of the Boys' and Girls' Charity School.

"On Wednesday evening next there will be a performance of Solemn Music, vocal and instrumental, in the College Hall, under the direction of Mr. Bremner. The vocal Parts chiefly by young Gentlemen educated in this Seminary, and the Words suited to the Place and Occasion, being paraphrased from the Prophets, and other Places of Scripture, upon the Plan of the musical performances in Cathedrals, etc., for public charities in England.

"The Chorus and other sublime Passages of the Music will be accompanied by the Organ, and the Intervals filled up with a few Orations by some of the Students."

In a report of the affair the Pennsylvania Gazette of April 18, 1765, states: "The whole was conducted with great Order and Decorum, to the Satisfaction of a polite and numerous Audience." The program was as follows:

ORATION

ACT I

Overture .... Stamitz
Air. Prov. III, from ver. 13 to 17, and IV, 8.

ORATION

ACT II

Solo, on the Violin
Overture .... Earl of Kelly
Air. Isaiah LV, 1, 2. John VII, 12.
Second Overture .... Martini

ORATION

ACT III

Overture in Artaxerxes ....Arne
Sonata, on the Harpsichord
Chorus Ps. XLVI from ver. 1 to 5.

New York came to the fore with a similar concert, given at Mr. Burns' New Room under the direction of William Tucky, on Oct. 28, 1766. The announcement states: "This concert will consist of nothing but church musick . . . accompany'd with a sufficient number of proper instruments. . . . N. B.—There will be more than forty voices and instruments in the chorus." On Jan. 9, 1770, Mr. Tuckey again conducted a "concert of church music," which included "A Sacred Oratorio on the prophecies concerning Christ and his coming; being an extract from the late Mr. Handel's grand oratorio, called the Messiah, consisting of the overture, and sixteen other pieces, viz., air, recitatives, and choruses, Never performed in America." This concert marked the first introduction of the "Messiah" to American audiences and on this account is especially noteworthy.

In 1772 William Selby came from London to accept the position of organist at King's Chapel, Boston. He at once became prominent in musical work and it was through his serious efforts that the way was paved for the inception of the Handel and Haydn Society. It was he also who first instituted the "Concert Spirituel" in America. The name originated in France in 1725, when Philidor, a brother of the composer of that name, obtained permission from the manager of the Opéra in Paris to give a series of concerts during the Lenten season. The request was granted on condition that during the evenings of these sacred performances no compositions in the French language nor any operatic melodies were to be sung. This Concert Spirituel later was performed in the Palace of the Tuilleries, and ever after became an institution of Lent, the Conservatory adopting it as a special feature for entertainment during the season. Selby introduced this feature to Boston in 1782, when he promoted a benefit concert for the poor of the city. This performance was announced as a "Musica Spiritualis, or Sacred Concert, being a Collection of Airs, Duetts, and Choruses selected from the oratorios of Mr. Stanly, Mr. Smith, and the late celebrated Mr. Handel."

In 1785 Selby founded, in Boston, one of our earliest musical organizations, which became known as the Musical Society. The following year this society gave a benefit for the unfortunates confined in the local prisons. This concert took the form of an elaborate liturgical-musical festival and was held in the Chapel Church. Its fame traveled outside the local environment and acted as a stimulus to the musical people of other cities. The program consisted of excerpts from the "Messiah" and other of "the late celebrated Mr. Handel's" oratorios, anthems, an overture of Bach's, and the regular Morning Service of the Church. So successful was this "Musica Spiritualis" that William Selby and the Musical Society hardly let a year go by before they again announced a "Spiritual Concert for the benefit of those who have known better days." There were not as many selections from the "Messiah" as in the preceding concert, but the "Hallelujah Chorus" again was included in the program. The Massachusetts Gazette published the program in full.

In 1789, during his famous inaugural tour, George Washington visited Boston, and the people of that city, anxious, perhaps, to prove that the community was æsthetic and artistic as well as patriotic and politic, arranged a concert as part of the plan for honoring him. The first part of the program contained, among other selections, "Comfort Ye My People," from the "Messiah" and "Let the Bright Seraphim," from "Samson," while the second part — to quote from a contemporary paper — consisted of "the oratorio of 'Jonah,' complete, the solos by Messrs. Rea, Ray, Brewer and Dr. Rogerson. The choruses by the Independent Musical Society; the instrumental parts by a society of gentlemen with the band of his Most Christian Majesty's Fleet."

A man prominent in the early concert life of Philadelphia was Andrew Adgate, and to him America owes its first concert performance on a grand scale. In 1784 Adgate founded in Philadelphia, by subscription, an "Institution for the Encouragement of Church Music." It was known first as the "Uranian Society," but in 1787 it was reorganized and adopted the name "Uranian Academy of Philadelphia." On May 4, 1786, the Uranian Society, under the leadership of Andrew Adgate, presented "A Grand Concert of Sacred Music," which took on a festival character. The following extracts from a lengthy review of the affair which appeared in the Pennsylvania Packet of May 30, 1786, will serve to show the unusual interest which it excited: "On Thursday, the 4th of May, at the Reformed German Church, in Race Street, was performed a Grand Concert of Vocal and Instrumental Music, in the presence of a numerous and polite audience. The whole Band consisted of 230 vocal and 50 instrumental performers; which, we are fully justified in pronouncing, was the most complete, both with respect to number and accuracy of execution, ever, on any occasion, combined in this city, and, perhaps, throughout America.

"The first idea of this concert was suggested to the trustees of the Musical Institution by the Commemoration of Handel in London and the Sacred Concert in Boston. This feast of harmony began with Martini's famous overture. Then followed a succession of celebrated anthems. Between the anthems the force of the band was interrupted and contrasted by two solo concertos. The whole concluded with the exertions of the full band in the performance of that most sublime of all musical compositions, the grand chorus in the Messiah, by the celebrated Handel, to these words 'Hallelujah! for the Lord God omnipotent reigneth,' etc.

"The decorum and method observed in conducting the whole harmonized with the precision and order necessary to the perfection of a musical performance. Nearly one thousand tickets were sold; at two-thirds of a dollar each."

This and the various other sacred concerts conducted in different parts of the country served to awaken an interest in choral music in particular and in concerts in general. In

Charleston, South Carolina, during Passion Week of 1796 a "Grand Concert Spirituale" took place, in which were rendered parts from the "Messiah," from "Samson" and from "Judas Maccabæus." The following year Norfolk, Virginia, heard a "selection of Sacred Music from the oratorio of the 'Messiah.'"

Some idea of the growth of concert life in America and of the men who were most instrumental in its development may be gleaned from the foregoing pages. In its early period concert giving was the result of individual effort, but through the exertions of these musical pioneers the societies which they founded later took up the work. The first musical society formed in this country was the St. Cecilia Society, founded by the music lovers of Charleston, South Carolina, in 1762. This organization, which still is in existence, did much to foster concert giving in Charleston in the early days. Although it always has been semi-private in character its labors nevertheless long served to disseminate an interest in music throughout the South generally. Until well on in the Nineteenth Century it formed the center of Charleston's musical life. For many years it gave its concerts fortnightly during the season, with a special annual performance on St. Cecilia's Day, Nov. 22. It had its own orchestra, which was formed of amateurs reinforced by a number of professionals engaged by the season. In the course of years this historically important organization has developed into a club of a social nature and the musical features consequently have dropped into the background.

Another important musical association still existing is the Stoughton Musical Society, which was the outgrowth of a singing school formed by William Billings in 1774. It took the name of "Singing Society" in 1786 with a President, Vice President, Secretary, and other officers. An account of the singing contest which the Stoughton Society waged with a body of singers from Dorchester, a neighboring parish, has been given in a previous chapter. While the St. Cecilia Society of Charleston antedates the Stoughton Society by some years the latter organization was of a different caliber and it probably was the first permanent body of singers established in America. It acted as an incentive to the formation of similar organizations, for there is record of many others coming into existence within a few years of its inception. The Stoughton Musical Society also is of special significance in that it formed the connecting link between the early singing schools and the later choral associations conducted for the purpose of oratorio singing.

The year 1815 marks the birth of the most famous choral society which America ever has produced. In the above mentioned year an elaborate concert, under the direction of Dr. G. K. Jackson, was given on Washington's birthday, February 22, in King's Chapel, Boston, in honor of the signing of the treaty of peace at Ghent on Dec. 25, 1814, This was one of the most important concerts that America yet had heard. There were two hundred and fifty singers in the chorus and an orchestra of fifty. The only previous musical event to compare with this festival attempt was the concert given in Philadelphia by Andrew Adgate and the Uranian Society in 1786. Within a few weeks of this Peace Jubilee, notice of a meeting of those interested in the matter was called to consider "the expediency and practicability of forming a society to consist of a selection from the several choirs, for cultivating and improving a correct taste in the performance of sacred music and also to introduce into more general practise the works of Handel and Haydn and other eminent composers." The meeting resulted in the formation of the Handel and Haydn Society, and on April 20, 1815, a constitution was adopted. Thos. S. Webb was elected first president and conductor. The first concert of the society took place on Christmas Day, 1815, the program consisting of numbers from Haydn's "Creation" and from the works of Handel. The chorus numbered about one hundred voices, ten of which were female, while an orchestra of a dozen pieces and an organ furnished the accompaniments. Three were nine hundred and forty-five persons in the audience and the concert realized the sum of five hundred and thirty-three dollars from the sale of tickets.

Up to the year 1818 the programs presented by the Handel and Haydn Society were made up of miscellaneous sacred selections, but on December 25 of that year the "Messiah" was given complete. So far as may be learned this was the first performance in America of the oratorio in its entirety. Haydn's "Creation" followed in the next year and in 1820 the "Dettingen Te Deum" of Handel was performed. According to the custom of the time, during the early years of its inception the Handel and Haydn Society in the distribution of parts gave the tenor to the women's voices, the air being taken by the men. This state of affairs continued until 1827 when Lowell Mason accepted the presidency of the society and brought about the proper distribution of parts. Up to the year 1836 the "Messiah" and the "Creation" were the principal works performed, although masses by both Haydn and Mozart were given as well as the larger part of Beethoven's "Mount of Olives." In 1836 Neukomm's "David" was performed for the first time and achieved a lasting popularity. Another work, "Mount Sinai," by the same composer, was given first in 1840 and also received many repetitions.

From year to year the repertory of the society was enlarged and persistent endeavor was made for a higher standard of performance. Until 1847 the president of the society acted as conductor also, but with the appointment of Charles E. Horn as leader the two offices became distinct. For one year, that of 1850, the posts were combined in the person of Chas. C. Perkins, but in the following season they were permanently separated. Following Mr. Horn came J. E. Goodson, G. J. Webb, and Carl Bergmann for one year each, after which Carl Zerrahn was appointed to the position which he held until 1895. B. J. Lang succeeded him and continued to occupy the post until 1899, when he gave way to Emil Mollenhauer, the present conductor, who brought about a thorough renovation in the affairs of the society. At the present time the active members number three hundred and ninety-five. Several concerts are given each season, usually on Sunday evenings, with an annual performance of the "Messiah" on December 25. The Boston Symphony Orchestra has furnished the instrumental accompaniments since its formation in 1881.

The efforts of the Handel and Haydn Society during its early life were not confined entirely to the performance of oratorio, for the society acted as sponsors to several musical publications as well. The first of these was the Bridgewater Collection, published by Brown, Mitchell and Holt of Boston. Later came the Handel and Haydn Society Collection, edited by Lowell Mason, three volumes of miscellaneous anthems, and several other works. The profits derived from these publications were used in defraying the expenses of the organization.

During his long association with the Handel and Haydn Society Carl Zerrahn exerted a highly beneficent influence on the progress of music in America. In addition to his work in connection with this historical institution he also acted as director of the Worcester Festivals and of the Salem Oratorio Society. He was instrumental in promoting many concerts in Boston; for some years he conducted the Harvard Symphony concerts, and in 1872 he led the chorus of twenty thousand voices assembled for the second Peace Jubilee. At the completion of his fortieth year of service with the Handel and Haydn Society Mr. Zerrahn was tendered a benefit performance and many well deserved honors and tokens of appreciation were bestowed upon him. After long and faithful service in the cause of music Mr. Zarrahn died in 1906.

It is impossible to make mention here of other than the most important and longest lived choral organizations which have existed in this country since oratorio first was introduced, but a paragraph cited from a copy of the Euterpeiad of Boston, dated May 12, 1821, serves to show that an interest in concerts and oratorios was fast developing in all parts of America at that early date. The article is headed "Musical Excitement" and states:

"During the last week we noticed the following Musical Performances that were to take place in the present month of May:

"A Concert of Sacred Music, by the Beethoven Society, at Portland (Me.), a grand Oratorio at Augusta (Ga.), under the direction of Mr. James Hewitt, formerly of Boston, a select Oratorio at Providence, by the Psallonian Society, under the direction of Mr. O. Shaw; a Grand Concert of Music, for the benefit of the musical fund at Philadelphia; the Grand Oratorio of 'The Creation' by the Harmonic Society of Baltimore; a performance of Sacred Music, by the New Hampshire Musical Society, at Hanover (N. H.), and in this town a Concert of Instrumental and Vocal Music for the benefit of Mr. Ostinelli; and the Public Oratorio by the Handel and Haydn Society of this Metropolis, for the benefit of the Howard Benevolent Society."

New York, although showing some interest in oratorio as early as 1770, fell behind the cities of Philadelphia and Boston in this respect in the earlier years of the Nineteenth Century. During this period New York was more active in giving encouragement to the ballad-opera. Nevertheless many attempts were made to keep alive the interest in oratorio, and in March, 1805, Dr. G. K. Jackson announced his intention of "having the oratorios performed under his own direction" at the French Church. The program was made up principally of selections from the "Messiah," the final piece being the "Hallelujah Chorus;" but, as was customary at this period, the oratorio portions of the program were interspersed with songs and anthems.

One must look to the Choral Society, founded in 1823, for the first serious work in oratorio in New York. The Choral Society was the offspring of a former organization, the Handel and Haydn Society. The latter was organized in connection with the raising of funds for the rebuilding of Zion Church. What it did and the nature of its concerts it is impossible to learn. The Choral Society, however, on April 20, 1824, gave an excellent program at its initial performance, in which were performed selections from the "Messiah," "Judas Maccabæus," the "Hallelujah Chorus" from Beethoven's "Mount of Olives," and Mozart's motet "O God, when Thou appearest." The chorus numbered fifty and the orchestra twenty performers under the leadership of E. C. Riley, with Messrs. Swindalls and Dyer as conductors. The Beethoven "Hallelujah Chorus" was heard for the first time and so enthusiastic was its reception that it was repeated. But the Choral Society soon dissolved, leaving the oratorio field to the New York Sacred Music Society.

This latter organization had its origin in the choir of Zion Church, which came into existence in 1823 as the Zion Church Musical Association. Application was made to the vestry by the choir for better remuneration for its services, or permission to give a concert by which to supplement the salaries. The application was not well received and consequently the choir resigned, and in order to continue the cultivation of sacred music the members organized the society before mentioned. On Feb. 28, 1827, the organization gave a concert for the benefit of the Greek fund. The chorus numbered sixty voices, and both the "Hallelujah" of Handel and that of Beethoven were rendered. But what makes this concert of particular interest is the fact that a professional soloist, Madame Malibran, was engaged to take part. This young singer, then only eighteen, was one of the distinguished soloists of Europe. A musical journal of the time in describing her singing of "Angels Ever Bright and Fair" in this particular concert of the Sacred Music Society says: "During the performance of the song, so silent was the audience that not even a whisper was to be heard. She performed it beautifully, as a matter of course, although the admirers of the simplicity of Handel had to regret the introduction of so much ornament. She was clad in robes of virgin white, and at the words 'Take, O, take me to thy care,' she raised her hands and eyes in an imploring attitude to heaven in so dramatic and touching a manner as to electrify the audience, and to call down a universal outburst of approbation, a very unusual occurrence in a church in this country."

As has been seen, oratorio already had been heard in New York in miscellaneous concerts of sacred music, but in 1831 the Sacred Music Society, under Mr. U. C. Hill, decided to take up the study of oratorio seriously and systematically. It is natural that the "Messiah," with which the members already were somewhat familiar, should be selected and on November 18 of the year mentioned the full oratorio was given in St. Paul's Chapel. The chorus numbered seventy-four voices with an orchestra of thirty-eight. The chapel was thronged, and the oratorio was repeated twice within the next two months. This organization which had given to New York its first complete performance of an oratorio continued to give annual performances of similar works until 1849. It also should be recorded that this society with a commendable spirit of enterprise gave a public performance of Mendelssohn's "St. Paul" within two years after its first performance in Düsseldorf.

In 1849 the New York Harmonic Society usurped the field hitherto held by the Sacred Music Society. Four years previously, however, it had found a rival in the Musical Institute which, under the direction of Henry C. Timm, made a specialty of the presentation of oratorios and cantatas. The chorus of this organization numbered one hundred and twenty voices, which was assisted by an orchestra of sixty performers. In 1846, two years after it was founded, the Institute gave a public performance of Haydn's "Seasons" and in 1848 Schumann's "Paradise and the Peri." But the Musical Institute, as had its predecessors, too soon ceased to exist, and a meeting of both professionals and amateurs was called to consider ways and means of uniting in one body those desirous of continuing the serious study of oratorio, and the birth of the New York Harmonic Society was the result. Rehearsals were commenced, H. C. Timm at first offering voluntary leadership, Theodore Eisfield later being elected conductor. The Harmonic Society gave its first public performance on May 10, 1850, the "Messiah" filling the program. This was repeated on November 9 of the same year with Jenny Lind as leading soloist. In June of the following year Mendelssohn's "Elijah" was performed in Tripler Hall, an auditorium which seated almost five thousand persons.

From the ranks of the Harmonic Society came the material for founding the Mendelssohn Union in 1863; then followed the Church Music Association, which was strong in the "society" element, its concerts, in which selections from oratorios were included, being most exclusive. Oratorio now had taken firm root in New York, and fortunately the genuine lovers of choral work, among them many Germans, met together and organized the New York Oratorio Society under the leadership of Dr. Leopold Damrosch. Its first meetings were held in Trinity Chapel; then the Knabe Piano firm generously offered the free use of its warerooms, afterward giving the use of an upper floor of the building as more commodious quarters. In Knabe Hall, Dec. 3, 1873, the Oratorio Society gave its first concert, when selections from the works of Palestrina, Bach, and from other classical composers constituted the program. In this concert there were but twenty-eight voices in the chorus. Within ten years the organization gave ninety-three public performances and rendered forty-four standard works or parts of such works.

In connection with the New York Symphony Society, which he organized in 1877, Dr. Damrosch in 1881 gave to New York its first May Festival, when a chorus of twelve hundred voices and an orchestra of two hundred and eighty-seven performers took part. In the organization of the chorus methods were pursued similar to those employed for the monster choruses in the Sydenham Crystal Palace, London. The nucleus of the chorus was the membership of the Oratorio Society itself, which was designated "Section A." An independent body of singers from other New York societies was designated "Section B;" "Section C" embraced

FRANZ KNEISEL. 1865-

Roumanian violinist, was born at Bucharest, where his father was a military band leader.

In 1886 Kneisel organized the famous "Kneisel Quartet," the performers being Otto Roth, Louis Svecnski, Alvin Schroeder and himself. This quartet is well known in London and in all the larger American cities.

Kneisel acted as conductor of the Boston Symphony Orchestra during the World's Fair in Chicago in 1893, and in 1905 became violin instructor in the Institute of Musical Art in New York.

the singers from Newark, New Jersey; "Section D" was composed of Brooklynites; "Section E" represented Jersey City; while "Section F" hailed from Nyack. In September, 1880, these individual sections began the study of the festival music under their respective leaders, and during the months that followed Dr. Damrosch himself visited each section at regular intervals. Later, these individual rehearsals were supplemented by mass rehearsals held in the Hall of Cooper Union, New York.

In connection with this festival Dr. Damrosch organized a chorus of young girls numbering over a thousand, under a special directorship, and a chorus of boys numbering two hundred and fifty, made up principally from the church choirs of the city, to take part in the afternoon performances. The concerts were held in the Seventh Regiment Armory, which was fitted up to accommodate ten thousand persons. The average daily attendance was about nine thousand. The soloists were Annie Louise Carey, Etelka Gerster, Myron W. Whitney, and Franz Remmertz. Artistically and financially the first May Festival in New York was a success, although the undertaking was severely criticized for its magnitude.

Oratorio found its way west of the Alleghenies at a comparatively early period. The Haydn Society was organized in Cincinnati in 1819. Previous to this time, however, there had been an active choral organization in the town, but serious oratorio work grew out of the enterprise of the Haydn Society. It came into birth with the incorporated city of Cincinnati itself, and it gave its first concert only four years later than did the Handel and Haydn Society of Boston. This particular concert was given in Christ Church, and the proceeds of the same were devoted to payment on the organ of the church. The program, while not an especially pretentious one, nevertheless yields sufficient proof of the ambitions of the musical people of the city. Haydn was represented by the chorus "The Marvelous Work," and Handel by the duet and chorus "Hail Judea," from "Judas

Maccabæus." In the notice of this concert which appeared in the Cincinnati Spy the writer states: "Public concerts of this description, although rather a novelty here, are quite common in Eastern cities and if well performed never fail to afford great pleasure to the audience." Then, after dwelling on the manner in which the several parts were performed, he adds: "This exhibition must have been highly gratifying to those who begin to feel proud of our city. It is the strongest evidence we can adduce of our advancement in those embellishments which refine and harmonize society and give a zest to life. We hope that another opportunity will occur for a further display of the talents of the Haydn Society. For their endeavor to create a correct musical talent among us they deserve thanks; but when to their efforts is added the disposition to aid the cause of public charities, or the services of the church, their claims to the most respectful attention and applause rise to an obligation on the part of the community."

This undoubtedly was the first encouragement of oratorio west of the Alleghanies. On Dec. 19, 1822, the Haydn Society gave its second concert, the program containing selections from Handel's "Israel in Egypt," from the "Messiah," and a selection from Mozart. It is seen therefore that there was a remarkable interest in oratorio in the chief city of the Ohio Valley even at the time when New York also was just beginning to develop a taste for this class of music.

Cincinnati's Haydn Society materially assisted in promoting an interest in music, so that other organizations soon were formed, among them the Episcopal Singing Society, and the Euterpean. The latter society gave a concert in the Cincinnati Hotel, on July 18, 1823, announced to take place at "early candle-light." This phrase serves to suggest something of the primitive conditions existing in Cincinnati at this period; yet its people were desirous of art culture, and anxious to develop the highest form of choral music by giving encouragement to oratorio, even under adverse conditions.

The Sacred Music Society, organized about 1840 under the directorship of Victor Williams, after giving concerts in which oratorio was mingled with other selections, later confined itself exclusively to the study of oratorio. It is impossible here to follow step by step the development of choral societies in Cincinnati. The city's May Festivals have become historic; the German singing societies, the coming of Theodore Thomas, and the enterprise of many leading citizens has made Cincinnati a truly musical city.

In May, 1873, there were gathered in Cincinnati thirty-six societies from the West and Northwest, over one thousand singers, with an orchestra of something over a hundred performers, and organ. This was the beginning. Theodore Thomas said: "It will send new life and vigor into the whole musical body of the West." In the performance of oratorio these May Festivals educated the people to a higher musical culture in choral music, besides cultivating a taste for the best in orchestral appreciation, and as Theodore Thomas predicted, its influence was felt in the "whole musical body of the West."

Chicago, with less than a quarter of a century to its municipal life, in 1858 had a society, the Musical Union, which took up the study of oratorio. This organization continued in existence until 1866. During these eight years it gave public performances of the "Creation," "Messiah," "Elijah," and other oratorios. After its disbandment, the Oratorio Society, under the leadership of Hans Balatka, sprang into existence. This society gave oratorio concerts during the winters of 1868, 1869 and 1870. Unfortunately the Oratorio Society was a victim of the fire. It lost its library, and its members scattered, Mr. Balatka going to Milwaukee. The Handel and Haydn Society of Boston generously came to its aid with a donation of books, including sets of the oratorios of the "Messiah," "Israel in Egypt," "David," and a number of miscellaneous collections, and the organization was revived with J. A. Butterfield as conductor. The churches offered their lecture rooms as recital halls, and on May 16, 1872, the "Messiah" was given in the Union Park Congregational Church. The chorus numbered one hundred and fifty voices, with an orchestra of twenty-two. The same program was repeated later in the Michigan Avenue Baptist Church. In January, 1873, the Oratorio Society again was a victim of fire, and again lost its library. Several efforts were made to hold the organization together, but ultimately it ceased to exist and left the field to the Apollo Club which had been organized in the summer of 1872, and which today, under the leadership of Harrison Wild, is the only organization in Chicago that gives public oratorio performances with any degree of regularity.

Chicago held its first Musical Festivals in May, 1882, with Theodore Thomas as director of music. The "Messiah" was rendered in its completeness on the second evening, May 24, with a chorus of nearly one thousand voices, one hundred and six of which came from the Arion Club, Milwaukee, and with an orchestra of one hundred and eighty, nearly fifty of whom were residents of Chicago, the remainder being collected from New York and Cincinnati. Of the ten soloists six were American by birth, each having attained fame abroad; of the remaining four, two were naturalized German-American citizens who already had won fame in the land of their adoption as well as in the land of their birth. The organist was Clarence Eddy, one of the most eminent of America's organ virtuosos, who had been a pupil of Haupt, and who had a phenomenal concert tour in Europe.

The State of Missouri has contributed much to the development of oratorio in the central part of the United States. St. Louis had its singing schools in 1837. In 1839 Charles Balmer, who later became well known as a music publisher, came to St. Louis. About the year 1845 Mr. Balmer organized the Oratorio Society, made up of singers from the various church choirs. Several concerts were given, and Haydn's "Creation" was performed as a whole. Later, in 1859, the Philharmonic Society was formed, with Mr. Balmer as vice-president. The chorus of this organization numbered about one hundred voices gathered from the various church choirs, and its repertory embraced the "Creation," the "Seasons," "St. Paul" and "Elijah." The war was disastrous to the Philharmonic, but in 1880 the St. Louis Choral Society was organized. This society in its first year gave four subscription concerts, Handel's "Messiah" representing the entire program of one of them.

Kansas is strong in choral organizations. It is said that there is hardly a town in the State which has not its choral organization. For seventeen years preceding the close of the Nineteenth Century the town of Lindsborg, with a population of little more than a thousand, gave Handel's "Messiah" on each Good Friday during the period. Of one of these oratorio performances a critic writes:

"Central Kansas, where hot winds sometimes blast the corn crop before it matures, and droughts and grasshoppers are of comparatively recent date, is not the eastern man's ideal of the place to find a musical people. Half of the United States supposes that the coyote's bark is the most musical sound to be heard in this region. Yet in this little town of less than fifteen hundred inhabitants Handel's oratorio, 'The Messiah,' was sung by a chorus of three hundred, two nights of this week in the auditorium of Bethany College. A pipe organ that cost five thousand dollars and an orchestra of thirty-four pieces furnished the instrumental music. The solos were by teachers and graduates of the college. The audience of seven thousand people came from the surrounding country and from towns up and down the Smoky and Solomon Valleys, and some across the Arkansas away to the South. Distance does not count for much in Central Kansas. . . . The history of Lindsborg, a settlement of music loving Swedish-Americans, its colleges and its great annual oratorio festival is the history of a struggle for higher education, and yet this great love for music is no uncommon phase in Kansas prairie life."

The earliest oratorio society of which there is any mention on the Pacific coast was organized by Rudolph Herold in San Francisco in 1860. The oratorio of "Elijah" was performed, the solos being taken by singers who came from

England to the East, and thence to San Francisco. Later, Mr. Oliver of Boston organized the Handel and Haydn Society, which became a strong force in promoting an appreciation for oratorio in the Golden Gate City. When it produced the "Creation" in 1862 it numbered two hundred and fifty voices. It also gave a performance of "Samson" in 1863. Five years later the "Creation" was given at St. James' Church by a chorus of eighty voices, with William McDougall directing. Parepa Rosa appeared in this concert. In 1887 the Oratorio Society presented Haydn's "Creation" on February 11, while the Handel and Haydn Society in April gave Mendelssohn's "Elijah," the chorus numbering one hundred and fifty voices. San Francisco must have given encouragement to oratorio performances at this period or two societies making a specialty of the same would not have attempted two oratorio performances within two months of each other.

Since oratorio in the Eighteenth Century kindled a love for higher choral work in New York, Boston, Philadelphia, and other cities of the East, gradually it has found favor with the public in almost every State in the Union. Handel's "Messiah" and Haydn's "Creation," together with other notable oratorios now are as familiar to the music-loving communities of America as to the people of Europe. The "Messiah" undoubtedly is the most frequently performed of any of the standard oratorios and it forms the annual Christmas offering of all the leading choral societies throughout the United States. Another great work, the St. Matthew "Passion" of Bach, also is rapidly becoming a fixture in the repertories of these societies. In addition to the performance of oratorio the various choral organizations have covered every department of vocal music — cantatas, glees, madrigals, and more recently a capella choruses. The study of the latter has been taken up principally by societies formed almost wholly of professionals.

At the present time almost every city of importance in America has one or more organizations devoted to the study and public performance of choral music. Some of these make a specialty of oratorio, while others give their attention chiefly to unaccompanied part singing. In addition to the time honored Handel and Haydn Society, Boston has several other excellent choruses. The Cecilia Society, organized in 1877 under the direction of B. J. Lang, gives several concerts each season. This society is noted for its initiative in the presentation of new and little known works. The Apollo Club is one of the best known male choruses in the country. Emil Mollenhauer has been the director since 1901, when Mr. Lang relinquished the post. The Choral Art Society, an organization which makes a specialty of ancient music and unaccompanied singing, was formed by J. Wallace Goodrich in 1901. A number of its concerts have been given in Trinity Church, where Mr. Goodrich is the organist and musical director. In addition to these better known societies Boston also has several large choruses made up chiefly of working people. Samuel W. Cole has been most active in this field and for some years has been the director of the People's Choral Union, a chorus of over four hundred voices.

In New York the Oratorio Society still holds first place among the choral organizations. Frank Damrosch is the present director. Mr. Damrosch also is at the head of the Musical Art Society, which is conducted along lines similar to the Choral Art Society of Boston, and of the Mendelssohn Club, a male chorus. The United Singers of New York and the People's Choral Union, both exceedingly large choruses, have been instrumental in creating an interest in choral music among the masses. Another New York organization, the Manuscript Society, devotes itself exclusively to the performance of works by American composers. Brooklyn has several excellent choruses, the most important of which are the Oratorio Society and the Choral Society.

In Chicago the Apollo Club, under the direction of Harrison M. Wild, covers the oratorio field and gives a series of concerts each season. The Mendelssohn Club, a male chorus, also directed by Mr. Wild, is one of the finest organizations of its kind in the country. In the Musical Art Society Chicago possesses an excellent body of singers, formed almost entirely of professionals, who make a specialty of unaccompanied works. Clarence Dickinson is the director. Cincinnati has its Apollo Club, which is noted for its performance of the larger choral works. The Loring Club, a male chorus, founded in San Francisco in 1876, also is well known for the excellence of its singing. It is impossible to enumerate the many excellent choral organizations existing at the present time in all parts of the country. From the Atlantic to the Pacific each of these units exerts an influence for the betterment of concerted vocal music in its own sphere and through its efforts enables the public to hear the highest type of choral music. A singing society never is conducted for financial gain; such organizations exist only for the pleasure and profit which they may give to those associated with them and to the general public.

No mention has been made thus far concerning the various organizations of foreigners existing from time to time in this country, but it must not be supposed that the efforts made by these societies have been of no moment, for they have exerted a most beneficent influence in the cause of music. However, so long as they have remained exclusive their influence has been restricted and has been felt only when the members have become absorbed by other and more catholic institutions. This fact remains true at the present time, for the many German and Scandinavian singing societies established in all parts of the country continue to cater almost exclusively to their own people and not to the public at large. One notable exception, however, is the Bach Choir of Bethlehem, Pennsylvania, whose influence has been broadspread and conducive of much good.

From the time of its settlement by the Moravians in 1741 Bethlehem has been a musical center. The community always has been noted for its musical life, but it was not until the latter half of the Nineteenth Century that it commenced to exert a pronounced influence on music in America, and this largely through the efforts of Mr. J. Fred Wolle. The event which brought Bethlehem into extreme prominence was the rendition on March 27, 1900, for the first time in America, of Bach's B Minor Mass under the direction of Mr. Wolle. The Bach Choir of eighty voices, which presented this great work, was organized in 1898. There was an assisting orchestra of thirty-nine and the soloists were engaged from Boston, New York and Philadelphia. The mass was presented in two parts, one in the afternoon and the other the same evening. Each session was announced by the playing of chorals by a group of twelve trombonists stationed in the belfry of the old Moravian Church, a method of announcement which had existed in Bethlehem from earliest times. The Bach cult organized by Mr. Wolle has given many of the great master's works and has succeeded in creating a new interest in these wonderful creations.

Among the oldest and best known of the associations of foreigners in America is the Deutsche Liederkranz of New York. This famous society was formed in January, 1847, as a male chorus, but in 1856 it was reorganized and women were admitted as active members. It has since continued to maintain a high standard of excellence, largely devoting itself to the performance of works by the German composers. Arthur Claassen is the present director. Another long established chorus is the Arion, a Männerchor which was organized in 1854 as an offshoot of the Liederkranz. Dr. Leopold Damrosch chiefly was instrumental in bringing this society into prominence, and under Julius Lorenz it continues to hold its place as one of the leading male choruses in the United States.

It is not in New York alone that these societies of foreigners exist, for in every large city in the country are to be found organizations representative of almost all the European nations. The German and Scandinavian singing clubs, however, are the most numerous. Milwaukee has a Musikverein which has been heard in choral concerts in that city since

1851. Each of the German and Swedish centers supports several male choirs. In Milwaukee alone there are over twenty such choruses. As a general rule the foreign residents of the United States take more interest in chorus singing than do the native born. The clubs and societies which they have established usually combine social affairs of some sort with the musical features. Although America has shown a more marked preference for instrumental music, especially for piano music, rather than for vocal, nevertheless wonderful strides have been made in choral singing. It is only when one stops to compare the concert life of today with that of a century ago that any idea of our progress can be realized. Our development has been rapid and sure and bids fair to continue along the same upward path.

OPERA IN AMERICA

Whatever progress America has made in operatic production may be ascribed almost wholly to New Orleans and New York, for it is in these cities alone that any lasting attempts have been made in the establishment of permanent opera. By permanent opera is meant the institution of a company regularly engaged in the presentation of opera in a house devoted exclusively to such an enterprise. While other cities for many years have enjoyed operatic performances they have been dependent largely on the New York organizations and on traveling companies. Even at the present time New York is the only American city which supports its own opera. New Orleans gave up the struggle years ago; and so, while steady progress has been made in other lines of musical endeavor, outside of the metropolis opera has made little headway, although the last year has been pregnant with promise.

The comparative failure of opera in America seems to rest with two features, viz., the enormous cost of production, and the caprice of the public. When finally the non-success of the matter is narrowed down to first causes the reason for failure is seen to rest with the public. If opera were wanted for its own sake, rather than for the exploitation of "stars," people would be content with good general ensemble, but such unfortunately does not seem to be the case. When this state of affairs becomes changed every city of prominence in America will be able to support its own resident company. In the past the country has had opera of almost every species — ballad-opera in English, Italian, French, German, and English opera, each taking its name primarily from the language in which it was sung.

The operas popular in England were the first to reach America. These were the ballad-operas, so designated because the songs therein were not set to music originally composed for them, but were adapted to the tunes of old ballads and popular songs. Such was the "Beggar's Opera," written by John Gay in 1727. The tunes, sixty-six in number, were arranged and scored by Dr. Pepusch, the overture itself being his own composition. The tunes were selected from the most popular of English, Scotch and Irish ballads of the day, and this familiarity with the music accounts, in a measure, for the widespread popularity of the opera itself.

So far as can be learned the "Beggar's Opera" was performed for the first time in America at the old Nassau Street Theatre, New York City, in December, 1750, nearly twenty-five years after its first performance in London. The theatre in which it was given was a two-story structure, and one marvels, in this day of wonderful electrical equipment, at the patience of our forefathers, who enjoyed opera amid an illumination of sputtering candles, six in front of the stage and another half-dozen suspended in barrel-hoops above the audience. Philadelphia first heard the "Beggar's Opera" in 1759, although other ballad-operas had been given in the city previous to this time. Even Boston, as early as 1770, enjoyed opera in disguise. The performance was announced as a "vocal entertainment in three acts." The program states: "The songs, which are numerous, are taken from a new and celebrated opera, called 'Lionel and Clarissa.'" Boston also heard the "Beggar's Opera" in an entertainment in which readings from the libretto and songs from the score formed the program.

The ballad-opera, like the French, Italian, and German opera which followed, first became familiar to the colonists by means of songs and selections which appeared with more or less frequency upon concert programs. These selections almost invariably were rendered by members of itinerant troupes during the period after the Revolution in which theatrical performances were placed under a ban. Thus in the Maryland Journal, on May 25, 1790, a concert was announced in which operatic selections form a considerable part of the program. Monsieur and Madame de Lisle's names appear as the leading vocalists, and one item of the program is announced as "an Opera Song by M. de Lisle with its accompaniments." Charleston, S. C., Williamsburg, Va., and Philadelphia audiences heard selections from Grétry, Dalayrac, and Gluck, becoming familiar with these excerpts long before the full opera made its appearance among them.

From 1793 to the close of the century Charleston enjoyed English opera, and after 1796 it became interested in both French and Italian works. This was brought about by a company of French comedians, refugees from the Island of St. Domingo. In the programs presented in the southern city there are found not only songs and selections from the operas by Arne, Atwood, Shield and others, but Rousseau, Grétry, Cimarosa and Paisiello also figure conspicuously. The original home of French opera in its entirety in America, however, was New Orleans. French families were in the majority there, and music had a strong hold on the everyday life of the people. In 1791 a company of French comedians settled in New Orleans and for twenty years gave regular entertainments, including opera.

In 1810, Paisiello's "Barber of Seville" was given in New Orleans. The following year there arrived from St. Domingo, John Davis, who conceived the plan of establishing a special home for opera in the city, and in 1813 the Theatre d'Orleans was built. It was a substantial building of brick and was equipped with all the scenic and mechanical appliances in vogue at the time in the best European theatres.

Here opera was performed three nights of the week, with plays in the French language on intervening nights. Within four years after its completion the Theatre d'Orleans fell a prey to fire, but Mr. Davis immediately arranged to erect a new opera house on the same site.

The second structure was even more pretentious than was the former one, one hundred and eighty thousand dollars being expended in its erection and equipment. It gave to New Orleans a prestige in the theatrical circles of the country, and its fame also traveled beyond the ocean until artists of real merit came over from Paris. The management was proud of the fact that here in the Crescent City, as nowhere else in America, French Grand Opera was being presented in all its completeness. This new opera house, which had arisen from the ashes of the former one, was opened in 1819, and for twenty-five years John Davis, and Charles Boudausquie who succeeded him, kept to the high standard which had characterized the performances of this playhouse from its incipiency. During four nights of each week, when the operatic season was in abeyance, French comedy, drama and ballet of the highest significance graced the stage. But the Theatre d'Orleans became the special home of opera, and every season a company from Paris gave an excellent repertory of the masterpieces being performed on the operatic stage of the French capital.

In 1842 New Orleans sent a fully equipped French opera company to New York; in fact, as the various companies passed to and from the city of New Orleans and Paris, New York frequently was given opportunity to enjoy French opera before the year in question, and Boston, in 1829, had been given its first taste of Italian opera by a French troupe en route to the Crescent City. For some decades preceding the Civil War, operatic companies, whether French, Italian, English or German, looked for reimbursement, after playing losing roles in other cities, to the gay and appreciative Louisiana capital, and today New Orleans still is something of an Eldorado for the better grade of opera companies.

During the twenty-five years in which ballad-opera held sway foreign operas were becoming familiar in adapted form. These were heard in America as given in London, the music simplified according to the whim of the adapter, who also undertook to add to or take away from both libretto and score of the original. The towns and cities in close touch with the European centers, as has been seen, enjoyed both French and Italian operatic music before the close of the Eighteenth Century. Outside of New Orleans these performances were given principally by English singers.

The presentation of Italian opera in its entirety in the United States begins with the coming of the Garcia family. Manuel del Popolo Vincente Garcia was then in the prime of life. He was a Spaniard by birth, and had won fame as a tenor singer and as a composer of operas not only in his own country but in Italy, France and England as well. His daughter, Maria Felicita, afterward known as Mme. Malibran, was his pupil, and had made her debut in London the year previous to accompanying her father to America. The principals of the company, besides Garcia and his daughter, were his wife, his son Manuel, Mme. Barbieri, Crivelli, and Angrisani. The company opened its season at the new Park Theatre, New York, on Nov. 29, 1825, with Rossini's "Barber of Seville," Garcia himself taking the part of Almaviva. It took the people of New York by storm. The orchestra itself was a revelation at this period, consisting of seven violins, two violas, three violoncellos, two contrabasses, two flutes, two clarinets, one bassoon, two horns, two trumpets, one pair of kettledrums, and piano.

After the novelty had worn off, however, the financial success was not so encouraging as was that from the artistic side. At first people went to the theatre to gratify their curiosity. The opera interested them for a time as something novel, but, failing to understand the language in which it was given, they gradually lost interest in the music. So after a year, playing at both the Park and Bowery theatres, and giving in all seventy-six performances, Garcia conceived the idea of going to Mexico. Here he met with splendid success during his eighteen months of sojourn, but on the return journey the company was held up by brigands and relieved of their valuables, including about thirty thousand dollars in gold.

From the time of the visit of the Garcia troupe during the season of 1825-1826, until 1832, New York heard many performances of opera given by English companies who made use of translations and arrangements of French and German and Italian works. Among the operas performed were Boieldieu's "Jean de Paris" and "Dame Blanche," Weber's "Der Freischütz" and "Oberon," and Mozart's "Die Zauberflöte."

In 1832 a second Italian troupe was brought to New York chiefly through the efforts of Lorenza da Ponte, an Italian poet who had written the librettos of several of Mozart's operas, and who at that time was a resident of New York. The company, which was under the management of the tenor, Giacomo Montresso, opened a season of thirty-five nights on Oct. 6, 1832, at the Richmond Hill Theatre. But the venture, excellent as it was from an artistic standpoint, resulted in financial failure. Notwithstanding this fact, in the following year Da Ponta again inaugurated a scheme which resulted in the erection of the first opera house in America devoted exclusively to such performances. This auditorium, which had been named the Italian Opera House, together with its site cost one hundred and seventy-five thousand dollars. Artists from Europe were employed to decorate its ceiling with mural paintings representative of the Muses; crimson silk draperies adorned its tier of boxes, while the furnishings of the pit were gorgeous in settings of blue damask, and the floors were laid with carpet. Italian opera here found its home in the New World of which it took possession with a carefully selected company of distinguished performers, and with an excellent orchestra. But the combined excellence of appointments, of singers, and of orchestral performers could not save it from financial wreck. In its season of eight months the treasury showed a deficit of over twenty-nine thousand dollars. The Italian Opera House remained in existence only long enough to ruin another manager, when it was given over to dramatic performances at the close of the season of 1834-1835, under the new name of the National Theatre, which soon after was destroyed by fire.

In 1844 Palmo's Opera House created new life in Italian opera in New York. Ferdinand Palmo, its projector, was a restaurateur who had accumulated some wealth as proprietor of the Café des Mille Colonnes on Broadway, and he now invested his savings in the new opera house in Chambers Street. This was not a pretentious structure by any means. On the contrary it was severely plain, but of good acoustic properties nevertheless, and with a seating capacity of about eight hundred. It was opened with Bellini's "I Puritani," the first performance, it is said, of this opera in the United States. But the scheme proved a failure, and his operatic venture ruined Palmo financially, and after again following his occupation as a restaurateur he failed to recover from his losses and finally died a dependent on charity.

It is said that Palmo's company, although good, was done to death by a formidable rival, the Havana Opera Company, which appeared in New York at this time under the musical directorship of Luigi Arditi, who in the previous year with Bottesini had gone to Havana from Italy. This company opened its season at the Park Theatre on April 15, 1847, and each season for many years it paid regular visits to New York, playing at Niblo's Garden, the Astor Place Opera House, and at Castle Garden after the destruction by fire of the Park Theatre in 1848.

Neither the efforts of Garcia, Da Ponte, Montressor, nor Palmo were in vain. The embers smoldered for a while but again were fanned into new life by the enterprise of Messrs. Foster, Morgan and Colles, who built the Astor Place Opera House. This house accommodated an audience of eighteen hundred and was opened on Nov. 22, 1847, with Verdi's "Ernani." It was built by subscription, on condition that Italian opera be performed here seventy-five nights a year for at least five years. But the enterprise never paid, and after five years' struggle for existence it closed its doors in 1852.

In the same year, despite the failure of each successive establishment which had attempted the production of opera on a permanent basis, a new scheme was started in New York. The idea of the promoters was the creation of an institution somewhat similar to the Boston Academy of Music. The charter stated that the new Academy was to be established "for the purpose of cultivating a taste for music by concerts, operas, and other entertainments, which shall be accessible to the public at a moderate charge; by furnishing facilities for instruction in music, and by rewards of prizes for the best musical compositions." The latter part of the plan never was carried out, but from the opening of the building on Oct. 2, 1854, until it was given over to theatrical performances in 1886, the Academy of Music remained the principal home of opera in New York. Among the men prominent in its management were Ole Bull, Max Maretzek, Max and Maurice Strakosch, Ullmann and Colonel Mapleson.

During the life of the Italian Opera House, Palmo's, the Astor Place Opera House and the Academy of Music, opera was produced in many other New York theatres as well. In 1837 the Seguin troupe began a series of performances of English operas and translations of French and Italian works. Three years later the Woods company revived the "Beggar's Opera" and also gave a number of adaptations of foreign works including "La Sonnambula" and "Fidelio." From year to year other English troupes appeared, and the Havana Italian Opera Company, under Señor Marty, visited New York for several seasons, playing at the Park Theatre and at Castle Garden. Maretzek, Strakosch and Ullmann all were prominent in operatic production, often in opposition to each other; indeed so fierce was the struggle that in 1859 all three impresarios took their companies on the road and New York was left without opera.

In 1855 the city was given a short season of German opera under Carl Bergmann, and on April 4, 1859, this conductor presented "Tannhäuser," the first Wagner opera to be heard in America. In 1862 another season of German opera was given at the Wallack Theatre by Carl Anschütz. The company, while not possessing any "stars," offered an excellent ensemble and played to audiences of true music lovers. But the enterprise was not successful financially and finally was given up. After the Civil War there came a distinct change in the opera field, the tendencies of the public turning to the French opéra bouffe and later to the lighter works of Gilbert and Sullivan. What has taken place in this direction has been discussed in a previous chapter.

While New York and New Orleans have been active in opera production other American cities have done little else than listen to the irregular seasons offered by the New York organizations on tour and by traveling companies. Philadelphia had its first taste of regular opera in 1827, when John Davis, to whom reference already has been made, brought a troupe from New Orleans to the Chestnut Street Theatre. The performances were given in French and so pleased the Philadelphians that the French Opera Company continued its visits each season for some years. In May 5, 1829, Italian opera first was produced in Philadelphia; and later, in 1833, the Montressor troupe came to the Chestnut Street Theatre and gave some excellent performances. At this period, in Philadelphia as well as in New York, Italian companies were found giving opera at regular intervals. In 1848 Max Maretzek was the leader of the orchestra at the Chestnut Street Theatre during the performance of the Italian Opera Company brought from the Astor Place Opera House, New York. This company was the most important of its kind to visit Philadelphia up to this time. Later Maretzek came there as manager with an Italian troupe, and gave performances which were artistic if not always remunerative.

In 1857 the Academy of Music was opened in Philadelphia, and became the temple of Italian opera. It retained its prestige for years; German, English and French opera performances also being presented here in turn.

Chicago first hear opera, at least one act of "La Sonnambula," on July 30, 1850. The performance was interrupted by an alarm of fire and consequently was discontinued. It was not until three years later that the city again was given a presentation of opera. On Oct. 27, 1853, the "Italian Troupe" opened a week's season with "Lucia di Lammermoor." The advertisement in the Democratic Press announces the members of the company as follows: "The grand prima donna, Signorina R. De Vries; the favorite tenor, Signor Pozzolini; the tenor, Signor Arnoldi; the comprimaria, Mme. Sidenbourg, late of Madame Albani's troupe; the unrivaled barytone, Signor Taffenelli, and the eminent basso, Signor Calleti. Also a grand and efficient chorus, and grand orchestra. This great company numbers over forty members, the whole under the most able direction of the distinguished maestro, Signor L. Arditi." This was a company of meritorious artists, and it really was the pioneer Italian opera troupe of the West. Since then Chicago's appreciation of opera, Italian, English and German, has encouraged the best companies to come and play regular seasons. Some few years ago a magnificent home for opera was built which unfortunately is used too seldom for that purpose.

Cincinnati inaugurated a home for opera in that city by a festival which took place on Feb. 22, 1859. A few weeks later, on March 15, Maurice Strakosch arrived with his company and gave the initial performances. The first opera presented was Flotow's "Martha."

San Francisco had its first taste of opera in 1853, when "Ernani" was given under the management of an Englishman, George Loder. Four years later came Signor and Signora Bianchi with an excellent troupe, reviving Italian opera and giving San Francisco its first extended season of grand opera. In 1862 the Bianchi troupe returned to San Francisco and opened a season at the Metropolitan Theatre. Among the works presented were "Norma," "La Sonnambula," "La Favorita," "Ernani," "Linda di Chamouni," "Il Trovatore" and others. Opera now came to San Francisco with some degree of regularity and the Bianchi troupe was a favorite for many seasons. As facilities for travel increased, impresarios looked toward San Francisco as a second Eldorado, and in 1881 Colonel Mapleson appeared with his star combination. Three years later the San Franciscans were being entertained by both German and Italian opera, and the opera seasons since have received excellent support. It is not necessary to speak of the introduction of opera elsewhere in America, for the same troupes which appeared in New York and Philadelphia also gave performances in Boston and other cities.

To return to New York, where opera was undergoing its struggle for existence, in 1878 Colonel J. H. Mapleson came from London to New York as manager of the Academy of Music. Colonel Mapleson was the first impresario to inaugurate the "star" system in this country, a system which long has militated against the production of good opera at reasonable prices. The season of 1878-1879 at the Academy proved extremely successful both artistically and financially, and in addition to the New York performances Colonel Mapleson took his company to all the leading cities in the East and as far west as Chicago. But after the first season matters did not go so smoothly and the birth of a rival of the Academy caused him to give up the struggle.

On Oct. 22, 1883, the Metropolitan Opera House, under the management of Henry E. Abbey, was opened with Gounod's "Faust." In the company were Nilsson, Sembrich, Scalchi, Trebelli, Campanini, Del Puente, Novara, Stagno and Capoul, with Campanini and Vianesi as musical directors. On the same evening the Academy of Music opened its season with Patti and a company which included Gerster, Pappenheim and Galassi. New York now was fairly ablaze with the meteoric shower of operatic "stars" and the day of fabulous salaries had begun. Thus began the struggle between the two houses which eventually closed the Academy and which brought a loss of $300,000 to the management of the Metropolitan. During the first season Abbey gave sixty-one performances, in which nineteen different operas were presented. Notwithstanding his financial failure he was asked to remain but declined, although some years later he again assumed control.

The Metropolitan directors then invited Mr. Gye of London to take charge, but he also refused. Dr. Leopold Damrosch now came forward with a proposition to establish German opera, and the directors decided to act on his suggestion. Within a short time Dr. Damrosch went to Germany, organized his company, and was back in New York. On Nov. 17, 1884, the season of German opera opened. The operas produced in thirty-eight subscription nights, five extra evenings and fourteen afternoon presentations were: "Tannhäuser," "Fidelio," "Les Huguenots," "Der Freischütz," "William Tell," "Lohengrin," "Don Giovanni," "Le Prophète," "La Muette de Portici," "Rigoletto," "La Juive," and "Die Walküre."

The advent of German opera and of opera in German at the Metropolitan gave a new trend to opera in the United States and fixed the position of the house as the operatic center of New York. Through the efforts of Dr. Damrosch the Wagner music-dramas assumed the prominent place they since have held in the repertory of the Metropolitan companies. On the death of Dr. Damrosch in 1885 E. C. Stanton was appointed manager, with Walter Damrosch as assistant, and Anton Seidl took up the musical direction. Under Seidl, "Die Meistersinger," "Tristan and Isolde" and the complete "Der Ring des Nibelungen" received their first presentations in America. After thirteen years of active Wagner propaganda in New York, Anton Seidl died in 1898.

In 1891 Abbey again assumed control of the Metropolitan, in association with Maurice Grau, and continued in charge until his death in 1896. Grau then undertook the sole management which he held until 1902, when he gave way to Heinrich Conried. The present year (1908) has seen another change and the season of 1908-1909 will see Giulio Gatti-Casazza, late of La Scala, Milan, installed as manager. During Mr. Conried's régime the Metropolitan was put on a much firmer financial footing. The season of 1903-1904 was made notable by the first production of "Parsifal" on any stage outside of Bayreuth. Another operatic event which attracted wide attention was the presentation of Richard Strauss' "Salome" during the past season. Since the time of Anton Seidl, Alfred Hertz, Felix Mottl and Gustave Mahler have been the leading musical directors. Of late years the Metropolitan Company has restricted its performances outside of New York to Boston, Philadelphia, Pittsburg and Chicago.

The season of 1908-1909 will bring radical changes in the management. Four men, with Gatti-Casazza at the head, will act as joint directors. Andreas Dippel, the tenor, will be the new administrative manager, while Toscanini, Hertz and Mahler will be the musical directors. It also is announced that in addition to these changes, the old system of having the manager share in the profits of the company will be abolished and the new managers will receive fixed salaries. Any profits realized will be used for the establishment of an endowment or pension fund, or for some similar purpose for the advancement of the Metropolitan Opera House as an art institution. The company will include Farrar, Fremstad, Gadski, Homer, Morena, Sembrich, Emmy Destinn, Selma-Kurz, Maria Gay, Bonci, Caruso, Grassi, Burrian, Goritz, Martin, Reiss, Scotti, Amato, Didur and Hinckley.

In 1906 a new opera company was inaugurated in New York which has proved a genuine success. On July 1, 1906, the Hammerstein Opera Company was incorporated, with Oscar Hammerstein at its head. The Manhattan Opera House was secured and after extensive operations was opened on Dec. 9, 1906, with "I Puritani." Since the opening performance Mr. Hammerstein's enterprise has steadily grown in public favor until it has caused the Metropolitan to look to its laurels. It has created a new interest in opera in New York and thus throughout America. In the course of its first season thirty-two operas, chiefly Italian and French, were produced at the Manhattan. Among the singers were the following: sopranos, Regina Arta, Pauline Donalda, Nellie Melba, Lina Pacary, Regina Pinkert, Gianina Russ, Gina Severina and Emma Trentini; mezzo-sopranos and contraltos, Mmes. Bresslar-Gianoli, Eleonore di Cisneros, Gilbert Leyenne, Giuseppina Giaconio, Anna Goaccomini, and Emma Zaccaria; tenors, Jean Altschefsky, Amadeo Bassi, Allessandro Bonci, Charles Dalmores, Francesco Daddi, Mario Venturino; barytones, Mario Ancona, Nicolo Fossetta, Renzo Minolfi, Maurice Renaud, Vincenzo Reschiglian, Mario Sammarco and Paolo Seveilhac; basses, Charles Gilbert, Fernando Gianoli-Galetti, Vittorio Arimondi, Herman Brag, Edouard de Reszke and Luigi Mugnoz. This cast, together with a chorus of one hundred gathered partly in Italy and partly in New York, and with an orchestra of seventy-five, was under the musical direction of Cleofante Campanini and Leandro Campanari. The latter did not remain long after the opening week, however, as Campanini was allowed to direct practically all of the performances.

The opening season, though late in starting, was a success in every way, financially as well as artistically, and the past one, its second, has shown no signs of cessation. Although during the first season the Manhattan did not attract its audiences so much from New York's four hundred as from among the middle class, the fact remains that the performances were given to crowded houses. The second season began on Nov. 3, 1907, and ran for twenty weeks, the regular subscription performances being given as before on Monday, Wednesday and Friday evenings and Saturday matinee. In the Manhattan chorus are about eighty

American voices, a fact which serves to show that it is no longer necessary to go to Europe for our singers.

From the appended table which Mr. Hammerstein prepared a judgment may be formed of the immense cost of operatic productions. "These figures are for any week of the season:

Orchestra	$ 4,500
Stage band	500
Chorus and ballet	2,200
Musical director, two conductors	1,700
Two pianists, two chorus masters	1,700
Stage manager, two assistant stage managers	450
Master machinists and assistants, eighty stage hands	2,000
Property man and twenty assistants	300
Chief electrician and twenty assistants	300
Scene painter and assistants	200
Costumer and assistants	200
Wigmaker and hairdresser	250
Doorkeepers, stage doorkeepers, cleaners	150
Hauling of scenery to and from warehouse	200
Heating and lighting of stage and auditorium	600
Advertising	2,500
Box-office men, telephones, press agent, ticket printing, etc.	1,500
Singers' salaries	27,000
Total	$45,000

"The passage of singers to and from Europe each season must be paid by the impresario, and these usually amount to about $15,000. To this table, of course, must be added the cost of scenery and the interest on the mortgage of the property."

The Hammerstein régime undoubtedly will work untold benefit in producing the competition which is absolutely necessary unless affairs are to stagnate. Among the innovations to be effected at the Manhattan during the season of

1908-1909 will be the substitution of pantomime for ballet for filling out the shorter operas. The New York and Philadelphia choruses and orchestras will be kept entirely separate, while the soloists will alternate between the two cities. Campanini will continue as conductor at the Manhattan. The Philadelphia performances will be directed by Giuseppe Struani of Rome. In addition to many of last season's soloists, including Tetrazzini, Melba, Mary Garden, Dalmores, Zenatello and Renaud, who have been re-engaged, the following new singers will appear: Maria Labia, Adele Ponzano and Mme. Lespinassa, sopranos; Doria, mezzo-soprano; Mareska Aldrich, contralto; Tacani, Columbini, Valles, Paoloa and Polese, tenors.

The presentation of grand opera in America always has been an uncertain financial proposition and many are the failures recorded in this field. Among the most recent attempts was that of Henry Russell with his ill-fated San Carlo Company. During the summer of 1906 Mr. Russell organized a troupe in London and played for some months at Covent Garden. In November, 1906, he brought the company to America and opened a successful season at the French Theatre in New Orleans. From here they went to St. Louis, afterward playing in all the leading cities both in the United States and in Canada. During this, their first season, the impression produced by the company was of the best. The principals, most of whom were Italians, although not known to the musical public, soon became well liked. The chorus was one of the best which had been heard for some time, indeed far above the average of the Metropolitan. A good orchestra with competent directors, attention to the details of operatic production, a general finish, and all this at moderate prices, combined to make the company a favorite at once. This was a most auspicious beginning yet it resulted in failure. During the first tour the company produced "Carmen," "Cavaleria Rusticana," "La Bohème," "Traviata," "Lucia," "Faust," "Gioconda," "Barbiere," "Les Huguenots" and one new opera, "Adriana Lecouvreur." Among the principal artists were Constantino, Maurel, Desana, Fornari, Olitzka, De Segurola, Bramonia, Albertieri, Claessens and Aleani.

At the close of the season Mr. Russell returned to Europe, and during the summer was engaged in adding all that was possible for the betterment of conditions in his company. He returned to the United States in the late fall with an exceptionally good chorus recruited from the leading European opera houses, an orchestra of sixty, a ballet of sixteen, and with the principals of the former year, to which he added Lillian Nordica Jane Noria, Ramon Blanchart and others less noted. But during the season of 1907-1908 ill luck seemed with them from the start. The company opened in Boston for a three weeks' season, thence to Philadelphia, Baltimore, Washington and Chicago. During this time owing both to the financial panic into which the country was plunged, and from the fact that Mr. Russell intrusted much of the management of affairs to other hands, affairs reached a crisis. In Chicago, though the best performances of grand opera which had been given in the city for years were presented at the Auditorium, the general public remained away. Though on the verge of a disruption Mr. Russell made strenuous endeavors to continue the season, but after three weeks, in which he sustained a loss of over twenty thousand dollars, the company proceeded to St. Louis and then to Milwaukee. From Milwaukee they returned to Chicago and played for one week at the Studebaker Theatre, later appearing in several of the western cities and finally disbanding at Cincinnati.

There is another opera company which has been heard by American audiences within recent years that has had quite a different history however. The record of Henry W. Savage's efforts show conclusively that opera in English, when fittingly presented, can be successful from the financial as well as from the artistic side. On May 6, 1895, the Castle Square Opera Company opened its first season at the Castle Square Theatre in Boston. After two years, during which time they played to full houses, Mr. Savage took the company to Philadelphia, where for the next two years they repeated their success of Boston. They then went to New York and for three years sang at the American. Here their success was such that Mr. Savage finally decided to take the Metropolitan Opera House, which had been losing money, and to present opera at popular prices.

During their stay in Boston none but the lighter operas such as "Bohemian Girl," "Fra Diavolo," "Maritana" and others of like caliber was presented, but Mr. Savage finally made up his mind to present the larger grand operas. "Carmen" was the first serious work given. Then came "Faust," "Mignon," "Lucia," "Aïda," "Rigoletto" and finally a grand presentation of "Les Huguenots." When Mr. Savage established grand opera in English at the Metropolitan Opera House an American chorus of eighty-five was engaged, with a ballet of thirty-six, and an orchestra which varied from forty-five to sixty. Among the singers engaged were the following: Zelie De Lussan, Frieda Stender, Grace Golden, Bessie McDonald, Rita Elendi, Phoebe Strakosch, Minnie Tracy, Ingeborg Ballstrom and Josephine Ludwig, sopranos; Elsa Marny and Louise Meisslinger, contraltos; Philip Brozel, Joseph Sheehan and Lloyd D'Aubigne, tenors; William Raull, Homer Lind, Chauncey Moore and Francis Rogers, barytones; and Lempriere Pringle, Clarence Whitehill, Leslie Walker, Harry Hamlin and Forest Carr, basses. There were two conductors, H. Seppilli and Richard Eckhold. The operas presented during this season were "Faust," "Mignon," "Tannhäuser," "Carmen," "Il Trovatore," "Lohengrin," "Gioconda," "Aïda," "Lucia," "Cavalleria Rusticana," "Romeo and Juliet," "Bohemian Girl," "Martha," "Traviata," "Don Giovanni," "Magic Flute," "Rigoletto," "La Bohème," "The Flying Dutchman," "Pagliacci," "The Jewess," "Der Freischütz," "Marriage of Figaro," "Paul and Virginia," "Daughter of the Regiment" and "Esmeralda."

In 1902 branches were started in Chicago and St. Louis, where good choruses and orchestras were established, while the principals alternated in the different cities. Many now well-known singers have come from these companies. The Chicago season opened on Dec. 24, 1901, and continued for over a year. It was an event of moment in the musical history of both Chicago and St. Louis, for it gave to the general public in these two cities their first familiar insight into grand opera.

Four years ago Mr. Savage engaged Walter Rothwell as conductor, and since that time his productions have continued on a high plane. His presentation of "Parsifal" in 1905 was quite on a par with that of the Metropolitan, the "Kundry" of Mme. Kirkby-Lund being especially notable. Two seasons ago he successfully produced "Mme. Butterfly," a work which has continued to make a strong appeal wherever sung. During the coming season Mr. Savage will present "Tristan and Isolde" in English with an eminent cast. One cannot but admire the commendable energy of a man, who, without any musical knowledge, could engage his singers and chorus, attend to all other details and make the prodigious success, both artistically and financially, which Mr. Savage has accomplished with his company. Through his venture opera in English apparently has become a fixture in our musical life.

In connection with the enterprise which Mr. Savage has so successfully conducted mention may be made of another operatic scheme of the same order which unfortunately never was realized. In 1886 an attempt was made to give grand opera wholly in English. With this end in view the American Opera Company was formed, and Theodore Thomas accepted the conductorship, for he saw in this plan a permanent engagement for his orchestra. It was a national enterprise, for its leading artists were gathered from twenty different cities, while the chorus represented twenty-three different States of the Union. A capital of two hundred and fifty thousand dollars was at the back of the organization, and its prospectus set forth the following distinctive features:

"First. Grand opera sung in our own language by the most competent artists.

"Second. The musical guidance of Theodore Thomas.

"Third. The unrivaled Thomas Orchestra.

"Fourth. The largest regularly trained chorus ever employed in grand opera in America.

"Fifth. The largest ballet corps ever presented in grand opera in America, and as far as possible American in its composition.

"Sixth. Four thousand new and correct costumes for which no expense has been spared in fabric or manufacture.

"Seventh. The armor, properties and paraphernalia, the handiwork of artisans employed solely for this department, and made from models designed by the best authorities.

"Eighth. The scenery, designed by the Associated Artists of New York, and painted by the most eminent scenic artists in America.

"In a word, the object of the American Opera Company is to present ensemble opera, giving no single feature undue prominence to the injury of others, and distinctly discouraging the pernicious star system, long since discountenanced in continental Europe."

This was a most commendable enterprise, but before two years had passed Mr. Thomas wrote upon the back of the program of his last performance, "the most dreadful experience I have ever had." In spite of the excellent performances the management had fallen in arrears. Mr. Thomas for months sacrificed his own salary in order that the orchestra might be paid; then, feeling powerless to avert the catastrophe, he left the organization on June 15, 1887. Feeble attempts were made to resuscitate it, but it was hopelessly swamped beneath a burden of indebtedness and finally was given up.

It has become quite evident that the country lately has shown a more marked interest in opera than heretofore, for many new plans are on foot for the season of 1908-1909. New York will have two permanent companies, the Metropolitan and the Manhattan. Philadelphia also will have the benefit of both of these organizations, for Mr. Hammerstein will open his new opera house in that city some time in the fall of 1908 and the Metropolitan management also purpose giving many performances in Philadelphia. Boston is to have its own opera house and company under the management of Henry Russell. In Chicago Max Rabinoff is promoting an organization which promises to become successful. The Savage English Grand Opera Company will continue to offer its excellent performances in the vernacular. So it is seen that interest in the matter is becoming more broadspread. What eventually will be the outcome of these endeavors is uncertain, but such earnest efforts will prove whether the American musical public really cares for the operatic art.

Although America has been privileged to hear the standard operas for over a century, and while her composers have won success in all other fields of musical composition, the country has not yet produced a serious opera by a native-born composer which has had any lasting success. Nevertheless many attempts have been made and prizes have been offered, but all without notable results. Whether the cause for this apparent failure lies in the works offered to the opera producers or whether it is because the public will not accept native compositions in hard to decide. Doubtless after some work of merit by an American composer has proven successful in the opera houses of Europe we shall receive it with proper respect, but so far nothing of the kind has taken place..

The first opera wholly composed in the United States, and therefore the first native composition of its kind, was founded on the story of William Tell, and was designated "The Archers; or The Mountaineers of Switzerland." The libretto was by William Dunlap, and the music by Benjamin Carr, an English organist and composer who became identified with the early musical life of Philadelphia. This opera was staged in New York on April 18, 1796.

Another native opera also came into existence in December of this same year, under the title of "Edwin and Angelina." The libretto, which was founded on Goldsmith's poem, was written by Dr. E. H. Smith, and the music by Victor Pellisier, a Frenchman then resident in New York in the capacity of horn-player in a theatre orchestra. Three years later "The Vintage," with William Dunlap as librettist and Victor Pellisier as composer, was performed in New York, meeting with good success.

Opera in more serious form first was attempted in the United States by William H. Fry in 1845. This opera, "Leonora," was founded on Bulwer Lytton's "Lady of Lyons." The Seguin Opera Company gave it its initial performance at the Chestnut Street Theatre, Philadelphia, in June, 1845, where it had a run of sixteen nights. It was well staged and excellently performed, but the expenses in connection with its setting ate up the receipts. Fry, who was a Philadelphian, completed another opera, "Notre Dame de Paris," after Hugo's famous drama, the libretto being the work of his brother, J. R. Fry. This opera was given three performances in the Academy of Music, Philadelphia, in April, 1864, and was well received. The orchestra was under the directorship of Theodore Thomas, then a young man of twenty-eight.

The next opera of merit to originate with an American composer was "Rip Van Winkle," by Geo. F. Bristow. The libretto, which was prepared by J. H. Wainwright, follows the legend by Washington Irving pretty closely until the second act, when it becomes a piece of pure invention. The Pyne-Harrison English Opera Troupe first produced it at Niblo's Garden, New York, on Sept. 27, 1855, after which it had a successful run of thirty consecutive nights. Bristow evidently aimed at producing a popular opera, and it really was the first lyric drama truly American in spirit, a fact appreciated by the public and received accordingly.

In later years several American composers have essayed their hand at grand opera but without lasting success. Among the better known works are: Frederick Grant Gleason's "Otho Visconti" and "Montezuma;" "Zenobia" and "Lucile" by Silas G. Pratt; J. K. Paine's "Azara." Geo. W. Chadwick has written a sacred opera "Judith." Louis Adolph Coerne has two operas to his credit, "Zenobia" and "A Woman of Marblehead," while Walter Damrosch also has written two, "The Scarlet Letter" and "Cyrano de Bergerac." Although many of these works reflect credit on their authors the fact remains that the successful American opera composer is still to come.

INSTRUMENTAL MUSIC, BANDS AND ORCHESTRAS

It is probable that the first instrumental music in America was heard in the Virginian colonies. Unfortunately there is no record regarding such matters; but it naturally may be supposed that the Virginian settlers, coming as they did of Royalist stock, brought with them some sort of musical instruments, even though the work of founding a new home allowed of little time for diversion. These southern colonists were of very different mold from the Pilgrim Fathers and were given to jollity rather than to piety. The known existence of dancing and dancing schools in the early life of Virginia presupposes accompanying instrumental music of some sort.

Knowing the aversion of the Pilgrims and the Puritans to instrumental music of any kind, it hardly is necessary to state that there is no record of any musical instrument coming with the early settlers to New England. The old inventories in the Probate Office of Essex County, Massachusetts, show lists of everything pertaining to household effects, but there is no mention of viol, lute, flute, cittern or harpsichord.

Of the first introduction of musical instruments into New England little is known. The earliest mention of the matter relates to the organ, but it may be supposed that the lesser instruments already were in use by the few musically inclined and perhaps less pious members of the community. If we except the instrument in the church at Quebec, to which the Jesuit Fathers in their letters of 1661 to 1664 frequently allude, it is believed that the first organ in America was brought over in 1694 by Kelpius and his party of Theosophical Brethren. Christopher Witt, an Englishman who had joined the community of Pietists established on the banks of the Wissahickon in 1704, was the first individual in America to own a pipe organ; he made it himself and could play upon it, as well as upon the virginal. One of the latter instruments, which had been in the possession of the Warner family for many years, was bequeathed to him in 1728. It probably was one of the first virginals brought to this country.

In 1704 the question of providing an organ for Trinity Church, New York, was brought up at a meeting of the vestry of the parish. From the fact that a consultation was held with Henry Neering, "organ maker," regarding the building of such an instrument, it is seen that there then were in New York persons capable of organ construction. The matter fell through at the time, however, and it was not until 1741 that the instrument really was installed. In the meantime Thomas Brattle of Boston had imported an organ from England and had had it installed in his home. Under date of May 29, 1711, Rev. Joseph Green of Salem notes in his diary: "I was at Mr. Thomas Brattle's; heard ye Organs." It was this same organ that was bequeathed to King's Chapel, Boston, and as has been stated elsewhere, this marked the introduction of organs into the churches of America.

When finally it was decided to install an organ in Trinity Church, New York, Johann Klemm of Philadelphia was engaged to construct the instrument. Klemm was a native of Dresden and had studied organ-building under Gottfried Silberman, who in his time had constructed forty-seven organs and who also was celebrated as a manufacturer

PATRICK SARSFIELD GILMORE. 1829-1892

American bandmaster of Irish birth. At the National Peace Jubilee in Boston in 1869 he organized an orchestra of one thousand pieces and a chorus of ten thousand voices, and at the World's Peace Jubilee in 1872 he doubled the number of instruments and voices—cannons, a powerful organ, a drum eight feet high, anvils and chimes of bells were added to the stupendous whole.

These performances were ultimately an influence for good music in America, but their immediate result was to make Gilmore's reputation international. He became quite a composer, and many of his works, military and dance music and songs, became very popular.

PATRICK SARSFIELD GILMORE. 1829-1892

American bandmaster of Irish birth. At the National Peace Jubilee in Boston in 1869 he organized an orchestra of one thousand pieces and a chorus of ten thousand voices, and at the World's Peace Jubilee in 1872 he doubled the number of instruments and voices—cannons, a powerful organ, a drum eight feet high, anvils and chimes of bells were added to the stupendous whole.

These performances were ultimately an influence for good music in America, but their immediate result was to make Gilmore's reputation international. He became quite a composer, and many of his works, military and dance music and songs, became very popular.

of pianos. When Klemm settled in Philadelphia in 1736 he dropped his Teutonic name and became known simply as John Clemm. He finished the organ for Trinity Church in 1741 at a cost to the parish of five hundred and twenty pounds sterling, or nearly three thousand dollars, a large sum in colonial times. This organ was of three manuals and had twenty-six stops. It 1763 it was offered for sale as Trinity was preparing to install an instrument imported from England. Klemm, its builder, died at Bethlehem, Pa., in 1762, at the age of seventy-two.

The first real impetus given to instrumental music in America came through the introduction of organs into the churches. In the parts of the country where formerly no instrumental music of any kind had been generally tolerated, the introduction of the organ acted as an opening wedge, and the sanction in the use of other instruments naturally followed. When, for financial or other reasons, the organ was not in use, other instruments such as the doublebass, cello, clarinet, flute and violin came to be used. From these sources sprang the desire on the part of the public for instruments and instrumental music. The instruments at first were used chiefly for the purpose of accompanying the voice, but gradually they came to take their place in the production of characteristic instrumental music.

In the early days there was a strong prejudice against any one devoting himself exclusively to music, but with the coming of the organ conditions underwent a change; for organ playing called for more than ordinary musical skill and for serious preparation on the part of the player. As none of the colonists possessed this necessary preparation, qualified organists were brought from England to fill the positions created by the adoption of organs in the churches. In addition to their services in connection with the church these men usually gave instruction in vocal and instrumental music and in dancing. Many of them also conducted shops where they kept music and musical instruments for sale. It is to these early church organists that the chief credit belongs for creating among the people a taste for instrumental music. Their efforts were not confined to organ playing alone, for many of them were excellent performers on the harpsichord, spinet, viol, and other instruments as well.

In 1713 a Mr. Price was engaged as organist at King's Chapel, Boston, and the following year he gave way to Edward Enstone, who was brought from England especially to fill this position. Enstone was engaged at a salary of $150 per annum, and finding this sum insufficient for his needs, on Feb. 21, 1714, he made application for permission to open a school as "Master of Music and Dancing," which petition promptly was vetoed by "ye selectmen." But Enstone opened his school notwithstanding, and the following year "ye selectmen" instructed the town clerk to enter "a complaint to Session." This was done in order, but the obdurate music master rather than the selectmen must have won the day, for the Boston News Letter bearing date of April 16-23, 1716, contains the following significant advertisement: "This is to give notice that there is lately sent over from London, a choice collection of musical instruments, consisting of flageolets, flutes, haut-boys, bass-viols, violins, bows, strings, reeds for haut-boys, books of instruction for all these instruments; books of ruled paper; to be sold at the Dancing School of Mr. Enstone in Sudbury Street, near the Orange Tree, Boston. Note: Any person may have all instruments of music mended, or virginals and spinets strung and tuned at a reasonable rate, and likewise may be taught to play on any of these instruments above mentioned; dancing taught by a true and easier method than has been heretofore."

Trinity Church, Newport, Rhode Island, was among the first to have an organ installed. Mr. Charles Theodore Parchelbel or Pachelbel — the name being written in different ways — assisted in setting up this instrument and he became the first organist of the church. Very little is known of Pachelbel except that in 1736 his name appears in connection with a benefit tendered him in New York. In the following year he again figures in a benefit concert given by the St. Cecilia Society at Charleston, S. C.

It is very evident that the organists in the early days had a hard struggle to make both ends meet, for a later organist at Trinity Church, Newport, John Owen Jacobi, wrote to a friend in Philadelphia as follows: "The want of instruments, together with the niggardliness of the people of this place, and their not having the taste for music, render it impossible for any one of my profession to get a competent maintenance here; and their feuds and animosities are so great concerning their government, that a man can take but little satisfaction in being among them."

In 1796 John L. Berkenhead, who was known as the "blind organist" was appointed to Trinity. He evidently supplemented his meager salary by giving concerts throughout the surrounding country, for his name frequently appears on the concert programs of his time. His star performance seems to have been the rendition on the harpsichord of a composition entitled "Demolition of the Bastile." The Salem Gazette in 1798 published a report of a concert in which it states: "The Bastile, by the Doctor, was admirably played on an elegant harpsichord belonging to a respectable family in that town." According to the advertised programs of concerts in and around Boston, Dr. Berkenhead must have demolished the Bastile many times with the aid of the harpsichord.

St. Philip's Church, Charleston, S. C., from 1753 to 1764, had as organist Benjamin Yarnold. He was followed by Peter Valton, Yarnold having gone to St. Mary's. In 1765 Valton's name appears associated with two lady vocalists in the giving of a concert, in which the instrumental music consisted of "concertos and overtures — likewise a concerto on the harpsichord." Peter Valton had been an organist in London, England, and on coming to America he found, as did all of our pioneer organists, that he was compelled to supplement his meager salary. This he did by opening a shop for "musical merchandise," selling spinets and other musical instruments. On Oct. 10, 1868, Valton advertises for "Proposals for printing by subscription, six sonatas for the harpsichord or organ; with an accompaniment for a violin." D. Salter was an organist in New Haven, Conn., in 1798, his name also appearing in concerts at Trenton and Brunswick the same year.

From 1763 to 1780 Philadelphia had a capable organist in James Bremner, who hailed from Scotland. Bremner opened a school of music in Philadelphia, teaching "young ladies . . . the harpsichord, or guitar" and "young gentlemen . . . the violin, German flute, harpsichord, or guitar." One of his most distinguished pupils was Francis Hopkinson, who assisted greatly in developing a musical taste in the Quaker City. Mr. Bremner also was a composer of some significance, and with Francis Hopkinson he did excellent service in fostering an early interest in what later became known as chamber-music.

In 1792 Raynor Taylor came from London to Annapolis, Md., as organist of St. Anne's Church. He became popular as a teacher of music, and in 1793 removed to Philadelphia, where he interested himself in organ playing and orchestral work. In the same year Benjamin Carr settled in Philadelphia. Carr had studied under the English masters, Arnold and Wesley, and was one of the best organists of which the town at that time could boast. He also was a composer of some talent.

As to the building of our first American organ; writers on this subject have claimed the honor for Boston, in the person of Edward Bromfield, and later, for Boston again, in the name of Thomas Johnstone. Bromfield was an amateur. He intended his finished instrument to have twelve hundred pipes; but it never was completed owing to the death of the young aspirant at the age of twenty-five. This instrument never was set up in any church. The date claimed for Bromfield's organ is 1745. Johnstone undoubtedly built the first organ in New England. This was set up in Christ Church, Boston, in 1752. But as has already been seen, the first organ built in America was the one constructed by Christopher Witt; and the first American built organ to be installed in a church was that constructed in 1741 by Johann Gottlob Klemm (John Clemm) for Trinity Church in New York.

Among the early settlements established in America by foreigners (in distinction to the English colonists) that of the Moravians at Bethlehem, Pa., takes first rank musically. When John C. Ogden visited Bethlehem in 1799 he wrote of an "organ with several pieces of instrumental music" which were used by the sisterhood. Again, he states: "Indeed, in almost every room we saw some musical instrument — an organ, harpsichord or forte-piano. These are in many private families in this settlement and other villages." At Nazareth, ten miles from Bethlehem, Mr. Ogden found that in the "large and lofty chapel supported by four octagon pillars — in front of the minister's chair and table is a large organ within a pew, which surrounds it, and is constructed for musicians." He also found an organ in the chapel of another small settlement, Easton. Owing probably to the exclusiveness and the retention of their own language, these colonies of foreigners played little or no part in our early evolution in music.

The organ made an early bid for popularity. In New York City, in 1756, Gilbert Ash built an organ for the City Hall, which at this time was used as a concert room. According to the New York Mercury of March 8, 1756, this particular instrument was heard for the first time in a charity concert, on the program of which is announced "a song in praise of music, particularly of an organ," as well as an organ concerto. This and similar musical entertainments, in which organ music seemed to be the chief attraction, ultimately led to the organ recital. The first of these entertainments deserving the designation was that given in Boston for the benefit of Peter Dolliver. It took place on Jan. 24, 1798, at the Columbian Museum, an institution which was established by Daniel Bowen in the same year. Mr. Dolliver, who for some time had been organist of the Universal Meeting

House, played several pieces on the organ, as did a Mr. I. Linley, who had offered his services. Miss Amelia Dolliver also played a selection and sang a song, her brother accompanying her on the clarinet.

The first pretentious concert organ set up in America was the one imported for the old Boston Music Hall. Through the enterprise of Dr. George B. Upham, the Music Hall corporation had been led to appropriate ten thousand dollars toward its purchase. This instrument was built in Germany and was brought to America in 1863, at a total cost of seventy thousand dollars. At the time of purchase it was expected that it would serve for many years, but it never was satisfactory, and when the Boston Symphony Concerts became so popular that space was a consideration it was sold in 1884 to the Hon. William Grover, who presented it to the New England Conservatory of Music. The Conservatory, however, could not see its way clear to building a hall of the needed capacity for the accommodation of so large an instrument, and the great organ which had done so much toward fostering a musical taste of a higher standard in Boston, and which its purchasers had thought might outlive the centuries, was doomed to the ignominious fate of being sold for about the value of the metal and lumber it contained — fifteen hundred dollars. The Music Hall organ was of four manuals; it had eighty-four speaking stops, and five thousand four hundred and seventy-four pipes. Its case was very massive, and this with the large front pipes imparted to it an imposing appearance.

There are several other American organs which have become widely known. That in the Mormon Tabernacle at Salt Lake City long had a wide reputation. It is a notable instrument not only on account of its size, which was unusual at the time it was installed, but because of the part it has played in educational lines. Unlike so many of our American organs, an instrument for the few, the Tabernacle organ always has been the people's instrument, and for years it has been the custom to give free recitals at least twice a week, when excellent programs are rendered. This famous instrument is of four manuals and has sixty speaking stops. It was built in 1873 under the direction of an English builder, Joseph Ridges, and within recent years was remodeled and added to by a Chicago firm.

Another organ which has been of educational value is that in Carnegie Hall, Pittsburg. This instrument has fifty-two speaking stops and four manuals. Since its installation it has been continually used for recital purposes. The late Frederick Archer inaugurated a series of free recitals, which were largely attended. Sunday afternoon concerts also were established, the average attendance being twenty-five hundred. Mr. Archer's successors still continue to follow the same plan. These concertos are unique in America, where, with the exception of a comparatively small number given in the churches, the organ rarely is used for concert purposes. Pittsburg indeed is fortunate in this respect, owing to the generosity of Andrew Carnegie, and it seems a pity that other philanthropists have not followed his example, for undoubtedly the king of instruments in this way could be made to give pleasure and profit to thousands.

America has produced some of the greatest organs of the world. That constructed for the St. Louis Exposition was the largest ever built. It had one hundred and forty speaking stops and over ten thousand pipes, but it lost much of its dignity because of its insignificant exterior. Few people realized that they were looking upon one of the marvels of the world in the form of a musical instrument while listening to the wonderful music produced from it by many of America's distinguished organists. There are several other American organs which also suffer through being obscurely placed. Judging from appearances one would hardly suspect that the Auditorium in Chicago contained one of the world's greatest instruments, yet it ranks seventh among them. Among other noted organs in this country are those in the Cathedral at Garden City, L. I., St. Bartholomew's Church in New York, Cincinnati Music Hall and Woolsey Hall at Yale University.

America has become famous for her wonderful organs. This could not have come to pass, however, save through the merits of the organists themselves. Our organists, from the early beginnings in the use of the instrument, up to the present time have received little enough of recognition for the influence which their efforts have brought to bear on our development in music. In the remote towns and smaller cities, where the "new church organ" gives opportunity for local interest in recitals and choirs, the organist usually is the leading musical spirit in the community and as such should receive due credit for the part he plays in our musical life.

From about the middle of the Nineteenth Century the melodion for many years was a favorite instrument in the home. The larger sizes had a pedal-board as well as a key-board. The tone was produced from one set of reeds, and though often pleasing was lacking in power. This little instrument, of direct American origin, was the forerunner of the cabinet or parlor organ, the first one of which was manufactured in 1861. In many provincial churches it served as predecessor to the pipe organ. It also was a veritable missionary in the home circle and schoolhouse in the cause of instrumental music. The reed organ at its earliest inception became the medium whereby people in the country, village and town became familiar with our popular airs, minstrel and plantation songs, and songs of the war. Time and the influence of those who endeavored to raise the standard of music gradually changed the inclinations of the lovers of music generally, and the player on the parlor organ became ambitious for music of a higher grade.

One reason why these instruments became so popular was because their cost was such that it fitted the pockets of the people, those who loved music but could not afford more expensive instruments. They danced to its gayer strains; they sang their hymns of praise to the accompaniment of the parlor organ; it was their music at the marriage feast; and to its muffled tones they bore their loved dead over the threshold. America has its traditions, and in the future many of them will be found lingering in and around the memories associated with the period when the parlor or cabinet organ was at its zenith.

Musical instruments such as flageolets, flutes, hautboys, violins and bass-viols were advertised for sale in the American colonies as early as 1716. It was in Maryland and Virginia that these instruments chiefly were used, for the people of the southern colonies were the first in America to enjoy a musical life. Owing to the dearth of newspapers in this section of the country, however, we have but meager records of the musical happenings of the time. The people in the South were extremely fond of dancing, and from some of the old advertisements it is seen that many of the dancing-masters also gave lessons on the spinet, the virginal, and later on the harpsichord. The spinet and virginal were smaller instruments of the harpsichord order.

The first American spinet was made in 1743 by Gustavus Hesselius of Philadelphia. Twenty-six years later the Boston Gazette published a notice concerning a spinet constructed by John Harris of that city, which it erroneously states to be the "first ever made in America." The earliest public mention of the harpsichord was in connection with a concert given in New York on Jan. 21, 1736, for the benefit of Charles Theodore Pachelbel. In announcing this concert the Weekly Journal states that Mr. Pachelbel will "perform the harpsichord part himself," with the "songs, violins, and German flutes by private bands." "A concerto on the harpsichord" is announced in a concert given in Charleston, S. C., in 1765 by Thomas Pike. Mr. Pike had come to Charleston a few months previously in the capacity of "dancing, fencing, and music-master." In the same year Hugh Maguire was teaching the young ladies of Annapolis to play on the spinet.

The first public notice of the use of the pianoforte appears in the New York Daily Advertiser of Feb. 25, 1791. It is announced that "Mr. Kullin, pianist, acquaints the public of his intention to give a benefit concert with the assistance of Mr. Capron and Mrs. Haye, lately from Paris, whose voice he had every reason to hope would be considered as a great acquisition to his concert." The announcement also states that Mr. Kullin will "perform on a Grand Concert Pianoforte, entirely of a new invention, and just finished by Messrs. Dodds and Claus of this city." It would be interesting to know something more definite concerning "Dodds and Claus." If they really constructed a pianoforte at this time they antedate the Chickerings (the reputed makers of the first American pianoforte) by some years. The latter firm produced, in 1837, the first grand piano with an iron frame in one casting. Jonas Chickering, the head of the firm, did much in his time for the cause of music in America.

From these early beginnings, America has come to take her place as the acknowledged peer of any country in the building of pianos. The wonderful growth of the piano trade, probably more than any other means, has tended to the popularization of music in America. From the position of an interesting curiosity the American made piano within a century has become the people's instrument par excellence. There is more piano music heard in this country today than that produced by all other instruments combined.

The St. Cecilia Society of Charleston was one of the most ambitious of musical organizations in Eighteenth Century America, and its active influence extended far into the Nineteenth Century. Its orchestra was formed partly of amateurs and partly of professionals, the latter being engaged by the season. The following advertisement, which appeared in the New York, Philadelphia and Boston papers, is indicative of the spirit of enterprise shown, and it must also have had its influence on the musical life of these cities:

"Charleston, South Carolina, April 11, 1771.

"The St. Cecilia Society give notice that they will engage with, and give suitable encouragement to musicians properly qualified to perform at their concerts, provided they apply on or before the first day of October next. The performers they are in want of are, a first and second violin, two hautboys and a bassoon, whom they are willing to agree with for one, two or three years."

In 1792 this same society wrote to Major Thomas Pinckney, then Minister to England, to buy and send out for it "one grand pianoforte and twenty pounds' worth of the best modern concert music." Josiah Quincy of Boston visited Charleston in 1773 and attended a concert given by the St. Cecilia Society. In writing of the affair he states: "I was passed from servant to servant and finally ushered in. The music was grand, especially the bass viol and French horns." He also adds that the "first violinist, a Frenchman, played the best solo (he had) ever heard." Then he tells that "the salary of this violinist was one hundred guineas" per annum; that "most of the performers were gentlemen amateurs." Then Mr. Quincy comments upon the "richness of the dress of both ladies and gentlemen;" that there were "two hundred and fifty ladies present and it was called no great number;" that the "ladies in taciturnity during the performance are greatly before our (Boston) ladies."

In 1773 the orchestral force of the St. Cecilia Society in its "Musical Festival," in which Gluck's overture, "Iphigenie en Aulide" and Haydn's "Stabat Mater" were rendered, was as follows: "One organ, twelve violins, three basses, five tenors, six oboes, flutes and clarinets, two horns, one bassoon, and two pair kettledrums, in all thirty." This early orchestra of thirty pieces, when measured by European standards of the period, was of fair size. Even in Beethoven's time the orchestra at Bonn numbered but twenty-two instruments.

There were many French musicians resident in Charleston at this period. There was "Citizen" Cornet, with his "orchestra of French Music" — probably the pioneer of the small orchestras devoted to social functions — announcing to the people of Charleston by means of the Gazette, that he had "established a Vaux Hall, after the Parisian manner, in which there will be dancing on Saturday." Then "Citizen"

Cornet announces that "the orchestra will attend at American or French societies, if required."

It was not until after the Revolutionary War that Baltimore showed a marked interest in instrumental music. On Sept. 28, 1786, Philip Phile, a violinist, was given a benefit in Baltimore. Phile's name is closely associated with orchestra work both in that city and in Philadelphia. To Baltimore, in 1791, came Alexander Reinagle, with a reputation as an excellent performer on the harpsichord as well as that of conductor and composer. He prepared good programs and added a dignity to the musical life of this southern city. In Virginia, before the close of the Eighteenth Century there were several cities more or less interested in bands of instrumental music or orchestras. Williamsburg, Richmond, Fredericksburg, Alexandria, Norfolk and Petersburg, all enjoyed a musical life.

Reference has been made in a previous chapter to the festival given by Andrew Adgate's classes in May, 1786, in Philadelphia, in which a chorus of two hundred and thirty voices and an orchestra of fifty took part. This undoubtedly was America's first pretentious orchestra. The festival was suggested by the Handel Commemoration Concerts given in Westminster Abbey in May and June of 1784.

Under the direction of Benjamin Carr, George Gillingham and others, a concert in which amateurs and professionals took part was given at Oeller's Hotel, Philadelphia, on April 8, 1794. This was the first of a series of six subscription concerts, taking place weekly, in which an orchestra was the chief feature of entertainment. It is interesting to note that in this particular concert the novelty was the playing by the full orchestra of Kotzwara's "Battle of Prague," a composition which enjoyed unrivaled popularity until the middle of the Nineteenth Century, when it gave place to the "Maiden's Prayer."

In 1790 an orchestra of ten was engaged regularly in giving open-air concerts in "Gray's Gardens," Philadelphia. This orchestra offered rather a high standard of music and seems to have been well appreciated. Here appeared a violin prodigy in the ten-year-old Louis De Duport, who had performed before the Royal family in France. The youthful violinist evidently was in much demand, for his name appears on many concert programs both in Charleston and in Baltimore.

Toward the close of the Eighteenth Century the theatres generally had engaged regular orchestras. On June 1, 1796, fourteen performers, members of various theatre orchestras, assisted Mrs Arnold, a well-known vocalist of the day, in a benefit concert given at Theatre Hall, Boston; and on May 15, 1798, Gottlieb Graupner, with the "assistance of the best musicians in Boston," gave an orchestral concert in Salem. Graupner came from Germany to America in 1795, and in October, 1796, his name appears in connection with a concert given in Norfolk, Virginia. The program states that he will play a concerto on the oboe, and as his name appears in a violin duet he evidently was a performer on that instrument as well. In 1797 Graupner moved to Boston, and in 1810 in conjunction with others he founded the Philharmonic Society, which was active until 1824. A writer of the time remarks that thc orchestra of this society "confined (their) work to the simpler fields of classical music. . . . Occasionally Graupner would insist upon trying a Haydn symphony."

Performers on various instruments associated with the orchestra must have been found in New York City in 1766, for in October of this year, William Tuckey, organist of Trinity, advertised for "gentlemen who play on any instrument to lend assistance" in a sacred concert. This particular concert was not held in a church, however, but was given at Burns' New Assembly Rooms. The instrumental music, and incidentally the orchestra work which William Tuckey zealously introduced and promoted in New York City, became the pioneer movement which later resulted in this city becoming a leader in orchestral presentation. To William Tuckey should be given the credit for awakening an early interest in instrumental music in general, and in orchestral work in particular.

The St. Cecilia Society, established in New York in 1791, was organized for the purpose of promoting instrumental music. This society had been preceded by earlier organizations, the Apollo and the Musical Society of the City of New York, both of which were pioneers in orchestral music. In 1799 there was organized the Euterpean Society, which combined social features with its amateur orchestra, its rehearsals becoming general assembly nights for musicians, literary men, and artists. Its public concerts were held in the City Hall and were followed by a ball and supper.

The first Philharmonic Society of New York was organized by the merging of the St. Cecilia and the Harmonical Societies on Dec. 9, 1799, and the first Philharmonic concert was held Dec. 23, 1800. This organization, while not keeping regularly together, during the earlier decades of the Nineteenth Century nevertheless exercised an influence upon the musical life of New York. The second Philharmonic of New York, which was destined to influence the orchestral work of other musical centers in the United States, was established in 1842. Its orchestra, at the inception of the still existing Philharmonic Society, numbered between fifty and sixty performers. In the meanwhile the old Philharmonic had been superseded by the Musical Fund Society, which latter also had its place in the development of orchestral music.

Two years before, the Boston Academy Orchestra had sprung into existence. This organization averaged from thirty to forty performers, with George J. Webb as its conductor. During its seven years of existence it made a brave endeavor to educate the people into an appreciation of classical music. Here, too, the first advance was made in the modern method of conducting, Mr. Webb using the baton instead of playing an instrument as was the custom with our earlier orchestra conductors. As a matter of fact European orchestral leaders did not adopt the baton until the beginning of the Eighteenth Century.

Owing to the presence of numerous German musicians Philadelphia early was privileged to hear both choral and orchestral music of the highest type. In 1820 an association known as the Musical Fund Society was organized with the aim of assisting its members and of diffusing musical culture in the city. It gave concerts of both secular and sacred music, founded a school and built a hall. At its first concert, given on April 24, 1821, there were heard choruses by Handel and Graun as well as Beethoven's First Symphony. This probably was the first performance of the latter work to be given in America. Unfortunately the Musical Fund Society did not receive the recognition it deserved and it was forced to cease its labors in 1857.

About the middle of the Nineteenth Century Europe was in an unsettled condition politically, and many musicians found it more conducive to the well-being of mind and body to cross the Atlantic. Notable among them were twenty-three professionals who left Berlin with letters from the English and American ambassadors. They first went to London, but receiving little encouragement they set sail for America, arriving in New York on Sept. 28, 1848. On October 5 they appeared under the designation of the "Germania Orchestra" in a concert at the Astor Place Opera House. The financial returns were anything but satisfactory, and the little band of artists, strangers in a strange land, passed on to Philadelphia, to meet with no better success. They then disbanded, but subsequently were called together to play at the presidential inauguration ball at Washington. From Washington they went to Baltimore, and here they not only were enthusiastically received, but substantially rewarded, in spite of the fact that a visiting European orchestra under Joseph Gungl then was entertaining the Baltimoreans. From Baltimore they went to Boston, giving concerts at New Haven, Worcester, and other large towns by the way. They were not at first well received at Boston, but afterward seemed to make a better impression. After playing at the Castle Garden concerts in New York, and during the summer season at Newport, they returned to Baltimore, remaining there during the winter of 1849-1850. In the summer following they made a very successful tour but returned to winter in Baltimore, and under the management of Strakosch, with Patti as soloist, they made a southern tour. Later they gave thirty concerts with Jenny Lind.

The Germania Orchestra became one of the strongest educators in orchestral work in America. In Boston, in 1851-1852, they were fairly successful, but in 1853-1854, their third time in Boston, they met with little success. The orchestra disbanded in 1854, but each of its leading members became a unit in the progress of American orchestral music. The fact that the Germania Orchestra received its best recognition in the South was because the people of the southern cities received an early educative influence in instrumental music. While the North still was debating on the question of church music the southern colonies had both sacred and secular music fairly well established, as English, French, German and Italian musicians early had found their way to the South and taken up residence there.

Save in the South, the Gungl orchestra, finely equipped as it was, gained little encouragement. This was in 1849, but four years later Jullien came with his orchestra of forty performers, some of them being soloists of the highest rank. Afterward he increased the number to ninety-seven. This was the largest orchestra America yet had heard, and it had its effect. It was an inspiration to our musicians and an education to the public.

These visiting orchestras left their influence and acted as incentives toward the formation of American organizations. In the past fifty years we have made wonderful progress in musical culture, especially in the way of a more general appreciation of orchestral music. The general American public, in contrast with the other English speaking peoples as a rule, is more interested in instrumental than in vocal music and this taste has tended toward our more rapid

THEODORE THOMAS. 1835-1905

Born at Esens, East Friesland, he was a self-educated musician who was the first American orchestral conductor, and according to some authorities the first conductor of his time.

He organized his first permanent orchestra in 1869 and made his first tour, going as far west as Chicago and St. Louis, and meeting with great success. In 1904, when Thomas was almost seventy years old, the magnificent hall built by the people of Chicago was finished and he conducted the dedicatory concert. This was his last appearance in public.

Theodore Thomas' success as a conductor was greatly increased by his genius for arranging orchestra programs which are recognized as models of their kind.

musical development. There is no question that the English themselves have been hampered through their adherence to choral music; and this preconceived taste has tended to retard their progress, for choral music has not kept pace with that written for solo instruments and for the orchestra. Owing to the American temperament and disposition instrumental music appeals more strongly to us, and it is in this field that the future of American music lies. It also is to this taste that our extraordinary progress is due.

In 1842, chiefly through the efforts of Uriah C. Hill, the New York Philharmonic Orchestra came into existence. This was the most important orchestral society which America up to that time had possessed. Mr. Hill became its first president and conductor. Its premier performance was given on Dec. 7, 1842, and was followed by two other concerts the same season. In spite of the fact that at the time Boston was favored with two orchestras New York now took the lead in the orchestral field, which place it has held up to the present. During the first seven years of its existence the New York Philharmonic had as many different conductors. In 1849 Theo. Eisfeld was appointed to the position, which he held until 1855. From 1855 to 1865 he alternated with Carl Bergmann, and in 1866 Bergmann assumed sole charge and continued to occupy the post until 1876, when he was succeeded by Dr. Leopold Damrosch. During the season of 1877-1878 Theodore Thomas conducted, to be followed by Adolph Neuendorf for two years, after which Thomas again assumed the position. Since this time the Philharmonic Society has had the services of other men of equally high aspirations. Anton Seidl, Walter Damrosch, and Emil Paur successively have occupied the post. Wassili Safonoff is the present (1908) conductor of this, America's first distinguished orchestral body.

The New York Philharmonic Society, under the direction of its many noteworthy leaders, has done much for orchestral music in America, and its educative influence has been widespread and lasting. During the years that Theodore Thomas was at the head of the organization he revived Bach's works and gave the first hearing of many compositions of the modern school. In the season of 1903-1904 the Philharmonic, with the aid of several wealthy patrons, inaugurated a series of concerts which enlisted the services of several of the best known European conductors. Colonne of France, Weingartner, Richard Strauss and Kogel of Germany, Henry J. Wood of London and Wassili Safonoff of Russia each appeared in one or more performances. These concerts attracted considerable attention to the work of the society and were the means of placing it on a more substantial basis. From its inception the Philharmonic Orchestra has been an important factor in our musical life and bids fair to continue on its successful career. The members elect their own conductor, give their concerts at their own risk and receive their remuneration from whatever profits may accrue. So far the dividends of each have not been large and as a rule are not equal to the salaries paid in the permanent orchestras of Boston and Chicago.

Another New York organization which has played a prominent part in the musical annals of that city, and of the country in general, is the New York Symphony Orchestra. This society came into existence in 1878, chiefly through the efforts of Dr. Leopold Damrosch, who was backed by several munificent music lovers. Twelve concerts, which were marked by broad and liberal programs, were given during the first season. The New York Symphony has been especially active in bringing forward works by American composers and many such compositions have received their first hearing at its hands. When, in 1885, Dr. Damrosch died, his son Walter took up the baton and without interruption continued the work begun by his illustrious father. Unfortunately the organization later got into difficulties and was forced to cease its labors, but after lapsing for some years it was re-established in 1903. At the present time, under the direction of Walter Damrosch, it is in better condition than ever before and gives promise of permanency.

When in 1847 the Boston Academy Orchestra broke up, a new organization, known as the Musical Fund Society, was formed by Thomas Comer. Its founder was not a man of high artistic ideals and consequently the music presented under his direction was of light order. Subsequently Geo. J. Webb assumed charge of the society and to some extent improved on the work of his predecessor. But the Musical Fund Society never attained to any eminence, and like its Philadelphia namesake it lasted but a few years, closing up its affairs in 1855. In the same year Carl Zerrahn, who had come to Boston as a flute player with the Germania Orchestra, instituted an organization which, under the title of the Philharmonic Orchestra, gave a series of concerts each year up to 1863. The Civil War caused music to languish at this time and for three years Boston was without any orchestra worthy the name.

In 1865 an orchestra was organized by the Harvard Musical Association with the object of maintaining high class orchestral concerts. The promoters announced that they did not purpose to make money but that their sole aim was to promote the taste for good music and to advance the progress of the art in Boston. The first concert was given on Jan. 28, 1866, and proved a success. Carl Zerrahn was the conductor, and he had under him the best orchestral body which Boston up to that time had possessed. Nearly one-third of the works presented by the Harvard Symphony Orchestra received their first Boston hearing at its hands. The association continued its labors until 1882, when it was found that the newly established Boston Symphony sufficed for the orchestral needs of the community. Mr. Zerrahn remained as director until its withdrawal from the concert field.

Those in charge of the destinies of the Harvard Symphony Orchestra were extremely conservative in the class of music given presentation and as a result many of the younger musicians chafed under the restraint. These progressive spirits wished to bring forward more of the works of the modern composers and as those in control continued to adhere rather strictly to the classicists a rival organization was the outcome. The new orchestra was established as an independent body in 1879 and was formed into a Philharmonic Society in the following year. Bernhard Listemann, Louis Maas and Carl Zerrahn were the conductors successively. The rivalry between the two bodies became most pronounced and continued until both gave way to a third and greater institution, the Boston Symphony Orchestra.

To the generosity and foresight of Henry L. Higginson, a Boston banker, is due the founding of this famous band; for he established it at his own risk and guaranteed its permanency. In the twenty-seven years of its existence the Boston Symphony has come to stand for the highest and noblest in the orchestral art and it is doubtful if it now is surpassed by any like organization in the whole world. From its inception as a philanthropic institution it has become entirely self-supporting, being the first orchestra in America to attain to this exalted position.

The Boston Symphony Orchestra began its career on Saturday evening, Oct. 22, 1881. Its first conductor was Georg Henschel, and during the opening season he had under him a band of sixty-seven men. Twenty concerts were given, each preceded by a public rehearsal after the plan first adopted in America by the New York Philharmonic. During the third season the organization gave twenty-six concerts, but after that the number was reduced to twenty-four, which has been the annual quota ever since. In 1884 Mr. Henschel resigned and Wilhelm Gericke of Vienna was appointed to the position. Gericke was just the man for the place, for he was a firm drill-master and not a musical radical by any means. Under his direction incompetent players were made to give place to those better qualified, and it is to his firm stand in this matter that the Boston orchestra has taken rank as a band of virtuosos. Mr. Gericke resigned in 1889 and Arthur Nikisch accepted the post, which he held for four years. Emil Paur then held the baton for five years, after which Mr. Gericke again assumed charge. In 1906 he gave way to Dr. Karl Muck who was "loaned" from the Berlin Royal Opera for two years. Max Fiedler of Hamburg has been appointed to succeed Dr. Muck and will enter on his duties during the season of 1908-1909.

For many years the concerts of the Boston Symphony Orchestra were held in the old Music Hall, but since 1899 they have taken place in Symphony Hall, which was erected especially for the purpose. In 1903 a pension fund was started for retiring members. This undoubtedly will act as an incentive to long and faithful service on the part of the players. In addition to its regular Boston season the orchestra makes many appearances throughout the eastern cities as well as giving a series of nightly popular concerts during May and June. The "Pops" as they are termed, are given under the leadership of prominent members of the band and have proved highly satisfactory. T. Adamowski, Max Zach and Gustave Strube at various times have acted as conductors.

There is one name which stands above all others in the history of orchestral music in America — that of Theodore Thomas — for unquestionably he did more to develop a taste for music of this class than any other. He felt, as he himself said, that what the country needed most of all to make it musical was a good orchestra, and plenty of concerts within reach of the people. With this end in view he called a meeting of the principal orchestra players of New York, laid his plans before them and asked for co-operation. On Dec. 3, 1864, he gave the first of the Irving Hall concerts, and with an orchestra of thirty, in the summer of 1865 he gave a series of concerts at Belvedere Lion Park. By 1867 the orchestra had been increased to eighty members, and the famous Symphony Soirées which he had instituted had given the organization a prestige beyond any other musical society, and what was more encouraging to the enthusiastic leader, the public were beginning to show their appreciation.

In the season of 1868-1869 Thomas traveled with his orchestra, but he could not venture far, for New York and

Brooklyn engagements filled up much of the time. But after 1869 he concluded to make a tour of the country, and with this end in view he reorganized his band and introduced it to Boston. The manner in which he was received in this city is well shown by the following extract from Dwight's Journal of Music of Nov. 6, 1869. It states: "The visit of this famous New York orchestra has given our music lovers a new and quick sensation. Boston had not heard such orchestra performances before; and Boston in the frankest humor gave itself up to the complete enjoyment and unstinted praise of what it heard. . . . Fifty-four instruments, picked men, most of them young, all of them artists, all looking as if thoroughly engaged in their work, eager above all things to make the music altogether sound as well as possible. . . . There was nothing which our people, our musicians, needed so much as to hear just such an orchestra . . . to show to us that, with all our pride in our own orchestra, we are yet very far this side of perfection, and must take a lesson from what is better done elsewhere. . . . We rejoice in the coming of this orchestra. It is just the kind of thing that we for years have longed for in view of our own progress here. We sincerely thank Mr. Thomas, first for giving us a hearing, under the best advantages, of a number of works which were new to us, but more we thank him for setting palpably before us a higher ideal of orchestral execution. We shall demand better of our own in future. They will demand it of themselves. They cannot witness this example without a newly kindled desire, followed by an effort to do likewise. With the impression fresh in every mind of performances which it is not rash to say may (for the number of instruments) compare with those of the best orchestras in Europe, improvement is a necessity."

From Boston the orchestra made its way west as far as Chicago, performing at every city en route and returning to New York by way of St. Louis, Cincinnati, Pittsburg and intermediate cities. In later years other tours were made, the last one taking in all the important cities between New York and San Francisco. Sixty-five concerts in all were given during this remarkable tour.

In 1890 Mr. Thomas decided to undertake the establishment of a permanent orchestra in Chicago. With this end in view he induced fifty prominent men of the city to each subscribe one thousand dollars a year for three years as the nucleus of a fund for the purpose. Mr. Thomas placed his enormous private musical library at the service of the new organization. For many years the Thomas Orchestra had a hard struggle for existence and again and again its sponsors came to the rescue. But the financial loss gradually lessened as the number of supporters increased until at the present time so liberal is the patronage that there no longer is a deficit. Up to the season of 1905-1906 the concerts were given in the Auditorium, but since that time they have been held in Orchestra Hall, another monument of Theodore Thomas' indefatigable labors. A series of twenty-eight public rehearsals and concerts now are given during each musical year. When Mr. Thomas died, in 1905, Frederick Stock was appointed to succeed him. Since his acceptance of the post Mr. Stock has steadily striven to raise still further the already high standard of the band under his direction and has been remarkably successful in his endeavor.

While Boston and Chicago are the only American cities having orchestras firmly established on a permanent basis all the leading cities are making steady progress in this direction. In addition to the Philharmonic and New York Symphony Gotham has several other bands of high attainments. The Russian Symphony Society under Modest Altschuler presents the works of Russian composers exclusively, and has exerted a broad educational influence in this respect. Frank Damrosch has done excellent work in connection with his Symphony Concerts for Young People. An orchestra under the direction of F. X. Arens, which offers an excellent series of concerts at low prices, has been extremely well patronized and has proved that there is a large public willing and anxious to avail themselves of the opportunity of hearing the orchestral masterpieces if placed within their reach. Another successful New York orchestra is formed of young professionals under the leadership of Arnold Volpe.

Since 1893 Cincinnati has had its own Symphony Orchestra which annually offers a series of concerts of a high order. Frank Van der Stucken has been the conductor since 1895. The Philadelphia Orchestra, which was inaugurated in 1898 by the late Fritz Scheel, has become one of the leading organizations of the country. On Mr. Scheel's death in 1907 Carl Pohlig was appointed to the position which he now so acceptably occupies. Pittsburg has supported an orchestra since 1895. Frederick Archer, Victor Herbert and Emil Paur successively have acted as conductors.

In addition to these larger and better known institutions there are many of lesser note which have exerted an uplifting influence in the individual communities in which they operate. Peabody Institute at Baltimore has an orchestra which for many years has given six concerts annually. The Minneapolis Orchestra under Emil Oberhoffer, and that of St. Paul under N. B. Emanuel, are rapidly coming to the fore. St. Louis has been more or less successful with a band which in 1907 called Max Zach from Boston to accept its leadership. Buffalo, Denver, Washington, Cleveland, Indianapolis, Detroit, New Haven, Kansas City, San Francisco, in fact all the leading American cities are moving in the matter of orchestral concerts given by their own organizations. It is a noticeable fact that wherever orchestral music has obtained a hold it has been largely instrumental in raising the standard in all other branches of the art. The pioneer educational work accomplished by all the leading orchestras of the country both in their home cities and in the places touched while on tour has been of inestimable value. In many of the smaller communities where it is possible to hear orchestral music of any grade only when a Musical Festival is held, the hearing invariably has tended toward an increased interest in music in general. Thus is seen what a prominent factor the orchestra has been in the development of music in America.

A vast change has been brought about in the orchestral music heard in this country during recent years. As heretofore the works of the classicists and romanticists form the basis of the orchestral literature. But the conductors of today as a general rule are not so loath to give new works a hearing as were their predecessors. Theodore Thomas was the first to take this broader view, and to him we owe our familiarity with Wagner and Tschaikowski. Brahms now occupies a place almost on a par with Beethoven. The Russians, Glazounow, Rimsky-Korsakoff and others are given frequent hearings. Richard Strauss and Mahler of the Germans, César Franck, Debussy and D'Indy among Frenchmen and the Bohemians Dvořák and Smetana occupy prominent places in the make-up of the modern concert programs. Elgar is about the only English composer to obtain any place; an Italian name rarely is seen; among the northerns Jean Sibelius has received most recognition. The Americans, Chadwick, MacDowell, Hadley and Converse, ever are attaining a more stable place. During his two years' stay with the Boston Symphony Dr. Muck has brought forward many works by American composers which have been favorably received. In addition to their purely orchestral presentations each of the larger bands during each season brings forward many soloists and thus adds to the pleasure of the concert performances. All of the leading singers, pianists, violinists, etc., who have appeared before the American public during the last half century, and even before, have been heard with one or other of the various orchestras of the country.

While the interest in orchestral music has been most pronounced and widespread it is only in the largest and most artistic centers that chamber-music has obtained any hold, and this only by ceaseless endeavor. Within recent years, however, an ever increasing public has been drawn to this, the most refined field of musical performance. The appreciation of string quartet music undoubtedly calls for a higher degree of culture than usually is found in the masses, and of necessity the growth in this branch of the art must be slow. Yet in spite of this fact every season witnesses the entrance of new organizations in this field and the outlook ever looks brighter.

From the data available it appears probable that the first public appearance of a string quartet in America was made in New York in 1843, when Uriah C. Hill, to whose efforts was due the founding of the Philharmonic Society, again showed his pioneer spirit. The quartet which Mr. Hill brought together, according to the report of the event, was not of a high order, and it remained for the Mendelssohn Quintet Club of Boston to first offer really artistic chamber-music. This club was formed in 1849 and made its first appearance on December 4 of that year. The members of the organization were August Fries, first violin; Francis Rziha, second violin; Edward Lehmann, viola and flute; Thos. Ryan, viola and clarinet; and Wulf Fries, cello. For nearly fifty years the Mendelssohn Quintet Club continued active, two of its members, Wulf Fries and Ryan, remaining to the last. It traveled all over the United States and presented chamber-music of a high order wherever it went. Another early Boston organization was the Beethoven Quintet Club, formed in 1873, and which was kept up for a considerable time.

In 1851 Theodore Eisfeld instituted a series of quartet soirées in New York, which were continued for several years. Some six years later William Mason with the assistance of Theodore Thomas, Joseph Mosenthal, George Matzka and Carl Bergmann entered this field and with the exception of one season (1856-1857) gave a number of concerts each year until 1869.

Since the establishment of orchestras throughout the country nearly every town of note has one or more chamber-music organizations. The first of the existing string quartets to attain wide celebrity was that formed in Boston by Franz Kneisel in 1884. The original members were F. Kneisel, E. Fiedler, L. Svecenski and F. Giese. Messrs. Kneisel and

Svecenski still occupy their respective places, while Julius Roentgen is the present second violin and Willem Willeke the cellist. The Kneisel Quartet now is recognized as one of the finest if not the finest organization of its kind in existence. It has performed most pronounced service in the field of chamber-music and deservedly occupies a unique place in the musical world.

Boston now is the home of several chamber-music associations of a high order. Among the best known are the Hoffmann Quartet, the Theodorowicz Quartet (recently formed), the Olive Mead Quartet, the Adamowski Trio and the Eaton-Hadley Trio. C. L. Staats is at the head of the Bostonia Sextette Club, composed of string quintet and clarinet. The Longy Club, a club composed of players of wind instruments, and which was formed in 1899, annually gives a series of chamber-music concerts. In New York there is the Flonzaley Quartet, the Marun Quartet, the Margulies Trio and the New York Trio. Chicago has two excellent organizations in the Heermann Quartet and the Chicago String Quartet. There are many other chamber-music clubs of lesser note which are working steadily to advance this truly artistic phase of music, and they gradually are attaining more and more recognition.

The most popular form of concerted instrumental music in this country undoubtedly is that of the military or concert band. It is a far step from chamber-music to band-music, for they are as widely separated as the poles. While the first finds favor only with the few the latter makes its appeal to the many, and the band often is listened to with pleasure where the delicate tones of the string quartet or other small combination of instruments would entirely fail to hold the attention. Another reason for the popularity of band-music, lies in the fact that as a rule it is of a much lighter order than that performed by the chamber-music organizations. America hears much of this music and it never fails to make its appeal. It is a noteworthy fact that there are over eighteen thousand bands, ranging all the way from the little company of village amateurs to the finest concert associations, in the United States today.

As early as 1767 there was a concert announced in New York to be given by the "Royal American Band of Music." In Philadelphia, in 1771, appeared an advertisement of a concert by a "full Band of Music, with trumpets, kettle drums, and every instrument that can be introduced with propriety." Boston also heard band-music in 1771, for on May 17 of that year Josiah Flagg solicited the patronage of the public to a vocal and instrumental performance in which the band of the Sixty-fourth Regiment took part. Two years later, on the occasion of a concert given for his benefit at Faneuil Hall, the opportunity was taken to remind the Bostonians that "Mr. Flagg has established and given instruction to the first band of a regiment of militia in their city."

The Salem Gazette of Jan. 16, 1783, contains an announcement to the effect that the "Massachusetts Band of Music, being at home a few days on furlough, proposes, with permission, to perform at Concert Hall, in Salem, tomorrow evening." In the same year there is record of Colonel Crane's band giving concerts at Portsmouth, N. H. The Revolutionary War acted as an incentive to band-music, and the public, accustomed to hearing fife and drum, gradually became interested in the performances of the military organizations. Many of the colonial soldiers marched to the field to the strains of fife and drum only, but the regimental bands of the British had suggested martial music of a more ambitious character, and America's military bands thus came into existence during the Revolutionary period.

In 1784 a concert was given in the State House at Providence, R. I., by an amateur band made up of the pupils of a Mr. Hewitt, who had come to the city some time previously. The organization afterward became a factor in the musical life of Providence. From 1786 until early in the Nineteenth Century many band concerts were given at Gray's Gardens and at Center House Tavern and Gardens in Philadelphia. It is said that at the beginning of the last century

West Point had one of the best bands in the United States. It consisted of five clarinets, two flutes, two horns, one bassoon, one trumpet, one trombone, one bugle and one drum. In 1821 a reed band was organized in Boston under the title of the Boston Brigade Band, which later was converted into one of brass instruments. In 1858 the reeds again were introduced and a concert was given in Music Hall. There were many earnest band-masters, and through their efforts this class of music was greatly advanced.

One of the finest institutions of its kind in America today is the Marine Band at Washington. It was first established in 1801, and therefore is one of the oldest in the country. Strangely enough, when originally instituted it was formed of sixteen Italians who were engaged by the officers of a United States warship stationed in Italian waters. When the ship returned to this country the band accompanied it, although it was not until 1838 that it was detailed to the Marine Corps at Washington. At that time the band was conducted by a fife major and so continued until 1854, when provision was made for a special leader and thirty players. In 1899 the number was increased to sixty; the leader was given the rank of first lieutenant and was allowed an assistant. During its long career the Marine Band has had eight conductors, Sousa being among the number. Scala held the post for forty years and firmly established the reputation of the organization. W. H. Santelmann has been the conductor since 1898. Not only has he raised the standard of the band itself but Mr. Santelmann also has succeeded in forming an excellent orchestra from among its members. The Marine Band now has a beautiful hall of its own situated in the Barracks at Washington, where it gives many highly artistic concerts. In addition to the Washington Marine, the United States maintains many other bands of a high order, that of West Point being the most notable.

Gilmore's Band was the first of the many excellent concert organizations with which the country now is familiar. Gilmore, who was an Irishman by birth, came to Canada as a member of an English band, and afterward settled in the United States. In 1859, when thirty years of age, he organized in Boston the company of players which afterward bore his name. Previous to this, however, he had been associated with the military, and during the Civil War he was stationed at New Orleans as band-master of the Federal army. While here he massed the army bands in a performance which was characterized by some realistic novelties, such as the firing of guns by electricity, the report occurring on the first beat of the measure, and causing something of a sensation with the audience. Reference has been made elsewhere to Gilmore's part in the National Peace Jubilees held at Boston in 1867 and 1872. In the first of these his own band participated and in the latter many foreign bands were heard as well. The Gilmore organization traveled extensively throughout the United States and Europe and was enthusiastically received everywhere.

Probably the best known concert band appearing before the public today is that presided over by John Philip Sousa. It was founded in 1892 by its present distinguished conductor and has remained a favorite ever since its formation. There are many other bands which have won well merited recognition throughout the country. Some of them, such as Frederick Phinney's, are termed "military," but the name does not necessarily imply connection with the army. It is used in distinction to those bands composed solely of brass instruments, the military bands having reeds in addition. Among other of the well-known concert organizations of this class are Brooke's, Feruello's, Creatore's, Pryor's, Innes' Orchestral Band, Duss' and the Ellery Band.

Band-music has obtained a tremendous hold on the American public, and it is indeed a small and unprogressive community which does not possess one or more companies of players. The larger organizations are made up almost entirely of professionals, while in the smaller ones the men are drawn from almost every station of life. The music played has an equal scope, ranging all the way from the popular march to the classic symphony. The programs of the concert bands very often compare favorably with those of the best orchestras, being drawn from the same sources. Wagner's works easily adapt themselves to band performance as do those of Puccini and others of the modern Italian School. The upward trend of band-music within recent years has been remarkable and shows an ever-increasing desire on the part of the public for music of true worth. Many compositions are heard by those attending band concerts which otherwise would remain entirely unknown except among the more cultured classes who are attracted to orchestral performances. Thus is seen the far-reaching educational influence which the various bands have exerted in this country.

In the smaller cities and towns every concert given by the larger orchestras and bands while on tour is looked upon as an important event by those interested in musical matters, and has acted as a stimulus toward the formation of local organizations. By this means many small companies of instrumental performers have been formed, each adding to the musical growth of the community. There now are scores of such associations connected with the schools, churches and theatres throughout the country, and each is doing its part, however small, in spreading an interest and love of the art. America has made wonderful progress in appreciation of instrumental music in all its phases within the last quarter century, and doubtless future years will show equal advancement.

AMERICAN MUSICIANS

America has witnessed a remarkable evolution in the art of musical composition. Starting with absolutely no artistic traditions, long hampered by the active hostility toward music displayed by the early Puritan settlers, thousands of miles distant from the art centers of Europe and for many years completely out of touch with them, intensely occupied in conquering and populating a continent, in spite of these overwhelming odds, America has produced many composers, performers, musical critics and instructors worthy of the name. When it is remembered that at the time our pioneer musicians were probably exhibiting their simple song tunes, Europe already had heard the masterpieces of Bach, of Haydn, of Mozart and of Beethoven, then and only then can one realize what has been accomplished within a century.

The real beginning of American music was the psalm singing of the Pilgrims and Puritans in New England. Before that time, the settlers in Virginia had brought over the music of the old country. They had even given concerts, but they in no way changed the music from its original form, so that it cannot be counted as an American product. Both the Pilgrims and Puritans looked somewhat askance at the divine art, questioning greatly its divinity. At first they objected even to hymns and permitted only the singing of psalms. They had only five tunes, taken from Ainsworth's collection. In 1640, The Bay Psalm Book was published at Cambridge, Mass. It was the first book printed in the colonies and was very carefully gotten up, such men as John Eliot and Richard Mather assisting in its production. At first the music was not printed with the words and the psalms were sung by the "lining out" method, in which the minister gave one line at a time, to be repeated by the congregation. In 1690, the music was printed with the words, an improvement which caused much discussion and opposition. In 1647, a few hymns had been added, causing another outburst of opposition from the elders of the church. The book was first used by the Puritans, and was adopted by the Pilgrims in 1692.

This singing of hymns and psalms led to the establishment of singing schools, the first being opened in Boston in 1717. An organ which was brought to the Boston Episcopal Church also helped to keep up the musical interest of the time. Choir singing began about 1750. However, it came into the churches so gradually that it evaded the opposition which usually met any change. The next step was concerts of secular music at which dancing was sometimes part of the program. Then collections of secular songs were made and about sixty books of them existed at the end of the Eighteenth Century. Efforts at composition soon began, though at first they were very crude. However, these early composers had a high opinion of themselves and claimed to be well grounded in their work. Their use of counterpoint on which they prided themselves, easily shows that they had no true idea of the art. The false idea that genius needed no tutoring and was above all restraint seems to have been uppermost in their minds. The need for "dry study" was barely felt. In the preface to his New England Psalm-Singing, William Billings, who was representative of his time, writes as follows:

"To all musical practitioners:

"Perhaps it may be expected by some, that I could say something concerning the rules for composition; to these I answer that Nature is the best dictator, for all the hard, dry, studied rules that ever were prescribed will not enable any person to form an Air any more than the bare knowledge of the four and twenty letters, and strict Grammatical rules will qualify a scholar for composing a piece of Poetry, or properly adjusting a Tragedy without a Genius. It must be Nature; Nature must lay the foundation, Nature must give the Thought. . . . For my own part, I don't think myself confined to any Rules for Composition laid down by any that went before me, neither should I think (were I to pretend to lay down the rules) that any one who comes after me were any ways obligated to adhere to them any further than they should think proper; so in fact I think it best for every composer to be his own learner."

From the above statement it is seen that the "air" was always the first consideration, and at the present day all that remains of the efforts of the early writers are a few psalm-tunes founded on these selfsame airs. Owing to the faulty and incorrect harmonization of the originals the arrangements of such of these tunes as now appear in some of our hymn-books are in altered form. Considering the time and environment in which they were written the early psalm-tunes and fuguing pieces show real merit. Had they been entirely deficient of value they would have been consigned to oblivion long ere this, and, such as they were, they served as the starting point for American musical composition. It is quite possible that they have the stamp of the country as it then was more clearly defined than have the works of our modern native composers. For with all our advancement, and excellent as are the compositions which have been produced within recent years by American-born musicians, with the possible exception of pieces of a popular order, they lack that inherent coloring and typicalness which make for nationality.

A man who was a tanner, a patriot of strong national sentiments and an enthusiastic music lover was William Billings, America's first composer. With regard to his physical appearance everything was against him. He is described as somewhat deformed, with one leg shorter than the other and with one arm comparatively withered, and added to these afflictions he was blind of one eye. Although his voice was strong, it was far from musical, being of a rasping quality. It is said that his first compositions were done between working hours and were chalked down on the walls of the tannery and on the sides of leather. In addition to his musical gift he was given to writing poetry, but he lacked the education necessary to make the most of his talent. His musical efforts also were hampered for a similar reason.

In 1770 he issued his first publication, under the following title:

"The New England Psalm Singer; or American Chorister, containing a number of Psalm tunes, Anthems and Canons. In four and five parts. (Never before published.) Composed by William Billings, a native of Boston, in New England. Matt. xii. 16; 'Out of the mouths of babes and sucklings has thou perfected praise.' James v. 13; 'Is any merry? Let him sing psalms.'

O, praise the Lord with one consent
And in this grand design,
Let Britain and Colonies
Unanimously Jine.

"Boston, New England, printed by Edes & Gill."

From an artistic point of view the tunes composed by Billings were anything but perfect, yet they contained an element of joyous spontaneity that was contagious and the approval of the public was won on account of this. About the time that the New England Psalm Singer appeared, English anthems of a fugal character were introduced in America and became extremely popular. This style of music seems to have made a profound impression on Billings and he is found voicing its praise in no uncertain terms. He speedily made use of it in the singing schools which he had established and his later compositions show evidence of a desire to emulate the writers of music of this class.

In 1778 his second publication, The Singing-Masters Assistant, was issued. This work won speedy popularity. It was carried to camp by the soldiers, affording them recreation and much pleasure. Billings' other published works comprise Music in Miniature, containing sixty-three pages of original composition and eleven standard tunes previously published; Psalm-singers' Amusement; Suffolk Harmony; and Continental Harmony. These, together with a few anthems, represent the life effort of America's first composer of music.

Crude as was his work when viewed in the light of today, Billings paved the way to higher achievement. It has been said with truth that he neither "borrowed, adapted nor stole" the melodies of others. Owing to his ungainly personality he was the butt of many jokes, still his enthusiasm awakened general interest in music, and his indefatigable persistence forced a reform in its development. To Billings was due the introduction of both the pitch pipe and the cello into the church as an aid to the choir.

Among the contemporaries and immediate followers of Billings were Holyoke, who was more scientific and better educated than Billings; Andrew Law, who is best known for his three musical publications, Tunes and Anthems, Rudiments of Music, and Musical Primer on a New Plan; and Kimball, who wrote Rural Harmony.

The spirit of the time was now becoming less severe, although music was still chiefly used for religious purposes. One of the first departures was the early orchestras, and the beginning of the Nineteenth Century saw practical musical freedom in America. In the early days, however, music had not been confined to New England. Philadelphia had become quite a musical center. It had seen the performance of a few operas, in spite of the opposition of the Quakers, and had a Musical Association as early as 1740. In New York the music was chiefly connected with the Episcopal churches. Baltimore and New Orleans were also musical centers but had no great influence.

The man, who to quote from Elson, "stands as the chief link between the early American composers and the school of the present," is Dr. Lowell Mason. He made a collection of the best sacred music and added some compositions of his own to it. This was published as The Handel and Haydn Society Collection of Church Music. Later he became conductor of the society. He also became well known as a teacher, and was the originator of teachers' conventions in this country. In Europe he would have ranked only as a mediocre musician, but he was far more advanced in his art than any other American of his time, and merits his title of "The father of American church music."

The first American classical composer, and the first American musician to have a foreign reputation was John Knowles Paine. He studied abroad and his mass in D was performed at Berlin in 1867. He brought out his oratorio, "St. Peter," in Portland, Maine, in 1873. His genius appears less hampered by form in his symphonies in C minor and in his symphony in A, called "Spring." His musical setting of "Œdipus Tyrannus" of Sophocles equaled many similar European works. He at first opposed the school of Wagner, but later used some of its best method in his opera, "Azara," produced in 1901. At the time he started working, he was the best composer of his time and the only one who attempted classical works.

The next American composer of reputation is George Whitfield Chadwick. His music has a tendency toward the dramatic and he wrote many overtures, the most famous being "Rip Van Winkle." He is regarded as the leader of the American School. His originality and deep knowledge of orchestration stamp his work as that of a genius. Among his best works are the concert overtures, "Melpomene," and "Thalia;" his third symphony; the D minor string quartet; and a cantata, the "Lily Nymph." Mr. Chadwick has written in almost all the musical forms, the list including three symphonies; several overtures, chamber-music; a comic opera, "Tabasco;" "Judith," a sacred opera; cantatas, and much instrumental and vocal music. His songs are of a high order and compare favorably with the best German leider. Elson says of him: "To hold the proper sonata form without becoming rigid is one of Chadwick's great gifts; he has reconciled the symmetrical form with modern passion."

Horatio Parker is another American composer who has used many musical forms. His work is rather scientific and undramatic and is not generally popular.

In the literature of sacred music, one name stands pre-eminent, that of Dudley Buck. His first Motette Collection, says Mathews, marks an epoch in American church music, the book being "notable because it was the first collection published in America in which modern styles of German musical compositions were freely used with unlimited freedom of modulation and addition of an independent organ accompaniment." As a concert organist, Buck made numerous and extensive tours. By means of these concerts and through his sacred compositions, he did notable pioneer work toward elevating the music of his time. His services as organist and choirmaster have been long and memorable. As a teacher he ranks with our leading instructors. Mr. Buck has written in all forms, but his fame as a composer rests chiefly on his church music and his cantatas. In religious compositions he freely makes use of dramatic effects, but they are so employed as in no way to lessen the grace and dignity of his works. A series of sacred cantatas, composed in his later years, are designed for the various church festivals and are called the "Christian Year." His large number of sacred compositions include anthems, hymns, offertories and a Te Deum. His organ music is of a wide variety, including two sonatas and the well-known "Triumphal March." Mr. Buck also has published Studies for Pedal Phasing, Influence of the Organ in History and an excellent hand-book for students and organists, called Illustrations in Choir Accompaniment. He has been by far our most prolific writer of church music, and not only the number of his compositions but their musical worth excites surprise at the amount of good work he accomplished.

An important element in American music is the college glee club, and it was in connection with such an organization at Harvard University that Arthur Foote first came before the public. One of his chief lines of work is choruses for male voices. He has been very successful, also, in his orchestral suite in D minor; his symphonic prologue, "Francesca di Rimini;" and his songs. "He has won his high place," says Hughes, "by faithful adherence to his own sober, serene ideals, and his genuine culture and seriousness. . . . I know of no modern composer who has come nearer to relighting the fire that beams in the old gavottes and fugues and preludes. His gavottes are to me the best since Bach."

William Wallace Gilchrist is essentially an American composer, never having studied abroad. Like Foote, his works are mostly for the voice, including solos, choruses, cantatas and religious music. While he is successful in this line, his orchestral work deserves even more praise. Other song writers are Van der Stucken, the chief composer of the West, Adolph Foerster and C. C. Converse.

The symphony is one musical form in which the American composers have not been particularly successful. Many have written symphonic poems, but the present day romanticism has not seemed suited to the dignified symphonic forms. However, Henry K. Hadley, a young musician, has brought out a very creditable symphony under the title "Youth and Life." It is full of healthy Americanism, is cheerful, uplifting and melodic. His other works have much the same character.

A distinctly American composer is Silas Gamaliel Pratt, whom Elson describes as "an example of the irrepressible Yankee in music." He had tireless energy and tried nearly all the greater musical forms, including operas, cantatas and overtures. Louis Adolphe Coerne has been classed as Pratt's opposite. He is devoted to his art for its own sake, and has, like Pratt, attempted nearly all the musical forms. He sometimes lacks simplicity but is always skilful and pleasing.

A composer whose works have a romantic and poetic character is Frederick S. Converse. He is best known for his musical interpretations of Keats' poems, Endymion's Narrative and the Festival of Pan.

The formation of definite musical groups or colonies has been important in the development of American music. Among these musical centers are Boston, New York, Chicago, St. Louis, Cleveland, Cincinnati and San Francisco. The New York colony is the largest, but the Boston colony seems to be the most progressive. "Boston has been not only the promulgator," says Hughes, "but in a great measure the tutor of American music." However, outside of these main centers, many smaller cities and towns can claim celebrated musicians and composers.

One of America's most gifted and most characteristical representatives is Edward Alexander MacDowell, who belongs to the New York group. The individuality of his music is equal to that of Chopin or of Beethoven. As a tone master and a painter of musical pictures MacDowell stands alone, and his ability to combine the greatest simplicity of composition with the most dramatic effect is indeed unique.

Although the greater number of MacDowell's compositions are of uniform excellence, only those better known to the public are here mentioned. Under this head the "Indian Suite," for orchestra, probably comes first. The themes are built on the music of the American Indian folk-songs, the treatment of which is most unusual and delightful. Vigorous and strong in construction, masterly in arrangement, it still possesses a refinement and delicacy that make it one of the very first American compositions for orchestra. The four piano sonatas, the "Tragica," simple, but a marvelously artistic statement of the tragedy as one of the facts of life; "Eroica," which bears the subtitle, "A Flower from the Realm of King Arthur," and is a musical version of an Arthurian story; the Norse sonata, a tone picture of almost barbaric splendor, dedicated to Edward Grieg; and the Keltic sonata, which mirrors all the glories of the Gaelic world, are his greatest works.

As a song-writer Henry T. Finck places MacDowell with the greatest of the world. In this smaller form of musical composition he has written some things that are wonderful bits of musical expression. In his smaller pieces for piano is seen another development of his genius, one which perhaps is more intimate than all others. A pianist of excellent abilities, he was able to give his own interpretation to these pieces as a sort of a key by which could be deciphered all the mystery and beauty of his larger works. His love of nature is charmingly expressed in his Woodland Sketches and Sea Pieces. In his Moon Pictures, suggested by themes from Hans Christian Andersen, one cannot help but feel the poetry, romance and charm which are there portrayed. MacDowell's leading characteristics as a composer were his vivid imagination and poetic feeling.

Another very original composer of this colony is Henry W. Loomis, a pupil and follower of Dvořák. Mr. Loomis has been especially interested in using music as a dramatic setting for recitations, pantomimes and the like, and he has been most successful in giving his work a vivid, and one may say, graphic coloring. He has composed two comic operas, "The Maid of Athens," and the "Burglar's Bride." He has also written some beautiful songs and some genre, or type pieces. He is unconventional and refreshing in his method. "His genius is the very essence of felicity," says Hughes.

A writer who wavers between the older classical school and the modern romanticism is Arthur Whiting. Philip Hale has said that "rigorous intellectuality" was the one aim of this composer. "You respected the music of Mr. Whiting," he continues, "but you did not feel for it any personal affection." His best work is for the piano and orchestra.

Henry Holden Huss is another active member of this eastern school. He has been described as a dramatic and lyric composer and his compositions are chiefly orchestral works and songs. His greatest fault is lack of simplicity.

Harry Rowe Shelley is a composer who has brought out some good religious compositions, namely, two cantatas, "The Inheritance Divine" and "Vexilla Regis," and a dramatic chorus, "Death and Life." He has also written an opera, "Leila;" overtures; symphonic poems and other compositions.

Other New York composers are Gerrit Smith, who is at his best in his songs for children; Homer Bartlett, an orchestral composer; C. D. Hawley, whose songs have fine lyric quality; John Brewer, another song-writer; Reginald DeKoven, who has composed some fairly successful comic operas and songs, and has attracted much public praise and also criticism; Victor Harris, a well-known accompanist and song-writer; William Mason; Arthur Nevin; J. Remington Fairland; Richard Henry Warren; and Carl Lachmund.

The Boston colony for some time claimed Ethelbert Nevin, although this composer was born in Pennsylvania and spent much of his time abroad. His excellent musical education was a great aid to his natural genius and shows plainly in his compositions. Nevin wrote many piano pieces and did little work for orchestra, but he will be best remembered by his songs. His child songs have a peculiar captivating charm and include some of Stevenson's best child poems. In Florence, Nevin composed his suite, "May in Tuscany," while his life in Venice inspired his well-known Venetian Sketches, The Sketch Book containing thirteen songs. His Piano Pieces is another popular work. "The Rosary," his best known song, reached a phenomenal sale. "Narcissus," his most popular piano piece, is contained in his Water Scenes, which work probably has made Nevin best known. His book, In Arcady; suite for piano, "En Passant;" a libretto, Lady Floraine's Dream, by Vance Thompson; a pantomime for piano and orchestra; a cantata and many songs and piano pieces have helped to make him the most popular composer in America.

Mr. Hughes in his Contemporary American Composers, writes, "It needs no very intimate acquaintance with Nevin's music to see that it is not based on an adoration of counterpoint as an end. He believes that true music must come from the emotions — the intelligent emotions — and that when it cannot appeal to the emotions it has lost its power. He also says: 'Above everything we need melody — melody and rhythm. Rhythm is the great thing. We have it in Nature. The trees sway, and our steps keep time, and our very souls respond.'"

America has indeed been rich in song-writers. One who belongs to the Boston group, is Frederick F. Bullard. He is best known for his "Song of Pan;" "The Sisters;" his settings to Richard Hovey's "Here's a Health to Thee, Roberts," "Barney McGee" and the "Stein Song," and several part songs. His harmonies are in some case monotonous, but in general his work is lively and original.

Homer Norris is a Boston composer who has turned his back upon German influence in favor of the French. He is chiefly a writer upon musical theory and is strongly opposed to emphasis upon form to the exclusion of emphasis on appeal. He has composed many songs. Other names in the list of successful song-writers are G. W. Marston and Clayton Johns.

The most famous member of the Chicago group of musicians, and one may say the most famous musician of the West, is Henry Schoenfeld. He is a follower of Dvořák and holds religiously to strictly national themes for his compositions, that is, like Dvořák he makes frequent use of the negro music. However, as Hughes says, "Schoenfeld negroes do not speak Bohemian." His piano pieces are his only published works.

Frederick Grant Gleason was a Chicago composer who tried the heavier musical forms. Prominent among his works are the operas, "Otho Visconti," and "Montezuma," of which he wrote both librettos and music. In these operas he closely followed the methods of Wagner. Another of his most successful works is his music to the "Culprit Fay." He was also a well-known critic.

Cleveland is by no means an unimportant center in the musical world. Its most celebrated composer is Wilson Smith, who has followed a line of happy medium in his compositions and thus is popular with both the masses and those educated in music. Mr. Hughes writes of him: "His erudition has persuaded him to a large simplicity; his nature turns him to a musical optimism which gives many of his works a Mozartian cheer. Graciousness is his key." He has composed several pieces based on the characteristics of Grieg, Chopin, Schumann and Schubert, and in these he has reached a high degree of excellence. However, his works along more original lines are also praiseworthy, especially his two Gavottes and his Minuet, Moderne, which has been described as "musical champagne." Some of his songs are also beautiful, "If I but Knew," being a favorite.

Other composers worthy of mention are Johann Beck, a musician who is making it his life-work to follow out the rules laid down by the old classic composers; the St. Louis song-writer, William Schuyler; and Ernest Richard Kroeger, also of St. Louis. Mr. Kroeger has shown much versatility in his compositions and is one of the few Americans who has published fugues. Mr. Kroeger says some of his ideas are entirely musical, while others are attempts to illustrate poems in tones, such as symphony, a suite, and overtures on Endymion, Thanatopsis, Hiawatha and Sardanapalus. He also has composed a group of sonnets on various themes; Twelve Concert Studies, which, Rupert Hughes says, "show the influence of Chopin upon a composer who writes with a strong German accent." An étude, "Castor and Pollux;" a Romanza; and other studies, Danse Negre and Caprice Negre resemble similar works of Gottschalk.

The far West has produced two composers of the first order, Edgar Stillman Kelley, who though born in Wisconsin, worked chiefly in San Francisco; and N. Clifford Page. Kelley first became known through his musical setting to

Macbeth. His comic opera, " Puritania," was also successful, and his Chinese suite, "Aladdin," is one of his best efforts. " Kelley plainly deserves pre-eminence among American composers for his devotion to and skill in the finer sorts of humorous music. No other American has written so artfully, so happily, or so ambitiously in this field," says Hughes. He has done artistic and masterly work in imitation of the Chinese. Nathaniel Clifford Page began writing operas in his childhood, the first produced being " The First Lieutenant." He has continued along the dramatic line of composition, writing much incidental music for dramas. Like Kelley, he studied the music of the Orient and used many Japanese themes.

Two names stand out pre-eminent among American women composers, Mrs. H. H. A. Beach and Margaret Ruthven Lang. Mrs. Beach's large works are her Gaelic Symphony, first given in Boston in 1896; a mass in E flat, sung by the Handel and Haydn Society in 1892; a Festival Jubilate, composed for the dedication of the Women's Building at the Columbian Exposition; also three cantatas, " The Rose of Avontown;" " The Minstrel and the King;" and " Sylvania." Mrs. Beach's piano works are many, some of the most important being a cadenza to the C minor concerto of Beethoven, six duets called " Summer Dreams;" concerto in C sharp minor; a Bal Masque Waltz; and a Children's Carnival and Children's Album. She has written over sixty songs, many of them surpassingly beautiful.

Margaret Ruthven Lang's first large work of note was the Dramatic Overture, performed by the Boston Symphony Orchestra in 1893. An overture, " Nitichis," was given the same year by Theodore Thomas in Chicago. These compositions are in manuscript, as is another overture, Totila. Of three arias, two were performed in 1896; " Sappho's Prayer to Aphrodite," for contralto and orchestra, was performed in New York; and "Armida," for soprano and orchestra, was performed at the Boston Symphony Concerts. The third is " Rhoelns," for barytone and orchestra. Among other compositions are a cantata for chorus, solo and orchestra; a string quartet, several compositions for violin and piano; piano pieces and songs.

American musical criticism has had an interesting history. The first so-called musical journals were mere literary efforts, full of flowery language. They contained much talk of Handel and Haydn, although at that time the people in America had only a very meager knowledge of these two great composers. The daily newspapers had no department of musical criticism. The pioneer musical critic of this country was John S. Dwight. He gave up the church to devote himself to literature, his musical writings gaining immediate attention. He was identified with the Brook Farm colony, where he taught German and the classics. At the conclusion of this venture he founded Dwight's Journal of Music, which proved an eminently successful publication, and of which he was editor-in-chief for fifteen years. His paper is the best American musical history of his time, and his writing in other lines is abundant. Among the contributors to the Journal were A. W. Thayer, Otto Dresel, Leonhard and Mathews.

Alexander Wheelock Thayer, another American critic, while serving as librarian at Harvard, conceived the idea of writing a biography of Beethoven. For many years all his endeavors were toward that end, and he was successful in achieving the finest and most authentic of the reviews of the great musician's life. In 1865 he was appointed consul at Trieste by President Lincoln, and in this capacity he served until 1882. During the first years of his consulate he published the first volume of the Beethoven biography. The second appeared in 1872, and the third in 1879. It is indeed pathetic that after these years of indefatigable endeavor Mr. Thayer was unable, on account of poor health, to finish the biography, this work being done by Dr. Herman Rieters, who had put the other volumes into German, in which tongue the biography must be read, as the English manuscript has never been revised.

Henry Theophilus Finck, also well known in musical literature, while pursuing his musical education abroad went to Bayreuth to attend the first Wagnerian Festival, of which he sent back accounts to the New York World and the Atlantic Monthly. He then sojourned in Munich and Vienna, studying psychology and anthropology, and always interested in Wagner. This interest finally deepened into a resolve to write a biography of the great composer. He had the advantage of knowing Wagner personally, and in 1893 published one of the most valuable studies of the great musician. In addition to his books Mr. Finck has done considerable work on the Nation and the Evening Post; is a successful lecturer and was at one time professor of musical history at the National Conservatory of Music. Besides Wagner and his Works, he has published Chopin and Other Musical Essays; The Wagner Handbook; Song and Song Writers; biographies of Anton Seidl, Edward Grieg and others; and a complete American edition of the four operas of The Ring of the Nibelung. Mr. Finck has a keen eye for new talent and is in sympathy with the more recent school of music.

Another American musical critic and writer interested in Wagner is Gustav Kobbé. He is a prominent contributor on musical and dramatic subjects to the newspapers and such magazines as the Century, Scribner's, and The Forum. Among his writings are The Ring of the Nibelung; Wagner's Life and Works; Plays for Amateurs; New York and Its Environs; My Rosary and Other Poems; Operas Singers; Signora; A Child of the Opera House; Famous Actors and Actresses and Their Homes; Wagner's Music-Dramas Analyzed; Loves of the Great Composers and Wagner and his Isolde.

Probably the best.known of eastern musical critics and an author of authority is Henry Edward Krehbiel. He prepared himself for the law, but abandoned this profession for musical journalism. In 1874, he became critic of the Cincinnati Gazette. Six years later he went to New York and became editor of the Musical Review and music critic of the

New York Tribune, which position he still holds. In 1900 he was appointed one of The International Jury of Awards at the Paris Exposition and later was made a Chevalier of the Legion of Honor. In addition to his editorial duties, his lecturing and magazine articles, he has written many valuable books on music. Among them are An Account of the Fourth Cincinnati Musical Festival in 1880; Notes on the Cultivation of Choral Music and the Oratorio Society of New York; Review of the New York Seasons from 1880 to 1890; Studies in the Wagnerian Drama; The Philharmonic Society of New York; How to Listen to Music; Music and Manners in the Classical Period. He has also translated the Technic of Violin Playing, by Carl Courvoisier, and has edited an Annotated Bibliography of the Fine Arts, and Lavignac's Music and Musicians.

Philip Hale is another eminent eastern critic. From 1889 to 1891 he was musical critic of the Boston Home Journal. In 1890 he accepted a position as critic for the Boston Post, and in 1891 went to the Boston Journal in the same capacity. Since 1897 he has been editor of the Boston Musical Record and was for some years correspondent of the Musical Courier. He has lectured throughout the country on musical subjects. Mr. Hale is known as one of the most brilliant and forceful writers in the interest of music connected with the American press. His articles are fair and judicious and also tinged with unique humor.

Louis C. Elson stands as one of the best writers on music in this country. His first journalistic work was on the Vox Humana, a paper devoted chiefly to organ music. About 1880 he was appointed editor of the Boston Courier. When abroad Mr. Elson was correspondent for the New York Tribune, the Evening Post, and the Boston Transcript. In 1888 he became musical editor of the Boston Advertiser. Mr. Elson has been successful as a director and has written numerous compositions of smaller forms, such as children's songs and operettas. He is best known, however, for his contributions to the musical literature of the country, which include The Curiosities of Music; History of German Song; The Realm of Music; The Theory of Music, Great Composers and Their Works; Our National Music and its Sources; European Reminiscences; Shakespeare in Music and a History of American Music, published in 1904.

One of the brightest writers of the younger generations is Richard Hughes. He became assistant of the Criterion in New York, and then went abroad to do research work for a large publishing firm. Fiction and verse, essays and criticisms, which have emanated from his versatile pen have been frequently encountered in the magazines, while several books, among them Contemporary American Composers, and a very popular one entitled Love Affairs of the Great Composers, have served to make him known as one of the liveliest and wittiest of musical authors.

William Smythe Babcock Mathews is a prominent Chicago critic and writer. In the decade following 1877 he was music critic on the Chicago Record, Tribune and Herald. In 1891 he brought out the magazine entitled Music, of which he was the editor, this being merged with the Philharmonic in 1903. Among his books are The Great in Music; Popular History of Music; Music and its Ideals; How to Understand Music; Complete School of Pedals; and many other valuable works of lesser scope. He is also favorably known as a piano teacher.

William Foster Apthorp is one of the best known of American critics. He was for five years critic of the Atlantic Monthly. In 1876 he became musical critic of the Boston Sunday Courier; in 1878 musical and dramatic editor of the Boston Traveler; and in 1881 he assumed the same position on the Boston Transcript, remaining there until 1903, when he went abroad to live. Mr. Apthorp was for a time program editor of the Boston Symphony Orchestra. He has also lectured at the leading American colleges. He is the author of several books, among which may be mentioned The Life of Hector Berlioz; Musicians and Music Lovers, and numerous translations.

Other American critics of note are James Gibbon Huneker and John Smith Van Cleve. In 1879 Mr. Van Cleve became music critic of the Cincinnati Commercial and was subsequently engaged upon the Cincinnati News-Journal. He went to Chicago in 1879 and gained recognition in that musical center. He now lives at Troy, Ohio, where he continues his activities as lecturer and writer. Mr. Huneker is very modern in taste and style, and his criticisms are delightfully pungent and vigorous. He has written a number of clever books, among them Mezzotints in Modern Music, also what is considered to be one of the best of the lives of Chopin. He is at present connected with the National Conservatory at New York.

Although nearly all of the American composers have been performers to a certain extent, there are some American musicians who are known almost entirely as performers. The greater number of these are organists and pianists. One of the first of these organists to win public favor was George Elbridge Whiting. He also ranks as one of the best American composers for the organ.

Samuel Brenton Whitney is another celebrated organist. He was first organist and director of music at Christ Church, Montpelier. After four years there, he held a similar position at St. Peter's, Albany, N. Y., then at St. Paul's Church, Burlington, Vt. He then became organist and choirmaster of the Church of the Advent, Boston, which position he still holds. Here he introduced the English Cathedral service. The choir of this church has become celebrated under his direction. Mr. Whitney has also been conductor of many choral societies in and around Boston, and has become identified with liturgical music and vested choirs, and a reverent performance of church music. For some time he was teacher of the organ and lecturer in the New England Conservatory, where he established for the first time a church-music class, in which not only vocal pupils were taught how properly to interpret sacred music, but pupils as well were instructed as to the management of the organ in the church service.

An eminent organist is Edward Morris Bowman. In 1862 he went to Minneapolis, Minn., where he became organist of the Holy Trinity Church and also taught music there. From 1867 to 1872 he was in St. Louis, Mo., as teacher, conductor and organist. He then spent three years of study in Europe under Franz Beudel; and studied piano and organ under Haupt, theory and composition with Weitzmann, and registration with Batiste in Paris. He returned to St. Louis, where he lived for thirteen years except for a trip to Europe in 1881, when he was the first American to pass the examination of the London Royal College of Organists. Since 1887 he has lived in Brooklyn, where he is organist of the Baptist Temple. For five years he was professor of music at Vassar College, and in 1895 organized in Brooklyn the Temple Choir of two hundred voices, which he still conducts. He was one of the founders of the American Guild of Organists and helped to found the American College of Music, which he served as president and trustee. Bowman also has served three terms as president of the Music Teachers' National Association. Besides being a very successful teacher he has published Bowman and Weitzmann's Manual of Musical Theory.

Hiram Clarence Eddy has an international reputation such as no other American-born organist can boast. Mr. Eddy has made many concert tours throughout this country and Europe, where his masterly playing elicited the highest praise from the leading critics. Haupt, Guilmant and others have all pronounced him a player of the highest rank, and by special invitation he played at the Paris Exposition in 1889 as America's foremost organist. Previous to that time he has played at the Vienna Exposition in 1873, and at the Philadelphia Centennial in 1876, and within the last few decades he has played at all the Expositions held on this continent. His influence in this country has been most marked in elevating the standard of organ playing and in widening the range of repertory. Mr. Eddy is organist and choirmaster of the Tompkins Avenue Congregational Church, Brooklyn, N. Y.

America can boast of three very prominent women pianists, viz., Fanny Bloomfield Zeisler, Julie Rive-King, and Myrtle Elvyn. Fanny Bloomfield Zeisler is one of the greatest living pianists. She was born in Austrian Silesia, but came to this country when but two years of age. She is thus an American by adoption. In the season of 1895-1896, Mrs. Zeisler gave fifty concerts in the United States and in the autumn of 1897 made a tour of the Pacific coast. While touring Great Britain and France in 1898 she received one of her highest compliments, an invitation to be piano soloist at the Lower Rhine Festival at Düsseldorf. Here the critics hailed her as one of the foremost pianists of the world. She has long been an integral part of the musical life of Chicago. She was a friend and admirer of Theodore Thomas and was for several years head of the piano department of the Bush Temple Conservatory in Chicago. In recent years she has taught privately, also appearing in recitals in the leading cities. Julie Rive-King made her debut in Leipsic in 1874, playing Liszt's second rhapsody and Beethoven's third concerto. She has made successful tours in America under the management of Frank H. King, whom she married. One of the youngest of America's pianists to obtain a world-wide reputation is Myrtle Elvyn. At the age of three and a half years she made her first public appearance, and at thirteen she appeared in public recitals, playing the highest grade of classical works. At eighteen she made her debut at Beethoven Salle at Berlin with the Philharmonic Orchestra and achieved an unqualified success. She later made a tour of the provinces, playing also in Germany, Austria, England, Holland and Belgium with Arthur Hartmann, the American violinist. She had written numerous piano pieces and songs.

Another famous American pianist and composer was Louis Gottschalk. Upon his first American tour he played many of his own compositions and directed his own orchestral works. A symphony entitled, "A Night in the Tropics," an overture, a cantata, and a portion of an opera was brought out at that time. He was received with lavish praise by his countrymen. Later he made a tour of Cuba and Spanish-America, and he lingered in the tropical clime for five years. Returning to New York in 1862 he made a tour of America from the Atlantic to the Pacific coast, and in 1865 he went to South America on a concert tour, where he died in 1869. His compositions like his playing are possessed of a warm and brilliant charm, but are not underlaid with profound intellect or feeling.

One of the few violinists of note that America can claim is Charles Martin Loeffler. He played in the Pasdeloup Orchestra in Paris and with other European orchestras, which gave him a practical knowledge of orchestration. He first came to New York, but in 1883 went to Boston to become second concert master and soloist in the Boston Symphony Orchestra, which position he resigned in 1903 in order to devote more time to composition. He has never toured alone but has been heard in most of the large cities of the country with the Boston Symphony Orchestra. He possesses a wonderful technique and plays with exquisite grace and largeness of style.

Francis Macmillen is a young violinist of America who promises to excel any of his predecessors. He has made several successful tours of the United States, and has played as soloist with many great orchestras, including that of Theodore Thomas of Chicago.

The development of instrumental music in America was much slower than that of vocal. The most active parts of the country in this musical line were New York, Philadelphia, and some of the other cities further to the South. New England was slow in developing it. The first instruments used were the organ and spinet. The first band was that of Flagg, started in Boston in 1773. Gottlieb Graupner, a German, established the first orchestra in Boston about 1810. It consisted of twelve members, gotten together with the greatest difficulty. It was called the Philharmonic Orchestra, and Graupner, who played the oboe, was its president. He also taught music and had a music store. He was one of the first men to introduce German influence in America. His orchestra lasted until about 1824.

In 1840 a larger orchestra was started in Boston by the help of the Academy of Music. This lasted for seven years. Philadelphia started a band in 1783 and in 1820 could boast of a musical organization called the Musical Fund Society. This society gave both instrumental and vocal music in its concerts and lasted until 1857. The first organization of the kind in New York was the Euterpean Society, which gave one concert a year. In 1842 one of the most important of American musical societies, the Philharmonic Society, was founded by Uriah C. Hill. Among the great leaders of this society have been Dr. Leopold Damrosch, Theodore Thomas, Anton Seidl, Walter Damrosch and Emil Paur.

The first really great leader in America was Theodore Thomas. Elson says, "He has done more to raise the standard of music in America than any other man." He began by giving chamber concerts in New York in about 1845 in partnership with William Mason. These concerts had a wide repertory and introduced many great composers in America. In 1864 Thomas began orchestra concerts, the Philharmonic Orchestra being his great rival. In 1877 and 1879 he became conductor of the Philharmonic Orchestra. In 1869 he had visited the West and gave some concerts in Chicago. He founded the Chicago Orchestra in 1890, fifty Chicago business men giving $1000 each toward its support. At first it was not successful, for the public was not sufficiently educated to enjoy the classical music which Thomas insisted upon playing. However, in time he was successful.

Henry L. Higginson was the founder of the Boston Symphony Orchestra, and its first conductor was Mr. Georg Henschel. The man who did the most for it, however, was its second conductor, Wilhelm Gericke. Its other great directors include Arthur Nikisch and Emil Paur.

The New York Symphony Orchestra was founded by Dr. Leopold Damrosch and succeeded from the first. It was re-established in 1903 by Walter Damrosch. Seidl Orchestral Society was another musical organization of New York started by Anton Seidl, an operatic conductor.

One of the most popular American leaders is John Philip Sousa, who began conducting orchestras at the age of sixteen. He was for a time conductor of the United States Marine Band. He founded his own band in 1892. He also has established quite a wide reputation as a composer, especially along the lines of military music.

While there are no government supported music schools in the United States musical education holds a high place here. All the public schools have music in their curriculum, and excellent private music schools are found throughout the country. Within recent years many fine music schools have also been established in connection with the state universities.

One of the first American musicians to be interested in musical education was Dr. Eben Tourjée. He did much to systematize the teaching of music and founded the New England Conservatory in 1870. Mr. Stephen Emery is a well-known instructor of harmony in this conservatory. Among its other celebrated teachers are Alfred B. Turner and Lyman W. Wheeler. Another New England music school was the Boston Conservatory of Music founded by Julius Eichberg. It is principally known as a violin school.

Theodore Thomas was one of the chief musical educators in the West. Another well-known teacher in Chicago is Mr. Emil Liebling. It is difficult to classify Mr. Liebling, for he is equally at home as lecturer, writer, teacher or concert performer. He has had excellent success as teacher, and has a large number of distinguished pupils to his credit. He has written numerous excellent compositions for the piano, and has edited a very valuable book of scales for the piano.

Among the other teachers worthy of mention are William L. Tomlins, Frank Damrosch, Hugh Archibald Clarke, John K. Paine, Albert A. Stanley, Horatio W. Parker, Karl Klauser, A. J. Goodrich, Percy Goetschius, Thomas Tapper, and others.

THE MUSIC TRADES

Whatever may be the state of musical culture in America, the standard of musical taste, or the value of American composition, there can be no question as to the importance of American achievement in the line of instrument making. The best of American instruments, in the matter of the piano for instance, serve as ideals for the followers of Cristofori's art in every country of the globe. And the principal improvements, which have placed the piano of today beyond comparison with its progenitors of half a century ago, have emanated from the brain of our own instrument makers. It sometimes is suggested that American initiative in this line is the initiative of the transplanted foreigner. This was well answered a few years ago, at a piano-makers' dinner in Boston, by Edward Everett Hale:

" What moral can we find in the circumstance by which Jonas Chickering's attention was turned from being a machinist in a cotton factory to enter upon the taking up of this industry in America? Why is it that a machinist in New Ipswich, or in New Hampshire, turns to making pianos? Does a blacksmith in Bulgaria turn to making pianos? Is there anywhere in Nijni-Novgorod or in Archangel, or in the center of Russia, where such a change of conditions is brought about? Is there any country in this world where a man turns about, as you see everywhere in this country, from the crude forms of manufacture into the making of pianos, or of watches, or of locomotive engines, or from every trace or indication of the profession he started in, excepting America? No. It comes in America because America is America, and because the constitution of America is what it is."

American inventiveness, so strikingly illustrated in the field of piano construction, of recent years has had full sway in the evolution of the phonograph for the reproduction and preservation of music, and the playing attachments for organ and piano, all of which were but faintly suggested many years before by the simple music box, which undoubtedly is the oldest of the self-playing musical instruments. The last word, however, has come from England in the Mills automatic violin player, a successful device which is to the violin what the pianola is to the piano.

Statistics speak most eloquently of the growth of the musical instrument industry in the United States. The census of 1860 was the first to treat the matter separately, and at this time there were reported to be two hundred and twenty-three establishments devoted to the manufacture of musical instruments and an invested capital of $4,431,900. The last census bulletin gives six hundred and twenty-five such concerns, and an invested capital of $72,225,379. The ratio of the improvement is commensurate, even the once despised street piano having come to be, except to the over-æsthetic, a source of joy.

A peculiar phase of the musical instrument industry lies in the frequency with which the founder of a house passes the business on to his sons, and they in turn to theirs. Undoubtedly the high degree of perfection attained is due to these commercial heirships and jealously guarded prestige.

America may indeed find just cause for self-complacency in her piano industry. In the eighty-five years since its actual beginning with Jonas Chickering it has had a phenomenal growth, and even more gratifying is the fact that the American instrument can take its place beside anything made in the world. The early perfection attained is more remarkable when we consider the skill, taste, and exquisite nicety which are positive requisites. Piano-making indeed is one of the pursuits which defy the labor-saving machine, and as the Scientific American observed not long ago, "the making of high-grade pianos is a field where the skilled artisan reigns supreme, and is likely to remain so to the end of time."

America shares with Germany the distinction of being most largely engaged in the piano-making business. Statistical reports of the year 1905 recorded two hundred and forty-nine piano manufactories in the United States, and an invested capital of $49,649,135. New York State leads with $15,504,312. New York City is the principal center in the United States for the manufacture of pianos, 82,532 uprights and nearly all the grands for the entire State being manufactured in that city in the representative year 1905. The State of New York reported the manufacture of 96,985 uprights, or more than one-third of the entire number reported for the United States. Illinois is a close second to New York with a capital amounting to $14,908,172, and Massachusetts follows next with $5,749,266. The annual output is over 250,000 per year, or as Edward Everett Hale estimated in his speech at the eightieth anniversary celebration of the founding of the house of Chickering, something like one new piano to every thirty-five houses in the country. The important patents taken out for the improvement of the piano from 1796 to 1896 do not fall far short of five hundred. The piano now is the most extensively used of all musical instruments, and its widespread use has very nearly killed the trade in cabinet and reed organs.

The rise and growth of the piano industry in the new world is an interesting chronicle. The history of the American piano (that is, of its direct antecedents) dates, as far as our knowledge goes, from the year 1743, for it was then that Gustavus Hesselius manufactured spinets in Philadelphia. In 1759 it was recorded that a man named Tremaine made a harpsichord of "a most agreeable and melodious volume and character," and also that a company of London actors made use of it at a benefit performance in the old John Street Theatre in New York.

It is generally believed that the first bona fide piano made in this country was one constructed the year of the beginning of the Revolution by John Behrent (sometimes called Belmont) in Philadelphia, which at that time was the principal seat of trade as well as the social and artistic center of the colonies. He announced it as "an extraordinary instrument of the name of pianoforte of mahogany in the manner of a harpsichord, with hammers and several changes." There were other claimants to fame about that time. In 1785 James Juliann of the same city appears to have produced "the great American piano of his own invention," and in the same year in New York, George Ulshoefer, a German, exhibited a piano of his own make in the coffee room of the City tavern, which he styled "George Ulshoefer's patent high-strung pianoforte." In the Quaker City Charles Albrecht made instruments before 1789, and the fame of their beautiful inlaid cases is not yet dead.

The New York Independent Gazette for May 23, 1786, announces the arrival of Charles Taws, an Englishman, "who builds and repairs finger and barrel organs. He also repairs and tunes pianofortes, harpsichords and guitars." Two years later Taws moved to Philadelphia and engaged in the trade in which two of his sons succeeded him. In 1729 John Isaac Hawkins, another Britisher, came to Philadelphia, where he invented the cottage piano which he called a "portable grand." This versatile fellow, according to one contemporary, was a civil engineer, poet, preacher, phrenologist and inventor of ever pointed pencils. In the year 1800 Thomas Jefferson, writing to his daughter from Philadelphia, remarks, "A very ingenious, modest and poor young man in Philadelphia has invented one of the prettiest improvements in the pianoforte that I have ever seen and it has tempted me to engage one for Monticello. His strings are perpendicular, and he contrives within that height to give his strings the same length as in a grand piano, and fixes three unisons to the same screw. It scarcely gets out of tune at all, and then, for the most part the three unisons are tuned at once."

The German Advertiser in 1790 speaks with satisfaction of the high state of perfection to which instrument making had attained in Philadelphia. The home-made article in two respects was preferable to the imported, for the American instruments were screwed together instead of glued, and London-seasoned wood was not adapted to the dry changeable climate of this country.

The art of clever advertising seems to have kept pace with the industry as the following notice from the first number of Louden's Register, issued Feb. 12, 1792, will show: "Messrs. Dodds and Claus, musical instrument manufactory, 66 Queen St., announces that the forte-piano is become so exceedingly fashionable in Europe that few polite families are without it. . . . The improvements which Messrs. Dodds and Claus have made in the forte-pianos have rendered it much more acceptable than those imported."

However, most of the pianos used in the new republic still were sent over by European firms, by the Broadwoods (the oldest firm of keyboard instrument makers in existence), by the Clementis, by the Longmans and others. The founding of the fortunes of the house of Astor by John Jacob Astor, the first, is said partly to have been achieved by the importation of pianos. In 1791 there were twenty-seven pianos in Boston, and all of these had been made in London.

It is quite possible that the first practical piano constructed in this country was made some time prior to 1803 by Benjamin Crehore, who lived in Milton, near Boston. Crehore made other musical instruments as well, such as violins, cellos, guitars, drums and flutes. There is a story that to sell his pianos, of which he made but ten or a dozen a year, Crehore put on them the imprint of London and Paris, which goes to show that human nature has suffered no serious change in the century just past. Morris Steinert speaks of Crehore's little shop as the training school of such men as John Osborne and the brothers Lewis and Alpheus Babcock, who served their apprenticeship there. It was during Crehore's activities that the first upright pianos were made, but a serious weakness was their inability to stay in tune. Crehore failed after a few years, and when his apprentices, the previously mentioned Babcock brothers, and Thomas Appleton, a pipe organ manufacturer went into business together, he became a workman in their shop. This firm, which received an addition in the Hoyts brothers, importers of musical instruments, dissolved during the panic of 1819. The Bents, William and Adam, also were prominent musical instrument makers in Boston in the early years of the Nineteenth Century. A press notice of 1800 speaks of William Bent as an "expert mechanic" whose new grand piano attracted much attention. Mallet & Shaw was another of the early firms.

The virtual founder of the piano industry in the United States — virtual because his instruments really were practical — was Jonas Chickering, of whom Hon. Robt. C. Winthrop proposed as a suitable epitaph: "He was a grand, square and upright man." Many of the prominent American piano firms have been founded by emigrants, a fact which also is true of France, the great French makers, Erard, Pleyel and Pape all having been foreigners. Chickering, however, was a thorough American. He was born in 1798 in New Ipswich, N. H., his father being a farmer and the village blacksmith. In his seventeenth year Jonas was apprenticed to a cabinet-maker. New Ipswich at that time possessed but one piano, an instrument made in London by Christopher Graner. Tradition has it that the piano once had belonged to Princess Amelia, daughter of George III. Whatever may have been its history, fate lurked among its strings and hammers. Some injury had befallen the piano so that it was not used and when the youthful Jonas, who had an innate understanding of mechanism, undertook its restoration, he discovered his vocation.

In 1818, when twenty years of age, Jonas Chickering went to Boston. Here he was apprenticed to John Osborne, one of the foremost piano merchants between the years 1815-1835, who in turn had been an apprentice of Crehore's. In 1820 a Scotchman named James Stewart entered into partnership with Osborne. Stewart was a piano-maker of ability, with a brain fertile for improvements, and he probably was the first manufacturer to export pianos out of the United States. While in Baltimore, previous to his Boston sojourn, he had shipped numerous instruments to Havana for the West Indian trade. After a short time Osborne and Stewart disagreed, and in 1823 the former entered into a partnership with Jonas Chickering, their shop being on Tremont Street. It is from this year that the founding of the great Chickering industry is dated. In two years Stewart returned to Europe, and in 1829 Captain John Mackay, the former partner of Alpheus Babcock, became Chickering's partner. Some of Jonas Chickering's greatest contemporaries were Nunns and Clark of New York, Boardman and Gray of Albany, and the Louds of Philadelphia. The Chickering factories, main office and warerooms still are located in Boston. Since the firm's formation over 100,000 Chickering pianos have been constructed, and the capacity of the factories is 5000 instruments per year. The patented improvements of the house are many and valuable and cover many points in piano construction. Let it suffice to say here that to the Chickerings is due, besides the introduction of the iron frame into both square and grand pianos, the invention of the circular scale for square pianos, the adoption of agraffes and the development and improvement of the action. They are one of the largest makers of artistic grand pianos in the world. Their use of the iron frame was particularly valuable, the variable American climate making the need of some such thing imperative. For the successful introduction of the iron frame Jonas Chickering has been called " the father of the piano as we know it today." After the death of Jonas Chickering in 1853 the business was continued by his three sons, Thomas E., C. Frank and George H. Chickering, all of whom were practical piano workers. Mr. C. Frank Chickering was one of the most accomplished scale draughtsmen of his time.

The fame and prestige of the Chickering piano is by no means confined to our own country. One hundred and twenty-nine first medals and awards have been acquired by these pianos, and in 1867, when the Chickering piano was shown at the first Paris exhibition, Mr. C. Frank Chickering was decorated with the cross of the Legion of Honor. Among the enthusiastic endorsers have been Liszt, Saint-Saëns, Gottschalk, Wehle, Gounod, Thalberg, De Pachmann, Carreño, Georg Henschel, von Bülow and an army of others.

Jonas Chickering was one of the founders of the Handel and Haydn Society of Boston and at one time was its president. For twenty-five years at least Chickering Hall in New York was the nucleus of the musical life of that city. The fourth Chickering Hall of the name was opened in Boston, Feb. 9, 1901. In 1893 the house of Chickering brilliantly celebrated its eightieth anniversary.

After Boston, Baltimore was the next to come into prominence as a piano manufacturing city. Its patronage came largely from the then prosperous Southern States, counterbalancing the eastern trade of the Chickerings. Notable among the Baltimore contingent was Joseph Hiskey, Conrad Meyer's master, who constructed pianos on the Vienna principle, which in substance consists in having the tuning pins above the keyboard, a sounding board extending over the whole instrument, and an iron plate, which holds the hitch-pin for the strings. Another feature of Hiskey's pianos was the application of four or five pedals to his square piano to produce the orchestral effect which at that time was a fad in Europe. Henry Gaehle was prominent among the Baltimore makers, and in 1841 he formed a partnership with William Knabe, who was born in Kreutzburg, Saxe Weimar, in 1797.

In course of time Knabe bought out Gaehle's interests. In this case, as in those of other great firms, the grandsons continue the trade of the grandfather.

Strange to say, New York, where now by far the greatest number of musical instruments are manufactured, at first was by no means at the front in the matter of piano manufacturing. But in 1850 a family of piano-makers named Steinway emigrated from Germany and settled in the city. Few men have had a history as remarkable as Henry Engelhard Steinway, founder of the company. Born on Feb. 15, 1797, in Wolfshagen, Germany, a small forest hamlet in the Duchy of Brunswick, Germany, the youngest of a family of twelve children, at the age of fifteen he was the sole survivor. The causes of this wholesale taking off were the Franco-Prussian wars of 1806 and 1812, and a bolt of lightning which had killed six persons, including young Steinway's father and three older brothers. The youth shouldered a musket at the call of the Duke of Brunswick and marched against Napoleon. He left the army at the age of twenty-one, and after his marriage in 1825 he settled as a cabinet-maker in the Harz Mountains. Soon he began to look longingly toward America as the land of opportunity. It was not, however, until about twenty-five years later, at the time of the political troubles of 1848, that the resolution became fixed, and in 1850 he started for America with his wife, three sons and three daughters. The eldest son Theodore C. F. Steinway, a great inventive genius, stayed behind, carrying on the piano business in Brunswick. Henry Steinway and the sons who were old enough worked at first as journeymen in New York piano factories, the father meantime intently studying business conditions. Three years later, in 1853, the year that Jonas Chickering died, Henry Steinway started modestly in business for himself. He was greatly aided to the successful career which awaited him by his sons, one of whom, Henry S., Jr., being possessed of remarkable originality. In 1855 the Steinways exhibited a square piano in which the American iron frame principle of a single iron casting was combined with a cross or overstrung scale, forming the foundation of the so-called Steinway system. Its novel feature made it not only record breaking but epoch-making. Both Charles and Henry Steinway died in 1866 and Theodore, the eldest son, disposed of his business in Germany, and became a partner in the New York firm. Henry Steinway, the father, died in 1871.

Eight men, members of the third and fourth generations of the house of Henry Steinway today are engaged in the industry he formed. A rule of the family is that every male member must learn his trade in the factories, expecting no shorter hours and no more favors than the other workers. Thus the members of the firm have intimate knowledge of the science of piano-building.

In addition to this splendid American establishment the Steinways also have a branch manufactory in Hamburg and a distributing house in London. In truth, the firm enjoys the distinction of being the leading firm of artistic piano-makers in the world, its products being in high favor with royalty and the greatest of the artists.

The firm of Mason & Hamlin was incorporated in 1854 for the purpose of manufacturing musical instruments and first became widely known for its cabinet organs. As times changed; the development of the Mason and Hamlin pianoforte (the house has clung to the old word with characteristic exactitude) was left to the younger generation and in this line has been achieved a success even greater than that of the Mason and Hamlin organs.

One of the foremost American piano firms is the Weber Company of New York. The founder of the house was Albert Weber, a Bavarian, who came to this country in 1845 at the age of sixteen. He learned piano-making in New York, working at his trade by day and giving music lessons at night. He entered business for himself in 1852, and the high standard set for his instruments, combined with profound business sagacity, soon brought to him not only prosperity but fame, national and European. Mr. Weber died at the comparatively early age of fifty, leaving his business interests in the hands of his son, Albert Weber, Jr. Albert Weber, Sr., was the originator of the term "baby grand," to characterize that popular bijou instrument.

The Blazius is manufactured at Woodbury, New Jersey, and marketed at Philadelphia. The product of this firm also includes the "Albrecht & Co." and the "Regent" pianos.

The Cable Company, Chicago, was established in 1880 and is the manufacturer of Conover Pianos, Cable Pianos, Kingsbury Pianos, Wellington Pianos and Chicago Cottage Organs. This company has a capital of $2,000,000.

The A. B. Chase Piano Company, New York and Norwalk, Ohio, was established in 1875. It is one of the few western firms to gain recognition in the eastern trade.

The Conover Piano is manufactured by the Cable Company of Chicago; first made in 1883 by J. Frank Conover, a piano expert of international distinction.

The Crown Piano is a well-known instrument manufactured by Geo. P. Bent of Chicago.

Also prominent among American pianos are the following:

Decker & Son, New York, established 1856, manufacturers of pianos of a superior quality. The late Myron A. Decker was one of America's oldest and most distinguished piano manufacturers. His son Frank C. Decker who succeeded him is an expert.

Fischer Piano, New York, made by the distinguished old house of J. and C. Fischer, which has been in existence since 1840. This house succeeded R. and W. Nunns, piano-makers, established in 1820. The elder Fischer came to America in 1839, having learned his trade in Italy. The career of this firm dates almost to the beginning of the American piano industry.

The Gabler Piano, New York. House established in 1854 by Ernest Gabler. At his death in 1883 his brother Emil Gabler succeeded to the management and later his nephew Emil Ernest Gabler, its present proprietor.

Haines Bros., Rochester, New York, one of the oldest established pianos in the market. The business now is controlled by the Foster Armstrong Company and is a component part of that corporation and of the " Big Four," one of the largest consolidations of capital and interests in the music trade.

Hallet & Davis, Boston, established in 1839. This instrument is widely known in trade. E. N. Kimball, Jr., C. E. Conway, secretary.

Hazelton Brothers, New York, established in 1849 by Henry and Frederick Hazelton. The firm now is controlled by Mr. Samuel Hazleton, a nephew of the founder, and his son, Mr. Halsey Hazelton.

Krakauer Bros., New York, established 1878. This old and reliable house was founded by Simon Krakauer, who came to America in 1853, and his son David. Messrs. Julius and Daniel Krakauer are the two surviving members of the original firm. All the members of the family are practical piano-makers and good musicians.

The Kimball Piano, Chicago, established in 1859; manufactured by the W. W. Kimball Company of great commercial strength, also manufacturers of reed and pipe organs and automatic attachments.

Kranich & Bach, New York, established in 1864. Their factories are among the most extensive in the country. Their chief improvements are the special spring used in the action, a newly patented grand action, and a patent fall board. This firm does a very large trade in small grand pianos.

Mehlin & Son, New York, founded by Paul C. Mehlin, a noted inventor and acoustic expert. The company is of high standing financially and commercially.

In the front ranks of American piano industries is the Henry F. Miller & Sons Piano Company, of Boston. This house was established in 1863. Among the art products of national manufacture this company represents the highest attainments.

The Sohmer, manufactured at Astoria, Long Island, warerooms and offices in New York, established in 1872. Hugo Sohmer, Joseph Kuder and George Reichmann, proprietors.

The Steck Piano, New York, established 1857. Founded by George Steck, one of the most noted piano experts of America.

The Stieff Piano, Baltimore, Maryland, established 1842. Chas. M. Stieff is the head of this conservative and reliable house.

Strich & Zeidler, New York, established in 1889. Proprietors, William Strich and Paul M. Zeidler.

Vose & Sons, Boston, founded by Mr. Hillard M. Vose in 1851. A piano enjoying the respect of musicians.

In the year 1908 Chickering & Sons, William Knabe & Co., and the Foster-Armstrong Company, joined in a corporation with stock valued at twelve million dollars, to be known as the American Piano Company. The incorporators were Ernst J. Knabe, Jr., president of William Knabe & Co., Baltimore; Charles H. W. Foster, president of Chickering & Sons of Boston; and George G. Foster, president of Foster, Armstrong Company, of Rochester, N. Y. The firm controls the manufacture and sale of these pianos: The Chickering, established 1823; the Knabe, established 1837; the Haines Brothers, established 1851; the Marshall & Mendell, established 1853; The Foster & Co., established 1892; the Armstrong, established 1893; the Brewster, established 1895, and J. B. Cook & Co., established 1900. The present output of these companies is about eighteen thousand pianos a year. The new company is one of the largest industries of its kind in the world.

It has been said previously that the best American piano can take its place beside any piano in the world, but more than this is true, for the best American piano has no equal, being almost perfect tonally. But unfortunately this cannot be said of the average American piano, which is not on a par with the average English, French or German instrument.

One of the greatest menaces to the American standard and a matter against which conscientious dealers are up in arms is the "stencil piano."

Many dealers in musical instruments engage with manufacturers of low-grade pianos for the wholesale purchase of their instruments under the agreement they may place upon the name-plate any name they may choose or invent, the true appellation being notorious for inferiority. When it is known that in a trade booklet exposing these "stencil" pianos over two hundred and fifty such brands are mentioned, some idea may be gained of the number of people hoodwinked into buying cheaply made instruments, which are dear at any price.

It is well known that organ music long was frowned upon by our Puritan forbears as a device of unholy origin, and when one of the first organs which appeared on American soil in 1713 was presented by Thomas Brattle to Queen's Chapel, Boston, there must have been much doubt and shaking of heads, for it remained seven months unpacked on the church porch before it was finally agreed to install it inside the place of worship.

The question of the construction of the first American organ already has been discussed under the heading, "Instrumental Music, Bands and Orchestras" of this volume and it is unnecessary again to review the subject, for the matter herein treated is confined to the organ trade. Organs are of two distinct types, the reed organ or melodeon, and the pipe organ. The former is of American origin. It is small and inexpensive, and is found in thousands of simple homes where pianos would be quite outside their owner's means. It was in 1854 that Henry Mason, youngest son of Dr. Lowell Mason, a pioneer of musical education in America, and Emmons Hamlin, a gifted mechanic, joined forces for the purpose of manufacturing musical instruments, and at once started to improve the melodeon as it then existed. They developed the instrument step by step until in 1861 they introduced practically a new instrument for which they coined and copyrighted the name "Cabinet Organ." These organs were distinctly in advance of anything at all akin to them then known, for it was but a few years before their introduction that Mr. Hamlin had discovered and perfected a feature of unique and distinct importance, namely that of voicing reeds. Previous to this discovery there had been prevalent a cry against all keyboard instruments, to the effect that they were monotonous in tone, but Hamlin's discovery was the means of bringing to the cabinet organ a most welcome tonal color. A large part of the demand for reed organs comes from the Southern States, where they still are extremely popular with the music-loving colored people. The Mason and Hamlin trade in reed organs is, with possibly one exception, the greatest in the country. In addition to their domestic sales, they do a large business abroad.

The words "Estey" and "Brattleboro" for many years have been synonymous. When either is mentioned, the other immediately is brought to mind. This comes about, of course, from the fact that the most important industry in Brattleboro is represented by this company, and also from the fact that Estey Organs are in use all over the civilized world, and each one bears, not only the name of the builder, but the address, Brattleboro.

The beginning of the Estey Organ industry dates back to 1846, and thus it has been in continuous activity for over sixty years. These have been years of development as constant as the manufacturing itself. After a score of years, or so, the Estey Cottage Organ was evolved, and the growth for the next two or three decades was phenomenal. These were the years just succeeding the Civil War. The Estey Organ Company by its many marked improvements and business enterprise has come to take high rank in its particular field. For over thirty years these organs have been exported in increasing numbers, and today there are very successful agencies not only all over Europe, in South America and in Asia, but also in Australia where there is a very great demand. Keeping pace with the growth of the trade, the builders have introduced continuous inprovements and advances, with the endeavor constantly to keep their product in the front rank. The third generation of Esteys now is in charge of the business, and is confidently expecting the next generation to take its place in due course of time.

Other notable makers are the Story and Clark Company of Grand Haven, Michigan, direct successors of Story & Camp, established in 1867, and the Farrand Company of Detroit, Michigan, established in 1884. The latter, in addition to its wide representation in this country, has a large foreign trade.

According to the census of 1905 there were at the time of its taking ninety-four establishments for the making of organs in the United States, with a capital of $7,203,878. In that year 113,065 reed organs were made to the value of $4,162,319 and nine hundred and one pipe organs to the value of $1,989,979.

The reed organ trade is centralized in Illinois, one might rather say in Chicago. In 1905, 57,219 reed organs were made in Illinois as against the same number in all the other states combined. The reed organ industry also exists on a large scale in Michigan, Indiana and Ohio, making the Middle West the principal seat of production. In the matter of pipe organs one does not find any such centralization, although more high-grade pipe organs probably are manufactured in Boston than anywhere else. Ohio and Illinois also contribute largely.

There seems to be an idea prevalent among manufacturers and dealers that the pipe organ is not profitable. A gentleman prominently identified with the firm of Lyon & Healy, Chicago, the largest supply house in the United States, stated: "We gave up our pipe organ business for the simple reason that it did not pay — the experience of many other builders. Then, too, when an organ has been installed there is continually something to be done. A firm has to act as godfather to it for the rest of its life."

The American pipe organ today too frequently is handicapped by the faulty construction, from an acoustic standpoint, of the buildings in which it is placed. The pipe organ industry differs from the trade in other musical instruments from the fact that, with the exception of some few small instruments, pipe organs are not made up in advance and exhibited in warerooms, but are built to order and adapted to the buildings for which they are intended. A good many organ plants are very small indeed, turning out only two or three, sometimes, in truth, but one organ a year.

One of the latest improvements to be effected in the greatest, if the least profitable of the instruments, is the electric action, which is operated either by a storage battery or by a small generator connected with the bellows motive power.

A large number of the world's finest organs are located in the United States. These, reckoned as to size by the number of their stops are as follows: The St. Louis Exposition Organ (the largest ever made), one hundred and forty stops; The Cathedral of Garden City, Long Island, one hundred and fifteen stops; The Auditorium, Chicago, one hundred and nine stops; St. Bartholomew's Church, New York City, ninety-eight stops; The Old Boston Music Hall, eighty-nine stops; Cincinnati Music Hall, eighty stops; Newberry organ, Woolsey Hall, Yale College, seventy-eight stops; Trinity Church, Denver, Colorado, sixty-seven stops; Plymouth Church, Brooklyn, sixty-four stops; Church of the Holy Family, Chicago, sixty-four stops; Ann Arbor, Michigan (from the Chicago Exposition) sixty-three stops; Grace Church, Chicago, sixty-three stops; Carnegie Hall, Pittsburg, sixty-two stops; Salt Lake City Tabernacle, sixty stops; Hebrew Temple, Washington, D. C., fifty-seven stops; Chicago Orchestra Hall, fifty-six stops; Boston Symphony Hall, fifty-six stops.

The oldest and perhaps the most prominent of the pipe organ builders in the United States is the Hook and Hastings Company. Its business from the start — over eighty years ago — has comprised the building of pipe organs and nothing else. The history of the house extends over a period beginning in the year 1827, when Mr. Elias Hook first engaged in the building of organs in Salem, Mass., with his brother George. Soon after, the two brothers established themselves in Boston and as E. & G. G. Hook earned a high reputation by means of their excellent work. In 1885 Mr. Francis H. Hastings became engaged with them and ten years later was admitted as a partner. Later the name of the firm was changed to E. & G. G. Hook and Hastings. In 1880 after the death of Mr. George G. Hook it was changed to Hook & Hastings. The next year Mr. Elias Hook died. In 1893 the company was incorporated under the laws of Massachusetts under the name and style of Hook and Hastings Company. This company has placed nearly twenty-two hundred instruments throughout the various sections of the country. Among the recent large organs built by it is the magnificent one for the First Church of Christ, Scientist, of Boston, Mass.

Brief mention of other firms prominent in the field would include some six or eight others. James Cole of Boston is a successful pipe organ builder. The Emmons Howard Company is a notable organ concern situated at Westfield, Mass. Its trade extends from Maine to South Dakota.

The Hutchings-Votey Organ Company, located at Cambridge, Mass., are successors to George S. Hutchings, an old established Boston builder of organs. The business of the late Hilbourne L. Roosevelt, a pipe organ builder of many valuable innovations, was merged with the Hutchings-Votey Company. Mr. Roosevelt built the organs in the Garden City Cathedral and the Chicago Auditorium.

The J. H. and C. S. Odell & Co., of New York City is an old firm, with an enviable reputation for its successful pipe organ building. The W. W. Kimball Company is one ranking high in the pipe organ field, as well as in that of pianos, reed organs, and automatic attachments. In the

Western States especially its instruments have been favorably received. Some of the finest examples of the organ builders' art to be found in the country are to its credit — William Wallace Kimball was the founder of the piano and organ industry of Chicago. His career as a wholesale dealer in pianos and organs began in 1864.

Also noteworthy in this branch of the music trade are the Hinners Organ Company, of Pekin, Illinois, a conservative and successful firm incorporated in 1902; George Kilgen & Son, established in New York in 1851 and removing to St. Louis in 1873, whose instruments are considered strictly high grade; the Estey Organ Company of Brattleboro, Vt., long famous for its reed organs, which began the manufacture of pipe organs in 1901; and the Austin Organ Company of Hartford, Conn. John T. Austin, who now is president of this company, originally went to work for the Farrand & Votey Company, of Detroit Mich., when it started business there and stayed with it until it bought out the Roosevelt Company of New York, at which time he invented and patented the universal air chest, and went with the Clough & Warren Company, which manufactured reed organs. This company built the first organ of the universal wind pressure type. The Clough & Warren Company continued building organs for some years under royalty. After its factory in Detroit was burned Mr. Austin started a company in Hartford, Conn., under the name of "Austin Organ Company." This business was steadily increased until in 1907 it reached nearly a quarter of a million dollars.

One of the oldest and most distinguished of the pipe organ houses is that of Henry Pilcher's Sons, which was established early in the Nineteenth Century in Louisville, Ky. Their instruments were found in many leading churches throughout the land. Henry Pilcher, the founder, began his organ building career in England in 1820 and established a business in this country in 1832. Henry Pilcher, the second, succeeded his father in 1856 and four grandsons of the first Henry Pilcher in turn have succeeded to its management.

The making of violins is not an important part of the musical instrument industry of America, at least in the matter of magnitude. For a good many years, in fact, there were no violin-makers of any distinction in America although they long have flourished in Europe. General attention was centered upon the piano, and other instrumental music was greatly neglected. An interest in the violin was aroused by the tours of Ole Bull, Vieuxtemps, and others. Now there are indeed a few violin factories turning out instruments which sell as high as fifty dollars each, but the better grades still are entirely hand-made, and as in the past, the makers are still striving to discover the delicate, elusive secrets of Stradivarius, Amati and Guarnerius.

Notwithstanding the splendid attainments in piano-making, centuries ago a higher perfection was attained by the violin, against which time makes warfare much less successfully. "A single workman, a cabinet-maker's bench, a few sharp tools, and glue pot over a fire" — thus some one has described the average violin-maker's establishment. Many days, or more truly weeks, are devoted to the making of a single instrument. It is curious to find the methods of violin making practically unchanged from the Sixteenth Century, in an age when the tendency is to reduce everything to a scientific basis. The census of 1900 reports only one thousand five hundred and three violins made that year, one-third of these in the State of New York.

The most important name connected with American violin making is that of Gemunder. They were two brothers, August and George, born in Ingelfingen, Württemberg, Germany, the former in 1814 and the latter in 1816. August came to the United States in 1846. He resided in Springfield, Massachusetts, for several years, removing to New York in 1865, where he became permanently established. It had been August Gemunder's specialty to copy violins of the famous Italian makers, but two years before he came to America a German musician suggested his making a violin according to his own ideas. The result was so admirable that he afterward used the instrument for a model. Many of the celebrated violinists have used Gemunder's violins, which resemble the old Italian models in tone and surpass them in power.

The younger brother, George, was a pupil of Baptiste Vuillaume of Paris. He came to the United States a year later than did his brother, it is said upon the advice of Ole Bull. He first located in Boston, the violins made during his residence there obtaining medals at the World's Fair in London in 1851. In 1852 he went on to New York. George Gemunder was especially successful in the model, finish and varnishing of his instruments. One of his most valuable discoveries was how to acquire results by means of natural woods, whereas Vuillaume and other makers of violins had thought it necessary to treat the wood chemically, destroying the resonance and in time rendering the instrument worthless. Gemunder has done much toward proving Oliver Wendell Holmes wrong in his genial reflection: "Certain things are good for nothing till they have been kept a long while, and some are good for nothing till they have been kept and used — of those which must be kept long and used I will name violins — the sweet old Amatis, the divine Stradivarius." For Gemunder's violins often are mistaken for Cremonas. A violin called the "Kaiser" was sent to the Vienna Exposition and the judges pronounced it an old Italian violin, declaring that it was impossible to secure its mellow tones from anything but an ancient instrument.

Knute Reindahl of Chicago is a successful maker of artistic violins, violas and violoncellos. He constructs his instruments from very old wood obtained from the ancient cities of Norway which he believes to be the only place in the world where woods of the requisite age and proper seasoning can be obtained. Among the violinists who endorse Reindahl's violins are Franz von Vecsey, Hugo Heermann, Sauret, Arthur Hartmann, Rosenbecker, Kubelik, Kreisler, and others.

Another fine maker of violins was J. C. Hendershot of Cleveland, Ohio. His instruments have been used by some of the best of the profession, among them Remenyi. The Hendershot collection of violins is very notable.

The census of 1900 reported the manufacture in the United States of 78,389 mandolins and mandolas, 78,494 guitars and 18,521 banjos. Dealers at the present time say that the trade in small instruments of this class has been virtually killed by the automatic musical instruments.

Wind instruments no longer are imported from Germany in wholesale fashion as they were a few decades ago. Now they are made equally well here, although in the matter of those made almost wholly by hand, the American manufacturer is at a disadvantage because of the cheaper labor in Germany. The value of the brass band instruments made in 1903 amounted to more than $300,000. In fact, the wonderful growth in popularity of the American-made band instruments has been a source of frequent comment not only in this country but throughout Europe. This in no small measure is due to the labors of Mr. Charles G. Conn of Elkhart, Indiana. Mr. Conn was born in Manchester, New York, in 1844, and remained there until 1850, when his parents came to Elkhart. At the beginning of his business career Mr. Conn recognized the crudities and imperfections incident to the manufacture of band instruments and their lack of uniform excellence. He noted that while one instrument might be entirely satisfactory another of a similar model would be absolutely imperfect in tonal results. This largely was due to the fact that the instruments were made by hand, and there were no means of securing uniformity. After many experimental years, Mr. Conn created a number of new manufacturing devices which made it possible for him to turn out instruments of uniform excellence. In addition to the brass band instruments, Mr. Conn is engaged in the manufacture of clarinets, flutes, saxophones, and other instruments of the orchestral family. The great factory at Elkhart, Indiana, has recently been enlarged, giving floor space as great as any half-dozen plants in Europe devoted to the manufacture of brass band instruments.

There are few matters which present as many different phases, beneficent and otherwise, as the automatic music reproductions, or upon which so many different opinions exist as to their ultimate effect upon the art of music. The greatest menace is the possibility that in providing ready-made music, general musical culture may come to suffer. Much of the drudgery of practise is palliated for the young by the hope of some day being able to fittingly interpret favorite scores. When these lie captive in scrolls on the top of the piano, ready upon attachment brilliantly to execute themselves, one strong incentive to application is absent, and the bleakness of scales and finger exercises is likely to become almost unbearable. Then, too, the ubiquitous parent, whose pride and joy for many generations have lain in the musical achievements of his offsprings, will not be so philosophical perhaps about the expenditure of money for music lessons, and the irksomeness of preliminary training when the thing can be done at once and perhaps much better by mechanical means. While this may save much misery from totally unmusical children and their associates, doubtless in this very fashion plenty of real talent has been discovered. It is not impossible that this phase of the matter is serious.

In the meantime, nevertheless, the phonograph, the self-playing piano and their kind are effecting a very evident elevation of the general taste in music. It has been said that "the people we do not like are the people we do not know." This maxim could even be applied more truly to good music. We love the music with which we are familiar; a feeling of possession, of self-satisfaction comes over us when the strains of something we can hum, or call by name assails our ears. The so-called mechanical music has brought the better class of compositions to popular attention. The people are surprised to discover that although familiarity may breed contempt for ragtime and other forms of light music, repeated hearings reveal new beauties in the finer things.

The increased demand for grand opera in part is directly traceable to the popularization of many operatic numbers by the talking machine. It places within the reach of provincial dwellers — those living on farms and in villages — the music of the finest operas, interpreted by the greatest singers. With the present high state of perfection to which the talking machine has been brought the tonal quality and the interpretation are excellently reproduced. People who are remotely situated may now hear an entire opera in their homes, for one of the latest achievements of the Victor Company has been to place the entire text and music of an opera upon the disks. In the preparation of the disks of "Pagliacci" (which was done at Milan) the composer, Leoncavallo, conducted the greater part, while the services of some of the best Italian singers and the chorus and orchestra of La Scala Theatre were employed. It is not too much to hope that within a few years there will not exist the thousands of people who not only have never heard an opera but who are quite unfamiliar with operatic music. The average American learns with astonishment that the Italian peasant often is familiar with operatic airs; but probably it will not be many years before the same fact will be true of his own countrymen.

The talking machine virtually has made the reputation of many vocalists and instrumentalists. But this is not the musician's only reason for gratitude. Music no longer may be wept over as the most evanescent of the arts. Future generations will hear Melba and Caruso sing and Kubelik and Paderewski play. Already the sentimental aspect of the affair has come to impress the world. Phonetic archives have been established in the last few years for the preservation of the voices of noted people. For instance, the British Museum holds among its treasures three of Melba's records, namely, "Voi che sapete" from Mozart's "Marriage of Figaro;" "Sweet Bird" from Handel's "L'Allegro," and "Caro Nome" from Verdi's "Rigoletto." On Dec. 26, 1907, with most impressive ceremony, there was a burial of records in the vault of the Paris Grand Opera House. Now that this once unthought-of perpetuation of sound lies within our grasp, our regret is keen that this marvelous invention did not antedate the days when Liszt and Chopin played and Lind and Mario sang.

Recently there originated the idea of utilizing the talking machine in the teaching of musical history. With selections typical of all styles and periods of music at hand, the lecturer many times may gain in impressiveness, and possibly a few years will bring the time when the instructor will deem the use of such means quite indispensable. As some one says, "It is coming more and more to be recognized that hearing great music is more useful in developing a great musical appreciation than hearing about it, just as in the study of English literature students are now expected to read selections from the great writers, whereas formerly they only read their lives and a criticism of their more important works."

America may be pardoned for taking a more than casual interest in the talking machine, for it was an American who discovered the principle — the undulation of sound — and made it practicable. The phonograph, which was the first machine to catch the sound waves, record them, and release them at the will of the operator, was invented by Thomas A. Edison in 1877. A part of the national responsibility is removed by the singular circumstance that within that same year, a Frenchman, named Charles Cros, filed with the secretary of the Paris Academy of Sciences a paper describing a very similar plan. Neither of these scientists had knowledge of the other's experimenting. Edison discovered the phonograph in an almost accidental manner while working upon a machine intended to repeat Morse characters. It was improved by him about 1889. "The phonograph (to give the Standard Dictionary explanation) operates by means of a thin diaphragm, set in vibration by the voice or other sound, and having a stylus which records the vibration on a rotating and advancing cylinder coated with wax, upon which latter is cut a faint, wavy line, sufficient to guide the stylus over the course again, agitating the diaphragm so as to reproduce waves of sound similar to those originally recorded."

An immense improvement has been made since the introduction of the first phonographs, which were awkward in size and rather indistinct in the matter of tone production. In 1866 a patent for a machine called the graphophone was issued to Prof. Charles Sumner Taintor of Washington, D. C., and to Rev. Chichester A. Bell, a brother of Alexander Graham Bell, inventor of the telephone, who, by the way, had lent his assistance in the present instance. This was similar in principle to the phonograph. Two years later Emil Berliner of Washington, D. C., received a patent for a sound reproducing machine in which a centrally apertured disk of zinc was used for receiving the record, i. e., the graphophone.

Quite as popular, though not as elaborate in principle, are the piano and organ players, attachments operated by pneumatic pressure or suction or by a combination of pneumatic and electric action. These usually are placed in the interior of the instrument. The air, passing through the holes of the perforated music paper and running over corresponding holes in a tracker board, is communicated by means of small tubes to the playing mechanism. A piano containing such a player may be played as the regular instrument, by hand. The player originally was an exterior attachment, felt plungers being arranged to strike the keys of the ordinary instrument. The organ is even more successfully manipulated by these attachments than the piano. These players have achieved an amazing popularity and may be found in homes all over the world. The increase in the manufacture of pianos is due, to a great extent, to the generous adoption of the player attachment. In the five years between 1900 and 1905 there was an increase of 233.9 per cent. in the manufacture of these attachments.

Probably the most ambitious and amazing of all the new musical inventions is the telharmonium, the result of many years' experimenting on the part of Dr. Thaddeus Cahill, of Holyoke, Mass. This electrical music, as it is explained in one of the musical journals, is music "generated at a central station in the shape of electrical vibrations, and thence distributed by means of wires to a thousand or several thousand hotels, clubs and parlors in each of which music is heard as if the performer were present in the room. The music is produced at the central station entirely by means of electrical apparatus and without the intervention of pipe, reed or string, and it may be heard wherever a wire may be run. The music rendered in hotel or parlor is not the whisper of the telephone, nor the characteristic sound of the graphophone or phonograph, but pure, clear notes and chords, as loud as if an orchestra were on the spot." To return to the phonograph: at the time of the last census there were only fourteen of these manufactories, but their capital reached the relatively immense figure of $8,740,618. The small number of these establishments and their magnitude is explained by the fact that the possession of the patents enables them to retain the right of sole production. One of the greatest items of expense with these companies is the cost of securing records of famous bands and singers. The manufacture of disk and cylinder records is increasing even out of proportion to that of the machines themselves. The sale of the machine is only the beginning of the transaction, for every owner desires to change and enlarge his library of records. The demand for records is much greater than the sheet music publishing industry. The principal centers for the manufacture of talking machines are Camden and Orange, New Jersey; Bridgeport, Connecticut; Toledo, Ohio; and New York City. The Victor Company of Camden, N. J., and The National Phonograph Company of Orange, N. J., are the largest in extent.

The present copyright laws, enacted when automatic music was in its earliest infancy and a factor scarcely worthy of consideration, are believed not to give composers sufficient protection against the "piracy" of these makers of the contemptuously called "canned music," and vigorous measures now are on foot for the amendment of these laws to provide for a royalty on music reproduced by automatic means.

The music publishing business has kept pace with musical activities in other lines. A pioneer in the music publishing industry in the United States was the late Oliver Ditson, who was born in Boston in 1811 and died there in 1888. When thirteen years old he entered the service of Samuel H. Parker, a publisher, and in 1834 became his employer's partner, the firm name being Parker & Ditson. In 1844 Mr. Parker withdrew, leaving Mr. Ditson in sole command, and in 1856 Mr. John C. Haynes, who had begun as an office boy like Mr. Ditson before him, became interested in the business, the firm assuming its present name, Oliver Ditson & Co. In 1867 a branch house under the management of a son, C. H. Ditson, was started in New York City, and a similar concern came into being in 1876 in Philadelphia under the name of J. E. Ditson & Co. The Ditson publishing house, which is one of the largest in the world, has a high standing abroad. Charles Healy Ditson now is president of the Oliver Ditson Company of Boston, succeeding the late John C. Haynes, and is treasurer of the C. H. Ditson Company of New York City.

Another important publishing house is that of G. Schirmer of New York City. Gustav Schirmer, the founder of the present firm, was born in Thuringia, Germany, in 1830. Both his father and grandfather were piano-makers to the Court of Sondershausen. He came to this country early in life, and his first experience in the music trade was with the house of Scharfenberg & Luis. In 1854 he became manager of Breusing's music business (founded in 1848 by Kerksieg & Breusing), and in 1861 he bought out the interest of Mr. Breusing in conjunction with a Mr. B. Beer. This partnership (Beer & Schirmer) was dissolved at the end of five years, when Mr. Schirmer obtained complete control of the business, which he held for many years. Six months before his death, which occurred on Aug. 6, 1893, the business was converted into a stock company, and continued under the direction of Rudolph E. Schirmer (president) and Gustave Schirmer, Jr. (secretary) until the death of the latter on July 15, 1907. The present head of the firm is Rudolph E. Schirmer.

An enterprise of great magnitude in which the house is engaged is the publication of a new edition of Musical Masterworks. This edition known as Schirmer's Library of Musical Classics, is not simply the equal of foreign editions of a similar character but in many respects their superior. A further undertaking of importance is the Collection of Operas and Operettas in vocal score, comprising over fifty numbers, and intended to include the standard works, new and old, of the modern operatic repertory. Foreign works are published in the original languages (when these are either French, German, or Italian) with English translations made expressly for the edition. The latest among the firm's major undertakings is the publication of extended contemporaneous compositions for full orchestra. The list already includes the names of representative American composers, such as Chadwick, Loeffler, Hadley, F. S. Converse and Schelling.

Another department, that of musical literature, was established in 1901 for the purpose of supplying the increasing demand for books relating to music. The stock of standard and current works in English, German and French on musical history, biography, criticism and theory is most complete.

One of the pioneer music establishments of America is the one bearing the name of the John Church Company, which was founded in Cincinnati in 1859 by Mr. John Church, born May 9, 1834, and died April 19, 1890. After eleven years' experience with Oliver Ditson & Co. of Boston, Mr. Church left Boston for Cincinnati in 1859, and in April of the same year raised the sign over the door at 66 West Fourth Street, which bore the name of John Church, Jr. From that time on the firm name has been a prominent one in the musical industries of this country. The trade name was changed in 1869 to John Church & Company. In 1872 the new firm purchased the book plates of Root & Cady of Chicago. This large purchase of plates of books famous the country over brought the firm into additional prominence as publishers of music books. The same year the firm purchased the stock and good-will of the Root and Sons Music Company, of Chicago, and has continued the business ever since under their name. In the same year (1872) a branch house was established in New York City.

As publishers of high-grade classical and standard music, the prints of the John Church Company are pre-eminent, and their distributions through their five establishments — Cincinnati, New York, Chicago, Leipsic and London — are numbered by the millions. In 1885 the company was organized as a corporation, with Mr. Church as president, at which time they entered the industry of piano manufacture, establishing a factory in Boston for the building of the now famed Everett piano. Two years after the death of Mr. Church in 1890, the company was reorganized, with a capital stock of one and a quarter million dollars, with Mr. Frank A. Lee as president and general manager, and has continued since under the same management.

The business of Clayton F. Summy of Chicago, publishers, importers of and dealers in music, was started August, 1888, and in 1895 was incorporated. The music published by the Summy Company has been of the better class and confined to the material used by the teaching and professional fraternity in general. It has been successful in bringing out a line of educational material for the child in music. Although of recent establishment the company ranks as one of the most important publishing houses in the country — certainly in the West.

A branch of the famous house of Novello, London publishers, established in 1811, is situated in New York City. They are particularly important as dealers in church music of a high class.

Other important publishing houses are those of Arthur G. Schmidt, Boston, Mass.; Theodore Presser, Philadelphia; the B. F. Wood Co., Boston; the Hatch Music Company, Philadelphia; E. Schuberth, New York; the Boston Music Company, Boston; White Smith, Boston; Carl Fischer, New York; S. Brainard's Sons Company, New York; Wm. A. Pond & Co., New York.

Among the large dealers in popular compositions are M. Witmark & Son, J. W. Stern & Co., Charles K. Harris, J. H. Remick & Co., and F. A. Mills, all of New York.

SUMMARY AND OUTLOOK

Owing to political and religious conditions, geographical position, and the utilitarian spirit always in evidence in young nations, in America music has had a hard struggle for recognition. Fate has been kind, however; all three obstacles at length have given way and a love of the art is becoming more and more general among all classes. Religious conflicts over music have subsided long since; the matter of distance from the art centers of Europe no longer is of moment; and the great wealth of the country is serving in good stead in attracting the best musicians from all countries to our shores, as well as assisting in the development of native talent and of musical productions in general. Having discussed in detail what America has accomplished in music since the coming of the early settlers it will be well now to take a rapid survey over the whole matter.

Of the music, if such it may be termed, native to this country there is little to be said, for it has undergone little or no change and has played no part in our development. Some few themes have been utilized by Edward MacDowell and others in their compositions, but in general the music of the aborigine, owing to its nature, has been looked upon as of no artistic value. The music of the negro, on the other hand, while of alien origin, has become a part of our heritage and has served as the foundation of our folk-music. Apart from its inherent worth it has proved of value through the use made of it by Dvořák, Chadwick, Schoenfeld and other composers.

The first music having any pretensions to artistry to be heard in America was the psalmody of the Puritans. Whatever its true status, as sung by the early settlers it was music of the crudest kind. This was our beginning. Then came the era of attempted improvement and the introduction of the mere rudiments of the art. Following this came our first real musical uplift with the advent of the singing master and the church organist. What the early English organists, such as James Bremner, William Tuckey and William Selby accomplished, hardly can be overestimated, for they implanted a knowledge of and a love for music of the better class among the general public. It was the efforts of such men as these which made further progress possible.

Owing to their efforts and those of their contemporaries music now began to assume a new trend and to be looked upon as something more than an adjunct to the religious services or of the dance. From the singing school sprang the choral society — such organizations incidentally aiding in the formation of orchestras. By means of these several factors by the beginning of the Nineteenth Century music had become firmly fixed in the life of the American people; but the art still was in its infancy.

The year 1815, in which the Handel and Haydn Society of Boston was organized, marks the beginning of important choral societies devoted to oratorio. Ten years later came Garcia with his troupe and gave to America its first introduction to serious opera. In 1840 the Boston Academy was founded, an institution which gave a mighty impetus to music education and which also brought about the formation of America's first properly conducted orchestra. In the field of composition the name of John K. Paine stands out as the first American writer to win success in the larger musical forms, his first great work being a mass which was performed in Berlin in 1867.

Since the time of these, our real beginnings in music, America has made wonderful strides in all branches of the art. Choral societies of the highest significance now are to be found in all parts of the country; opera has obtained a firm hold; orchestras have been established on a permanent basis in many of the larger cities; excellent educational advantages are to be had everywhere; and our composers have won recognition through the intrinsic worth of their works. But in spite of what has been accomplished America still lacks the spirit necessary for the development of her own resources. The country continues to look to Europe, and it must be said, of necessity, for her conductors required for the highest positions, for the majority of her opera singers, and for her orchestral players. It is in the latter field, perhaps, that our shortcomings are most pronounced, for at least ninety per cent of the performers in the leading American orchestras are foreigners. All these discrepancies arise from the narrow lines assumed in our musical education, where the efforts largely are directed toward solo playing rather than toward general musicianship. The facilities also are lacking for preliminary training in ensemble playing. Back of all there is seen in the American music student the unwillingness to make haste slowly and to undergo the routine work necessary for future achievement.

But notwithstanding our deficiencies much has been accomplished and the outlook ever is growing brighter. That it is possible for Americans to occupy prominent places in the musical world clearly is evident, as a glance at the list of well-known artists now before the public will show. In every phase of the art, as singers, pianists, organists, teachers, etc., they have demonstrated that America is capable of producing as great talent as any country of Europe.

For the present status of opera in America one still must look chiefly to New York. Other cities, however, recently have shown a desire to support their own companies. Philadelphia and Boston both are to have houses devoted to opera given by resident troupes, while Chicago also shows evidences of a like venture. Henry W. Savage's Company is the only one of note which presents grand opera in English, and judging from its past successes it long should continue in the field. Mr. Savage has performed a work of lasting benefit through his excellent presentation of opera in all parts of the country. It is just such productions as these which the country needs for its educational advancement in the operatic art.

There hardly is an American city which does not support an orchestra devoted to works of symphonic character. Boston, Chicago, New York, Philadelphia, Pittsburg and Cincinnati have established orchestras on something like a permanent basis, while in fact all the leading American cities are moving in the same direction.

In the matter of musical education the country has reached an enviable position. More attention is paid to music in our public schools than is shown in the schools of any country of Europe. The same conditions exist in our higher institutions of learning. The general musical education of the public at large merely is a matter of time, for America now is privileged to listen to the greatest artists of the world. Owing to the immensity of the Union and to the constant absorption of myriads of unlettered foreigners the process necessarily is slow. But eventually our development must come from within, being assisted by our own rapidly unfolding genius and by the European pedagogues and artists attracted to our shores. Another factor which is proving of benefit is the establishment of musical libraries in connection with our public institutions. Through the munificence of a few public spirited men who have become interested in the musical uplift of their respective communities, Boston, Chicago and Philadelphia have been the first American cities to profit thereby.

The outcome of the ever-increasing interest in music has resulted in the trade in musical merchandise assuming immense proportions. Statistics show that upwards of $39,000,000 was spent during the year 1907 for pianos alone.

It is indeed rare that some musical instrument is not found in an American home. The twenty thousand and more bands in the United States utilize the output of numerous makers of band instruments. A phase of the music trade which has developed practically within the last decade is that which is devoted to the production of mechanical piano players, phonographs, gramophones, etc. Although this "canned music," as it has been somewhat satirically described, has been frowned down upon in some quarters, nevertheless it doubtless will prove of benefit in the long run. By means of the pianola and other piano playing devices the field of music has been opened to those who otherwise would be debarred from any but occasional hearings of the best piano literature. The same conditions apply to the gramophone and phonograph except that the repertory largely is taken from concerted instrumental numbers and from vocal sources. These reproductive instruments also should prove of value in the years to come in the matter of preserving a more or less accurate tonal record of the art of our present day singers. Finally, the music trade has resulted in the formation of publishing houses devoted to the publication and sale of the vast quantities of music called for by the devotees of the art.

Our ultimate goal, which lies in the realm of composition, already has been sighted, and although as yet there are no signs of anything approaching an American school, the productions of our native composers have won recognition by their intrinsic merit. What is to come we know not, but judging by the accomplishments of the last half-century America is destined to become a true home of art. We have the talent, and we have the facilities for its development; perhaps the way is made too easy. But after all, the way is found not by the American nor by the European but by the genius. If heartache and tears be necessary for his unfolding they are found in America or elsewhere. The past was good; let us hope and work for the future.

SELECTED BIBLIOGRAPHY

Apthorp, W. F. — Musical Reminiscences of Boston thirty years ago. (See his By the Way, Vol. II., pp. 48-82.)

Armstrong, Mrs. M. F. and Ludlow, Helen W. — Hampton and its students, with fifty cabin and plantation songs arranged by Thomas Fenner.

Armstrong, W. G. — Record of the Opera at Philadelphia.

Baker, Theodor — Über die Musik der Nordamerikanischen Wilden.

Banks, Rev. L. A. — Immortal Songs of Camp and Field, the story of their inspiration together with striking anecdotes connected with their history.

Beale, James — A Famous War Song. (John Brown's Body.)

Bibliotheca Sacra. Vol. XXXVI. New England Psalmody.

Brooks, H. M. — Olden Time Music, a compilation from Newspapers and Books.

Catlin, George — Letters and Notes on the Manners, Customs, and Condition of the North American Indians. 2 vols.

Curtis, Natalie, ed. — The Indian's Book; an offering by the American Indians of Indian lore, musical and narrative, to form a record of songs and legends of their race.

Dickinson, Edward — Music in the History of the Western Church. Chaps. 11 and 12.

Drake, F. S. — The Indian Tribes of the United States. 2 vols.

Earle, Alice M. — The Sabbath in Puritan New England.

Elson, Arthur — Music Club Programs from All Nations. (Chap. 12. America.)

Woman's Work in Music. (Chap. 9. America.)

Elson, L. C. — The History of American Music.

The National Music of America and its Sources.

The Realm of Music. (Pp. 290-292. Our National Anthems.

French, Florence — Music and Musicians in Chicago.

Finck, H. T. — Songs and Song-Writers. (Chap. 8. English and American song-writers.)

German Opera in New York. (See his Chopin and other musical essays.)

FitzGerald, S. J. — Stories of Famous Songs. Chaps. 1 and 8.

Fletcher, Alice C. — Indian Story and Song from North America.

A Study of Omaha Indian Music. (In the archæological and ethnological papers of the Peabody Museum. Vol. I., No. 5.)

Gilmore, P. S. — History of the National Peace Jubilee and Great Musical Festival held in the city of Boston, June, 1869.

Goldstein, Max — Der Stand der öffentlichen Musikpflege in den Vereinigten Staaten. (In Dammlung Musikalischer Vorträge, ed. by Paul Graf Waldersee. Vol. II., No. 15.)

Gould, N. D. — History of Church Music in America.

Griggs, J. C. — Studien über die Musik in Amerika.

Hood, George — History of Music in New England.

Hughes, Rupert — Contemporary American Composers.

Johnson, J. C. — The Introduction of the Study of Music into the public schools of America.

Jones, F. O. — A Handbook of American Music and Musicians.
Kobbé, Gustav — Famous American Songs.
Krehbiel, H. E. — Notes on the Cultivation of Choral Music and the Oratorio Society in New York.
The Philharmonic Society of New York.
Review of the New York Musical Season, 1885-1886 to 1889-1890.
Lahee, H. C. — Grand Opera in America.
Lavignac, Albert — Music and Musicians, with additions on Music in America.
Madeira, L. C. — Annals of Music in Philadelphia and History of the Musical Fund Society from its organization in 1820 to the year 1858.
Maretzek, Max — Crotchets and Quavers; or Revelations of an Opera Manager in America.
Marsh, J. B. T. — The Story of the Jubilee Singers; with their songs.
Mathews, Washington — Navaho Legends. (In The Memoirs of the American Folk-Lore Society. Vol. V.)
Mathews, W. S. B.— A Hundred Years of Music in America.
Mathews, W. S. B., ed.— The great in Music. (See chapters on American composers.)
Mees, Arthur — Choirs and Choral Music. Chap. 9.
Nason, Rev. Elias — A Monogram on Our National Song.
Newell, W. W. — Games and Songs of American Children.
Paine, J. K., Thomas, Theodore, and Klauser, Karl, eds. — Famous Composers and their Works. 3 vols. (Vol. II. Music in America.)
Perkins, C. C. and Dwight, J. S. — History of the Handel and Haydn Society of Boston, Mass., from the foundation of the Society through its seventy-fifth season, 1815-1890.
Pike, G. D. — The Jubilee Singers and their campaign for twenty thousand dollars.
Preble, G. H. — History of the Flag of the United States of America. (National and Patriotic Songs. Pp. 715-768.)

Ritter, F. L. — Music in America.

Sagard-Theodat, F. G. — Le Grand Voyage du Pays des Hurons.

Salisbury, Stephen — An essay on the Star-Spangled Banner and National Songs.

Scharf, J. T. — History of Baltimore City and County from the earliest period to the present day. Chap. 38.

Scharf, J. T. and Westcott, Thompson — History of Philadelphia, 1609-1884. Vol. II., Chap. 33.

Scharf, J. T. — History of Saint Louis City and County. Vol. II., Chap. 38.

Seidl, Anton — The Music of the Modern World. Vol. I.

Smith, Nicholas — Stories of Great National Songs.

Sonneck, O. G. — Bibliography of Early Secular American Music.

Early Concert Life in America (1731-1800).

Francis Hopkinson, the first American poet-composer (1737-1791) and James Lyon, patriot, preacher, psalmodist (1735-1794), two studies in early American Music.

Spillane, Daniel — History of the American Pianoforte; its technical development and the trade.

Strang, L. C. — Celebrated Comedians of light opera and musical comedy in America.

Trotter, J. M. — Music and some Highly Musical people.

Upton, G. P. — Musical Pastels. (The First American Composer. Pp. 59-71.)

Wallaschek, Richard — Primitive Musik. (Chap. 1. America.)

Warren, Charles — The Place of Music among the Æsthetic Arts Defined, and its value as a Part of Free Common School Instruction considered. (In Circulars of Information of the Bureau of Education. No. 1, 1886.)

White, R. G. — National Hymns; how they are written and how they are not written, a lyric and national study for the times.

Wilson, G. H., ed. — The Boston Musical Year Book. 10 vols.

Winsor, Justin, ed.— The Memorial History of Boston including Suffolk County, Mass. 1630-1880. Vol. IV., Chap. 7.

PERIODICALS.

Ditson & Co.'s Musical Record — Sept., 1878 to Dec., 1890.

Dwight's Journal of Music — 41 vols. April 10, 1852 to Sept. 3, 1881.

Étude — Vols. 1-24. 1883-1908.

Folio; a journal of music, art, drama and literature. 1875-1885.

Music — W. S. B. Mathews, ed. — 22 vols. Nov., 1891, to Dec., 1902.

The Musician — 1896-1908.

The Musical Courier — Jan., 1880-date.

The Musical Leader and Concert Goer — Vols. I.-XVI. 1895-1908.

The Musical Review — Vols. I.-IV. 1891-1894.

Musical World — Vols. I.-XXVII. 1863-1890.

The New Music Review and Church Music Review — (Official organ of the American Guild of Organists.)

New York Musical Pioneer and Chorister Budget — J. B. Woodbury, ed. — 16 vols. 1855-1871.

Southern Musical Journal — March, 1879 to Dec., 1882.

SONGS.

Allen, W. F., Ware, C. P., and Garrison, Lucy M., eds. — Slave Songs of the United States.

Brown, J. D., ed. — Characteristic Songs and Dances of all Nations. (America. Pp. 185-216.)

Chamberlain, D. B. and Harrington, K. P., comp. — Songs of All the Colleges.

Curtis, Natalie — Songs of Ancient America.

Eggleston, E. C., ed.— American War Ballads and Lyrics; a collection of the songs and ballads of the Colonial wars, the Revolution, the War of 1812, the War with Mexico and the Civil War. 2 vols.

Fagan, W. L. — Southern War Songs; camp fire, patriotic and sentimental.

Fenner, T. P. and Rattibun, F. G. — Cabin and Plantation Songs as sung by the Hampton students.

Hughes, Rupert, ed. — Songs by thirty Americans, also biographical sketches of the composers represented.

Morris, G. P. — American Melodies.

Our War Songs, North and South.

Redall, H., and Buck, Dudley, eds. — Songs that Never Die. Famous Words and Melodies Enriched with Valuable Historical and Biographical Sketches of Renowned Authors and Composers.

Stevens, C. Wistar — College Song-Book. A collection of American college songs with pianoforte accompaniment.